The New History of Scotland

General Editor
Jenny Wormald

Advisory Editors
G.W.S. Barrow and Christopher Smout

6

The New History of Scotland

* Publication 1981

Integration, Enlightenment, and Industrialization

Scotland 1746 – 1832

Bruce Lenman

Edward Arnold

First published 1981
by Edward Arnold (Publishers) Ltd
41 Bedford Square, London WC1B 3DQ

British Library Cataloguing in Publication Data

Lenman, Bruce
  Integration, enlightenment, and industrialization:
  Scotland 1746–1832 (The New history of Scotland)
  1. Scotland — History
  I. Title   II. Series
  941.107   DA815

  ISBN 0-7131-6314-3
  ISBN 0-7131-6315-1   Pbk

To Philip Haffenden

Printed in Great Britain by Richard Clay (The Chaucer Press) Ltd.
Bungay, Suffolk

Contents

Preface

I must record my profound gratitude to the editors of this series, first for the invitation to contribute to what I have found to be an intellectually challenging enterprise, and secondly for the help they have given me in shaping my work. Jenny Wormald displayed exemplary patience with a laggard author and contributed shrewd comments when the manuscript finally appeared. However, I single out Christopher Smout for special thanks. His detailed reading of my text proved immensely helpful and his lucid, courteous, and economical suggestions improved the structure of this book more than I would have thought possible without affecting its fundamental character. To Marjorie Nield I am, as ever, deeply indebted for her typing. To my old tutor Philip Haffenden, who has permitted me to dedicate this book to him, I cannot offer anything as magisterial as his own studies of New England in the British Empire. As an Imperial historian I have so far been of little credit to him. However, I do think that in an era of supreme crisis for the British Atlantic Community, such as the period covered in this book, there is a case for looking at the most deferential of the British provinces, as well as at the troublemakers.

Bruce Lenman
University of St Andrews

1

Scotland After the '45: The Structure of the Economy and of Society

The defeat of the Jacobite army commanded by Prince Charles Edward Stewart at the battle of Culloden, fought a few miles to the west of Inverness in April 1746, finally laid to rest an issue in Scottish politics which most Scotsmen as late as 1744 assumed had been settled 30 years previously. By 1746 it was clear that the throne of Great Britain was irreversibly transferred to the House of Hanover, represented by George II. Even Prince Charles's brother Henry, 'Duke of York', appreciated the realities of the situation. In 1747 he effectively retired from dynastic politics by accepting a Cardinal's hat in the Roman Church. By 1750 everyone wielding significant power in Scotland was Hanoverian, by conviction or resignation. By definition they all accepted the Act of Union of 1707 and the authority of the King in Parliament in Westminster. Repeal of the Union had been a Jacobite aim.

The Union settlement had offered guarantees for certain institutions and rights which were regarded as essential to the identity and continuing local autonomy of Scottish society. Such were the Scottish universities, the presbyterian settlement in the Church of Scotland, the distinctive Scottish legal system and court structure, and the powers and privileges of the royal burghs of Scotland. Given the lack of any concept of legal restraint on the unbridled authority of the sovereign King in Parliament none of these guarantees were ultimately secure but most of them were respected for a long time. The great exception was a direct result of the '45. The Act of Union guaranteed those heritable jurisdictions and offices which in the extreme form of a regality converted areas into sub-kingdoms virtually excluding the King's Writ. A consensus that these jurisdictions had contributed to Jacobitism produced the Abolition of Heritable Jurisdictions (Scotland) Act of 1747. Already in decline, the jurisdictions which covered perhaps half Scotland were swept away. By 1750 Scotland had, just, left its medieval past behind. It remains to examine its demographic, economic, social, and cultural structures on the eve of an era of rapid change.

Demographic and Economic Foundations

Arguably the size and distribution of the population was the most significant single area of change in the rapidly-evolving pattern of human life in Scotland between 1750 and 1832. Certainly it is only after 1755 that we can begin to speak about Scottish population statistics with any degree of confidence. It was in that year that Dr Alexander Webster, Minister of the Tolbooth Kirk in Edinburgh, produced his 'Account of the Number of People in Scotland, 1755'. A former Moderator of the General Assembly of the Church of Scotland, Webster had built up close links with parish clergymen and schoolmasters. Despite the indirect way in which he calculated his results, modern scholarship has not seriously shaken the standing of his estimate that Scotland's population came to 1,265,380 souls.

If a million and a quarter is roughly the right order of magnitude in 1755, informed guesses would suggest that this was something like a peak figure which in previous centuries would have been eventually cut back by dearth and demographic crisis of the kind that struck in the 'ill years' of the 1690s. This cycle of expansion and contraction was, however, decisively broken in 1739–41, when severe harvest deficiency was contained by extensive poor relief measures, substantial grain imports, and above all by the existence of accumulated wealth capable of tiding Scotland over the crisis. There was a sharp regional famine in the Highlands and Islands in 1782–3, but again imports staved off total disaster. Better coastal and inland transport had already virtually unified Lowland grain markets.

Growth was so marked that the first official census in 1801 gave Scottish population, despite significant emigration, as 1,608,000. The figure represents a retained population increase of just over a quarter in roughly 50 years, or an average of 0.52 per cent per annum since 1755. Thereafter the rate of population growth in inter-censal decades accelerated. In 1811 the population was 1,824,000, representing an increase of 1.27 per cent per annum in the period since 1801. In 1821 a population figure of 2,100,000 reflected 1.42 per cent per annum growth in the previous decade – the highest ever recorded. By 1831 the population of Scotland was given as 2,374,000, which implied a 1.23 per cent annual expansion since 1821. In the next decade the annual rate of increase fell to just over 1 per cent.

A higher and higher percentage of these people were crowding into the Central Lowlands, that transverse band of relatively fertile low-lying, often sandstone-based soils which lies between the older and harder rocks of the Highlands and Islands and the lower, but still relatively infertile hills of the Southern Uplands. All the bigger Scottish Towns, from Aberdeen to Dundee, and from Edinburgh to Glasgow, lay within the narrow central belt which even in 1750 had a disproportionate share of the population. At that date the Highlands and Islands, covering 70 per cent of the land surface of Scotland had a population of 652,000, or 51 per cent of the total figure. The Central Lowlands, with a little over 14 per cent of the country's area, possessed in its 464,000 people some 37 per cent of the population. With a similar area the Southern Uplands held only 149,000 people or roughly 11 per cent of the total. Highland population did grow overall between 1755 and 1832 but by 1832 it was clear that growth in these counties was lagging decisively behind that in the Central Lowlands. Indeed by 1831 many individual parishes in the Highlands and Islands already had declining populations, and one Highland county, Argyllshire, had a similar overall trend.

Scottish urban units were known as burghs. They came in two types: royal burghs and burghs of barony. Royal burghs were self-governing, albeit under narrow and totally self-perpetuating oligarchies whose precise composition was defined by the 'sett' or constitution of the burgh. Originally only royal burghs could conduct overseas trade or retail imported commodities. Burghs of barony, dependent on a feudal superior, had much narrower trading rights and restricted self-government. The Act of Union both confirmed the privileges of royal burghs, and authorized all Britons to trade where they wished in the Crown's dominions. It was an unstable position, and by 1743 a decisive legal case (between Kirkwall and Stromness in Orkney) had started a 15 year journey ending in the House of Lords and the destruction of the royal burghs' monopolies.

Though there were about 70 royal burghs and roughly 200 others, only approximately an eighth of the population in 1750 was urban. In the next 70 years urban growth was swift. Glasgow's population of 27,451 in 1755 grew to 147,043 by 1821. Edinburgh (including Leith) started with 52,720 people in 1755 and grew fast enough still to be bigger than Glasgow in 1801 when Glasgow had 77,385 indwellers and Edinburgh 82,560. However, by 1821 Edinburgh with 138,235 inhabitants had fallen behind its great western rival. Aberdeen and Dundee, the traditional rivals for third place amongst the burghs also grew swiftly. Aberdeen had 15,730 inhabitants in 1755. 27, 519 in

1801, and 44,796 in 1821. Dundee grew from a figure of 12,477 in 1755 to 26,084 in 1801 to 30,575 in 1821. What was remarkable was the fact that Paisley, a smallish place of 6,799 people in 1755, had swept ahead of both Aberdeen and Dundee by 1801, when it had 31,179 of a population, and it held its lead with 47,003 in 1821. Old county towns and secondary seaports grew at a gentler rate. Perth had 9,019 people in 1755, 14,878 in 1801, and 19,068 in 1821. Stirling had 3,951 in 1755 and 5,271 and 7,113 respectively at the two later dates. Yet it is important to remember that if in 1821 the urban fraction of the population had increased to about a third, this still left two-thirds of the national population in rural communities.

Traditional historiography saw the eighteenth-century rural scene as dominated by a gradually mounting tempo of Improvement. Improvers like John Cockburn of Ormiston (1679–1758), and John, Earl of Stair (1673–1747), were seen as starting a process which reached maturity under leaders like Lord Deskford, later Earl of Findlater (1716–70), and Sir Archibald Grant of Monymusk (1696–1778), at which stage it had reached the proportions of an Agricultural Revolution. Yet, it is now clear that in the period of not very buoyant agricultural prices before 1750, self-conscious Improvement was a rich man's non-paying hobby, not a universal fever. Cockburn of Ormiston himself became insolvent and sold his estate in 1747. Empirical adaptation and gradual change, on the other hand, can be traced far back into the seventeenth century, especially on estates in Lothian near the big Edinburgh urban market.

Commercialization and specialization, along with social instability, came early in the south-west of Scotland, in Dumfries and Galloway, where the rapid expansion of the black cattle trade to England stimulated enclosure of land by dry stone dykes to form large cattle parks. By the 1720s resentment by the excluded tenant farmers had bred agrarian violence. Elsewhere premature attempts at restructuring rural society just failed. For example, from 1737 the Duke of Argyll, advised by the great lawyer Duncan Forbes of Culloden, tried to squeeze out the clan gentry or tacksmen in his country, on the ground that they held their tacks or leases too cheaply and that their sub-tenants, if turned into direct tenants of Argyll, would pay more than ever had the tacksmen. Apart from gravely undermining the military cohesion of Clan Campbell during the 1745 rebellion, the experiment did not even pay. Tenants bid high in public auction for farms, but no more cash rent was collected than under the tacksmen. The balance simply accumulated in the form of arrears.

Successful change tended to be gradual and to respect commercial realities. Scottish agriculture was strongly commercial. Though farmers produced much of what they ate and wore, inter-regional trade was essential. The Highlands, for example, always produced a substantial surplus of animal products, ranging from skins to butter and cattle on the hoof. To supplement their own inadequate hardy grain crops (mostly oats and barley), Highlanders traded with the Lowlands, which in normal years produced a grain surplus. A series of market towns on the Highland margin such as Dingwall, Inverness, Kirriemuir, Dunkeld, Crieff, Dunblane, and Dumbarton catered for this trade. A similar form of specialization sustained regional trade between the Orkney and Shetland Islands. Orkney produced a grain surplus of hardy cereals such as oats or bere (a primitive barley). The lairds of the much bleaker Shetland Isles were masters of a very commercial local fishery, but it was still true, as had been said by the Reverend John Brand in 1700, that 'as Zetland could not well live without Orkney's Corns, so neither could Orkney be so well without Zetland's Money.' Surplus fish, turned into cash, were exchanged for vital foodstuffs.

In 1750, even in the relatively advanced Lowlands, many farmers still lived in fermtouns or hamlets. They held grazing in common and cultivated as individuals scattered plots in the arable area, which was divided into infield and outfield. Only the infield received any systematic manuring. Mixed farming was universal, though the balance between crops and animals varied from area to area. Much rent was paid in kind, but landlords usually converted the bulk of this to cash in the nearest urban market. Especially in arable areas from 1600 onwards there had been a steady drift towards consolidation of estates into single-tenant farms usually held on a lease of nine or more years. Improvement did not start only after 1707.

As Daniel Defoe pointed out in his *Tour Through the Whole Island of Great Britain* published in 1724–6, the huge flow of black cattle from the Highlands was ultimately geared to meeting London's need for meat. The cattle marts or trysts at Crieff, and after 1770 at Falkirk, were simply points of organization and departure on the road to Smithfield meat market in the metropolis. Highland rents were often settled in drovers' bills. In the Southern Uplands an increasing emphasis on sheep farming was directly connected with the raw material needs of the Scottish and northern English woollen industries. The finer branches of Scottish woollens, in decline before 1707, were destroyed by English competition after that date, but coarser woollens survived, and Scottish wool flowed into England alongside cattle on the hoof. Between 1745 and 1770 the pace of rationalization, specialization, and change in the Scottish countryside accelerated in response to urban demand for food and raw materials, a demand often rooted in industrial growth.

Industry in Scotland in 1750 was heavily dominated by textiles. The Board of Trustees for Fisheries and Manufactures in Scotland (set up by legislation in 1727) had rightly identified linen as the most promising growth industry and the scale of expansion in this trade may be gathered from the fact that the amount of linen made for sale in Scotland rose from 2,000,000 yards valued at £103,312 in 1728 to 36,000,000 yards valued at £1,403,767 by 1815. Production doubled roughly every 25 years between 1750 and 1800, excluding the large quantities consumed within manufacturing households. Spinning yarn was a widely-dispersed female trade. Lowland merchants even bought yarn in the more accessible Highland glens. Weaving, on the other hand, was and remained concentrated in the countries of Fife, Angus, and Perthshire on the east coast and Lanarkshire and Renfrewshire on the west. The Board of Trustees tried by offering prizes and importing foreign experts to stimulate advances in technique. Its grants did help those involved in the expensive business of creating bleachfields, but linen was a winner, with or without the Board.

The growth of the linen trade was nevertheless heavily dependent on protective tariffs and export bounties. The temporary withdrawal in 1753 of a bounty on the export of coarse linens, the staple of the Tayside industry, led to a sharp depression in Angus in 1754–5. The first signs of the grouping of looms under one roof on a scale worthy of the name of factory can be discerned in ports like Montrose, Arbroath, and Dundee, where exports were always vitally important to local textile manufacturers. Growth resumed with the restoration of the bounty. London merchant houses absorbed a high proportion of Scots output, much of it for export to the colonies, so increased foreign competition and political disturbance in the American market triggered off another depression in 1772–4.

Though much rent was paid out of the price of webs of linen, the landed classes were more directly interested in mining. Coalfields occur at intervals throughout the Central Lowlands south of the Tay. Mines around 1760 were usually simple affairs worked by the landlord or a single tacksman or leasee. Apart from pits in the vicinity of the large Edinburgh and Glasgow markets, most Scots pits were on or near tidal water and were linked to saltworks where the culm or small coal was used to evaporate salt water in great iron pans. Drainage, like winding, was effected by horse power. Only half a dozen primitive steam engines seem to have been at work in Scottish mines around 1760. After that date coal prices began to move up due to increased domestic demand, with population growth and the exhaustion of Lowland peat; increased industrial demand; and significantly greater agricultural demand for lime produced in coal-fired kilns.

Chemical works such as the Prestonpans sulphuric acid works established in 1749 by Dr John Roebuck and Samuel Garbett consumed a deal of coal, but were insignificant compared with the demand from ironworks. Charcoal was for long the only acceptable smelting fuel. Several Lancashire firms even set up blast furnaces in Inverness-shire and Argyll between 1729 and 1775, to smelt imported ore with local timber. Scotland never ceased to import Swedish malleable bar iron, but in 1759 the Carron Iron Works near Falkirk opened — the first works to use local coal to smelt nearby ironstone in its furnaces. However important as a precedent, Carron had no comparable rival for 20 years.

The Scottish economy around 1750 was in some ways more poised for expansion than rapidly expanding. Even so widespread an industry as brewing showed this. Private brewing was universal but the seventeenth century had seen the emergence of a tendency towards concentration of commercial brewing within specific regional centres. Between 1700 and 1750 this trend accelerated. Edinburgh, with its large domestic market and nearby fuel supply from Lothian coalmines surrounded by barley-producing farms was pre-eminent. However excise returns suggest a short-term downward trend in production between 1720 and 1740. If the underlying trend was still upwards, and recovery came fast after 1740, it is still true that it was only in the 1760s that sustained expansion set in, and as late as 1765 foreign-going exports of ale and beer were, at 40,000 gallons per annum, a tiny fraction of total production valued at a mere £2,000.

Social and Cultural Structures

The relationship between the economy and contemporary social and cultural structures is only very crudely represented by the analogy between foundations and superstructure. In reality the relationship is infinitely more complex. Nevertheless it remains a fact that the social and political structure of Scotland in 1750 reflected broadly the realities of contemporary economic power, and that the very significant political changes which occurred at the start of the third decade of the nineteenth century were, to put it mildly, in some measure a recognition of fundamental shifts in the balance of power and influence within Scottish society, shifts ultimately determined by the pace and nature of economic changes in the period between 1750 and 1832.

Around 1750 Scotland was still overwhelmingly an agrarian country dominated politically by its landowning class. At the very top of that class stood the peers. The Union Roll, which listed Scots titles in existence in 1707, contained 154 entries. In the Westminster House of Lords there were only 16 elected Scottish representative peers. The right to vote for them depended on being listed on the Union Roll, itself subject to debate and adjustment. Nineteen peers involved in the '15 rebellion had their names removed, as had those convicted of treason after the '45, though the latter were subsequently restored, with one exception. Between 1711 and 1782 Scots noblemen who acquired a peerage of Great Britain from the Crown after 1707 were, most inequitably, excluded from the House of Lords. One reason for this partisan ruling by the Lords was the political subservience of Scots peers who notoriously allowed the government to virtually nominate the so-called Scottish representative peers.

At the very top of the Scots peerage were a knot of magnates most of whom managed before 1800 to achieve ducal status. Such were the Dukes of Hamilton, Queensberry, and Buccleuch in the Lowlands, or the Duke of Argyll and the Duke of Atholl in the Highlands. In the north-east of Scotland the ducal house of Gordon was a power to be reckoned with in both Lowland and Highland areas. Not too far behind these mighty personnages came noblemen like the Marquis of Tweeddale or the Earls of Rothes, Haddington, Hopetoun, Glasgow, Glencairn, or Seaforth, all possessed of extensive estates and great influence. Below the 40 or so earls came the holders of the comparatively modern title of viscount, and the holders of the lowest peerage title in Scotland — that of Lord.

The Scottish baronage comprised all tenants-in-chief of the Crown below the rank of viscount holding in free barony. The baron court was the only heritable jurisdiction to survive 1747, though with reduced powers. All lords were barons: not all barons were lords. The term 'laird' was vaguer, embracing barons and landlords who were not barons. It peers were few, lairds were legion in the Lowlands while in the Highlands tacksmen, often relatives of clan chiefs, held substantial blocks of property on generous leases or tacks, subletting to the peasantry and acting as a laird class. Tacksmen often lent money on mortgage or wadset to their chief. Wadset was also common in the Lowlands, and since few landlords had enough surplus revenue to pay off outstanding debts, a wadset secured on land constituted virtual ownership. Ownership therefore occurred well below the level of laird.

Scotland between 1750 and 1832 was governed by a North British version of that 'open aristocracy based on property and patronage' which governed England. There are indications, as in contemporary England, that the landed élite tended to become more exclusive as time went on. In theory a successful merchant could buy an estate as the first step towards establishing a landed family, and this was a continually occurring phenomenon especially in Stirlingshire, Ayrshire, and the Borders. In the county of Angus behind the city of Dundee, on the other hand, very few such families were ever established before the Victorian period. By the late eighteenth century it was notorious that the merchants of the city of Perth found it extremely difficult to buy land in Perthshire anywhere near Perth itself. Glasgow merchants in the western Atlantic trades in the late eighteenth century were an exception because of the sheer weight of wealth they could accumulate. Successful Edinburgh lawyers could afford properties in the Lothians. However, at a humbler level it is clear that many of the independent proprietors established during the great sixteenth-century boom in the feuing (i.e. perpetual leasing) of ecclesiastical lands had by 1750 been bought out by bigger proprietors. A small minority escaped this fate by rising to become large landlords themselves.

Dominant and stable as they were, the aristocracy and gentry were not a caste. Primogeniture sent younger sons out into many careers, while in theory an able or lucky man could rise to any noble rank. The landed interest dominated the highest level of the legal profession. Throughout the eighteenth century some 90 per cent of entrants to the Faculty of Advocates (barristers entitled to plea before the central courts in Edinburgh) were from landed families. Any advocate rising to the top of his profession as a Senator of the College of Justice automatically joined the *noblesse de robe* with the judicial title of a Lord of Session. In control of politics, and entrenched at the top of the legal system, the landed interest could and did use its power and property to construct elaborate vertical chains of patronage and dependence tying society together under its lead.

That leadership was in no way challenged by the burghal oligarchies, themselves a small, closed and increasingly unpopular self-perpetuating caste. Each royal burgh had a 'set' or constitution peculiar to itself but in all of them the retiring town council elected the new one, with predictable results. Even where, as in Dundee, it was normal usage that the provost serve only for two years at a time, the result was that in the late eighteenth century Alexander Riddoch, the dominant figure on the council, simply had to find a crony to act as front and provost every alternate two years. For the merchants in the smaller burghs the lairds in the landward area were often by far the biggest customers for trades ranging from wine importing to building contracting. The Adam family of architects started under William Adam as general builders in Kirkcaldy, and the proprietor progressed through contracts for country houses and resulting patronage to Master Mason in North Britain to the Board of Ordnance.

Deference and obedience were what was expected of the lower orders, the bulk of the people, divided into Highland peasants and Lowland countryfolk and townspeople. The Highland peasant was marked off by his Gaelic tongue and usually by his poverty. Because of the absence of middling classes and towns in the Highlands, the gentry and tacksmen had to act as entrepreneurs and even as bankers. By 1750 clans survived only as sentiments. The reality had been crushed and then made illegal with the abolition of heritable jurisdictions and military tenures. Highland tenants usually lived in hamlets or clachans surrounded by strips of ground suitable for arable farming beyond which lay the extensive common grazing. Legally, the joint-tenure of the clachan was precarious. Leases were rare. The law recognized no customary right.

Cattle and sheep represented the main form of exportable surplus, and were far too precious to eat, except on rare occasions. Meal (often bere), milk, after 1750 increasingly potatoes, and fish made up the staple diet. Even so, meal had to be imported and it was reckoned that in districts like Lochaber the cost of imported meal represented half the cash surplus derived from livestock. Household possessions were seldom worth more than £5 all told, and of this a fair proportion (between £1 and £2) might be the wooden couples which held up the turf roof over the boulder-walled, earth-floored hut. Rent, when paid, was not high. Life was lived on the margin.

In Orkney townships or tunships as they were called operated a system of agriculture very like that of the Highlands but producing in a more favourable landscape surpluses of grain in the form of oatmeal or bere which a remarkable class of merchant-lairds exported to nearby areas like Shetland or sold to the many ships which put in at an Orcadian anchorage as they swung round the north of the British Isles between Orkney and Shetland. Shetland had its own class of merchant-lairds who had risen on the ruin of the class of immigrant Scottish lairds who had asserted control over Shetland in the late sixteenth and early seventeenth centuries. Keeping their tenants deliberately at the margin of survival on what were known as fishing tenures, Shetland lairds forced them by threat of eviction and by debt-bondage to concentrate on fishing for fish which had to be handed over to the laird who cured and exported them. Division of farms to secure more hands for the boats ensured that agriculture was incapable of sustaining the population for more than part of the year.

In the Lowlands too there was increasing emphasis on the absolute property in land held by landowners, a concept underlined by seventeenth-century Scottish legislation giving landlords extensive powers to reorganize and consolidate lands lying in runrig (i.e. jointly farmed with arable in strips). Main tenants rented direct from a landlord. Sub-tenants or cotters rented gardens and dwellings from main tenants. Below them came the landless — domestic and field servants and beggars. Wage payments were mostly in food and access to land. They appear to have been at a subsistence level, but after 1750 part-time industrial activity was more available to help poor households supplement their incomes. With consolidation of farms accelerating after 1760, many substantial tenant farmers controlled 100 acres or more, and could exploit the numerous urban and village markets of the Lowlands. Early in the eighteenth century their inventories already show an impressive range of domestic utensils and furnishings as well as the odd sign of luxury such as a piece or two of silver, or a set of drinking glasses.

There were plenty of craftsmen in the countryside but the biggest concentrations of skilled workers were naturally to be found in the burghs. Organized in powerful, and until the end of the seventeenth century restructive guilds, their standards of living, though below those of the ruling merchant oligarchy, were comparable with those of prosperous Lowland tenant farmers. In the course of the eighteenth century these craftsmen lost their ability to exclude the work of outsiders from town markets, but their inventories show that they enhanced their modest prosperity. Below them the journeymen and casual labourers of the burgh were usually so close to the margin of subsistence that their notorious propensity to riot over rising food prices is perfectly understandable.

What is interesting is that the forms of social control used by the aristocracy, gentry, and merchants to manage so many poor and hard-used people relied very little on constantly available physical force. There was no effective police force. The army was not usually visible. Patronage, and the public theatre of their ruling style were reinforced by the inculcation of deference and seemly obedience by kirk and school. The Kirk By Law Established — the Church of Scotland, Presbyterian in governance since 1690 — had few rivals. Roman

Catholics survived only in traditional pockets in the Highlands, Islands, and north-east, and may have numbered under 20,000. Episcopahlains had suffered dreadfully because of their association with Jacobitism, and were in sharp decline by 1760. The landed classes tended to be attracted more by Anglican than by Scots Episcopal views and traditions. In 900 parishes and in the burghal kirks, the Church of Scotland ruled.

It was a hierarchy of courts, with the annual General Assembly in Edinburgh at its apex. In the parishes the kirk session still managed to operate a remarkable moral discipline on all but the gentry and nobility. The latter nevertheless often supported ecclesiastical discipline. After all, with the restoration of lay patronage in 1712 they nominated clergymen themselves and could influence Crown patronage. Clerical demands for augmentation of inadequate Stipends were crushed in 1749–50. By 1752 that group of clergymen known as Moderates, who favoured lay patronage and were anxious to reach a dignified accommodation with the ruling political oligarchy, had emerged to preach compromise and elevated social morality.

Inevitably, the tensions generated by so blatant an attempt to ignore the radical implications of Presbyterianism, and to come to terms with an aristocracy which usually neither belonged to nor wholly approved of the Church of Scotland bred schism. Lay patronage was the issue which precipitated the Original Secession of 1733, led by a Stirling clergyman, Ebenezer Erskine. Other secessions followed. Moderates preferred such people out of the Established Kirk, which they then found easier to manage. Its authority over schools, next to the pulpit the most effective means of mass communication, was never shaken.

Nor, be it said, was it very rigid. Virtually every Lowland parish had a parochial school. Heritors or landowners had to bear its cost, which explains the miserable 100–200 merk[1] salary range for the teacher or dominie, who usually doubled up as session clerk and often led praise as precentor on Sunday. Subject to visitation by the local presbytery, such schools provided good cheap elementary education for all classes and both sexes, as well as preparing promising lads for university. Burgh high schools were effectively secondary schools usually stressing Latin. They were controlled by town councils nearly all of whose members were elders of the burghal kirk and who also licensed the adventure or charity schools which taught elementary subjects. We simply do not know what sort of literacy rates this system produced. In the Gaelic Highlands with huge poor parishes and few schools most people were illiterate, that is clear. The Lowlands probably had literacy levels higher than most of England (outside London) and higher than most Continental countries (but not Sweden). The Society in Scotland for Propagating Christian Knowledge tried after 1709, and more effectively after 1766, to bring literacy in English even to some Highlanders.

Compared with Oxford and Cambridge, Scotland had many universities. There were three fifteenth-century foundations, St Andrews, Glasgow, and King's College, Old Aberdeen, as well as two post-Reformation foundations, Edinburgh University and Marischal College in New Aberdeen. They varied enormously in size. St Andrews had about 150 students in 1730. In 1776 the smaller of the two Aberdeen universities, King's, had 50 students, while Marischal had 207. Glasgow, which was very much the university of Presbyterian Ulster as well as of western Scotland rose from about 500 to about 1,000 students between 1700 and 1800. Edinburgh University, controlled and aggressively sponsored by the town council, was always a few hundred larger than Glasgow. The century saw a complete swing in all the universities from a system whereby regents taught the entire curriculum, to one where specialist professors taught individual subjects. Professors' incomes depended largely on class fees and the age range amongst their pupils was vast. The tradition of completing university studies abroad, usually in Holland, was still alive in 1750, especially in law and medicine.

Presbyterian clergymen of the Established Kirk dominated the universities, being almost invariably Principal and holding many chairs. The Chancellor of a Scottish university was usually a great noble. St Andrews even elected the Duke of Cumberland, the victor of Culloden. Intellectual boldness never deviated into social radicalism in Scottish academic circles. Like the Convention of Royal Burghs, the Scottish university world was automatically deferential to great aristo-cratic politicians. Scots nobles resented not being as rich as English aristocrats, but benorth Tweed the landed interest was truly lord of all it surveyed.

1 A merk was 13s. 4d. or two-thirds of a pound so 100 merks was £66 13s. 4d., but this was of course in pounds Scots which survived as a unit of account for decades after 1707 and were worth a twelfth of the same value in sterling. In sterling £66 13s. 4d. becomes £5 11s. 1d.

2

The Age of Islay 1746 – 1761

Scotland between 1746 and 1761 was a developing society, econom-
ically, socially, and culturally. Its development was, however, profoundly conditioned by the fact that it took place within a relatively
unchanging framework of political power derived in its forms from
two main sources. The Act of Union gave Scottish politics new parameters within which to work. The supreme prizes of the electoral
system were the 45 seats in the House of Commons and the 16 places
for representative peers in the Westminster House of Lords allocated
to Scotland. In terms of population Scotland was, and remained for
the best part of 200 years grossly under-represented, but contemporaries in 1707 thought more in terms of relative wealth, and in those
terms Scotland was over-represented. The actual figures were a compromise seldom argued about before the end of the eighteenth
century. What was controversial was the way in which Scotland's
representatives were chosen.

The 'Sixteen Peers of Scotland' were nominally elected by the free
vote of those Scottish peers on the Union Roll but in practice for 60
years after the Act of Union there was no chance of a nobleman being
elected against the wishes of the King's Ministers. Indeed the greatest
of Scottish magnates tended to give up the idea of even standing if he
could not secure official backing, as did a Duke of Atholl in a by-
election of 1722 'since I found that the Court does unanimously joyne
for the Earl of Findlater'. The London government drew up a list of
peers before a General Election, or nominated an individual before a
by-election, and that list or person was returned. Discontent with a
system which so blatantly used government influence to turn an election into something like a nomination from London came to a head as
early as 1734 when a committee of malcontent peers openly protested
against 'money given to many, promised to more; offers of pensions
places, civil and military preferments, acts of grace, reversals

of attainders' offered to those willing to support what was unctuously referred to as 'the King's list'. After a brisk contest, the malcontents lost and for another 30 years peers' elections were suspiciously unanimous. Even more suspicious was the solidarity with which the bulk of peers denounced anyone who, like the Earl of Buchan in 1768, protested against the system. The fact that the 36 other noblemen present on that occasion publicly and solemnly denied that there was such a thing as a King's list is perhaps the most convincing possible tribute to its reality and importance.

In elections to the House of Commons the second main source of rules for the Scottish political game came into play. This was the electoral regime of the pre-Union Scottish state, for its franchises and electoral machinery were carried over into the post-Union period, modified only when modification was unavoidable. The outstanding modification was the reduction of constituencies from 159 to 45. Thirty constituencies were allocated to the shires and 15 to the royal burghs. This grossly over-stated the significance of the burghs with the inevitable result that a high proportion of the burgh seats were pulled into the aristocratic politics of the surrounding shires. Edinburgh alone had a seat to itself. All the other burgh seats represented constituencies of four or five burghs organized in what were known as districts of burghs. Much ingenuity was expended on these arrangements which only became operative, after the Septennial Act of 1716, at very lengthy intervals for the purpose of a General Election, or in a specific constituency at the time of a by-election. At these times the crucial question was who had the right to vote.

In the counties the determining legislation was an act of 1681 of the Scots Parliament which had extended the franchise to feuars (virtual proprietors subject to fixed annual feu duty), and any others owning land to the value of £400 Scots (£33 6s. 8d. Sterling) annual rent, and had also carefully preserved the old-established freeholder franchise based on the holding of land valued at 40 shillings annual rent provided the land was 'of old extent'. The last phrase was vital for it confined the right to vote at a 40 shilling valuation to holders of land recorded in an obsolete medieval taxation schedule. Legislation of 1743 insisted that this minimum holding 'of old extent' had to be proved by a legal document known as a retour of date prior to 16 September 1743. The freeholders of a county, meeting at their annual head court, had to maintain a list of qualified freeholders and this was crucial, for to vote in or represent a county a man had to be on that list. In the burghs the franchise was confined to the town council. The councils sent delegates to a meeting of representatives of burghs in a given electoral district of burghs, so to control a seat a candidate needed a majority of the four or five burghs involved to support him. Open bribery was very common in the burghs and physical violence not unheard of as a means of influencing voters. As for the counties, the manufacture of fictitious votes rapidly became after 1707 both a lucrative industry and a fine art for Scots lawyers. Before the Union there had been a reasonable procedure for appealing to Parliament or to the Court of Session against such malpractices. After 1707 no effective check existed. The legislation of 1743 tried to curb abuse in the compilation of the list of freeholders, but it too proved ineffective.

The discontented peers of 1734 made no bones about the fact that they saw the hand of a specific government manager behind the manipulation of the peers' election. That manager was Archibald Campbell, first Earl of Islay, and younger brother to the then Duke of Argyll. Between the corrupt and unrepresentative nature of the franchise and the susceptibility of the Scottish governing classes to government influence, Scotland in the mid eighteenth century was a machine politician's paradise. Only a few thousand men had the franchise and of these only a tiny fraction were capable of independent choice. No London government wanted to see a single Scottish politician establish himself as the essential channel of government favour and patronage in Scotland. That man would thereby acquire countervailing power against his English masters. On the other hand, only a Scot could hope to have the intimate knowledge of the Scottish aristocracy which was needed to distribute favours wisely and above all to work out which claimants could safely be disappointed of their hopes of government bounty. Islay undoubtedly acted as Scottish man of business to Sir Robert Walpole during the last period of that domineering politician's reign as First Minister at Westminster, but Argyll himself was in fulminating opposition to Walpole by 1740. After Walpole's fall his successors resumed a policy of balancing the two leading Scottish factions — the Squadrone, and their rivals the Argathelians (or Argyll's party), led after 1743 by Archibald Campbell who succeeded as third Duke of Argyll in that year but who will be referred to here by his better-known name, Islay.

For Islay the '45 was traumatic but immensely profitable. The Squadrone Secretary of State for Scotland, the Marquis of Tweeddale, made such a botch of the crisis that he stood out in an administration covered with well-earned odium for the bungling incompetence with which it handled the rebellion. Tweeddale actually resigned in 1746 just ahead of dismissal and with him went his office. The Secretaryship of State for Scotland was not resurrected again before 1885. Clan Campbell had not exactly covered itself with laurels during the campaign but under Major-General John Campbell of Mamore, who succeeded Islay as fourth Duke of Argyll in 1761, it did enough to underline its extreme soundness, from the point of view of Westminster. By 1747 Islay was backing, very unenthusiastically, the Heritable Jurisdictions Bill, and bargaining with Henry Pelham and his brother the Duke of Newcastle, who had assumed at Westminster the mantle of Walpole. Islay collected £21,000 compensation for his own abolished jurisdictions (three times as much as anyone else) and reached a tacit working arrangement with the Pelhams, based on his own massive territorial base and his supremacy in the minutiae of Scottish politics. It was always a delicate relationship. Islay had to be discrete. His position was always resented by Newcastle, that greatest of patronage-mongers, and yet it survived the death of Henry Pelham in 1754. Newcastle himself said in 1761 that Islay died 'the absolute Governor of one of His Majesty's Kingdoms'.

It was an exaggeration. Islay could not, for example, secure the Lord Presidency of the Court of Session for his candidate Charles Erskine. In 1748 Henry Pelham compromised by giving the Lord Presidency to Robert Dundas, and compensating Erskine with the Lord Justice Clerkship. Nevertheless, it is clear that Islay controlled most government patronage in Scotland in exchange for delivering a phalanx of MP's and Representative Peers well disposed to the administration. In 1747, for example, only 10 Scots MP's were 'unsound' as compared with 23 six years before where John Duke of Argyll and the Squadrone were united in opposition. Between 1747 and 1761 Islay quietly dominated the scene, often from London. In Scotland his chosen, and very able, man of business, Andrew Fletcher Lord Milton, Lord Justice Clerk 1735–48, attended to the day-to-day running of the system. Within the framework of what contemporaries openly called Islay's vice-regalty significant developments in Scottish economic and cultural life occurred. The Scottish world of Islay was still generally conservative but change was in the air.

It was primarily a world made safe for Whig, Hanoverian landlords, and for their dependents. Of that there was never any question. Islay himself had sufficient flexibility of mind to grasp, when he succeeded to the ancestral dukedom in 1743, that Duke John's offensive against the Campbell tacksmen, designed to squeeze them out as 'useless mouths', was not only failing to produce higher real returns from the Argyll estates, but was also unpicking the seams of Clan Campbell as a military unit. Islay threw the policy into reverse. However, one major result of the '45 was the forfeiture of the estates of a large number of proven rebels. Mostly but not exclusively these estates were situated in the Highlands. There was a general determination after the '45 to act firmly to ensure that there was no recurrence of Jacobitism and for a time these estates became the vehicle of policies designed to 'civilize' the Highlands by turning them into models of 'the Protestant religion, good Government, Industry and Manufactures and the Principles of Duty and Loyalty to His Majesty, his Heirs and Successors'. To this end an act was passed in 1752 annexing 13 of the forfeited estates 'unalienably' to the Crown. From these islands of economic, political, and spiritual virtue beneficent influences were supposed to spread through the Highlands. The state itself seemed determined to replace the ducal family of Argyll as the principal catalyst of social and economic change in the Gaelic-speaking regions.

In practice developments failed to live up to these exaggerated expectations. Interest in official circles faded extremely quickly after 1752, so that the appointment of Commissioners to manage the forfeited annexed estates had to wait until 1755. The Duke of Argyll was inevitably one of them, but His Grace never went so far as to attend one of their meetings. Due to legal complications several of the annexed forfeited estates only came under the control of the Commissioners as late as 1770. Like the managers of many modern nationalized industries, the Commissioners were given objectives to aim at which proved ultimately contradictory. They were to endeavour to encourage economic and social change in the direction of a more commercially-oriented, modernized, reorganized Highland agriculture, but they were also warned that it was imperative to encourage loyalty to the House of Hanover among the tenantry. This latter injunction deprived them of the single most effective device for compelling tenants to modernize their social relationships and agricultural methods − a steady screwing up of real rent levels.

What the legislation of 1752 did do was give the government a permanent administrative structure for a huge chain of Highland estates previously in Jacobite hands. Both in the wording of the act and in the behaviour of the Commissioners an ideology of improvement and assimilation to Lowland patterns was emphatically asserted. The time was not ripe for such over-simple plans. The numerous mineral surveys carried out at considerable expense by the Commissioners were unable to locate any significant commercial mining prospects. In 1760 virtually the only saleable Highland commodity was still cattle. Nevertheless, there was a very real sense that a Hanoverian, Whig ascendancy had come to stay in the Highlands and the confidence of its protagonists was well expressed in the protracted creation of the Duke of Argyll's own new house at Inveraray on Loch Fyne. Roger Morris planned there in 1745 — 6 the first major neo-Gothic house in Scotland, a great crenellated square block with circular angle-towers and a clear-storeyed central hall which completes the medieval image as it rises above the roof-line like a central keep. Islay also had plans for sweeping away the old burgh of Inveraray, inconveniently close to the ducal seat, and recreating it in a neo-classical mould further away but it is typical of his era that only a couple of the new buildings were completed in the 1750s.

In general, the period 1746 — 61 saw the confirmation of the authority of a Whig landed ascendancy rather than the use of that authority to produce drastic change in the patterns of daily life among the lower orders. Another very good illustration of this point is the struggle for formal control of the funds used for poor relief in Scotland which came to a head in the years 1751 — 2. Established in the late sixteenth century along lines broadly similar to those of the Elizabethan poor law in England, Scots poor relief was based on the parish, seems to have been reasonably liberal in its view of those entitled to relief, and made free use of both voluntary and compulsory stenting or assessment for the raising of a poor rate when the kirk session of the parish found that its funds from other sources were inadequate to deal with the problem. Stenting involved the levying of a tax for a period which could be short or long, half to be paid by the heritors or principal landowners of the parish, and half by the other inhabitants who were inevitably almost all heritors' tenants. Mounting resentment amongst landlords, who could be and often were Episcopalian absentees, at the idea of a kirk session full of the virtually propertyless disposing of large sums of money resulted in a series of test cases before the Court of Session. That court was political in the sense that its members owed their seats to their known loyalties to Westminster politicians, so it is hardly surprising that its verdicts reflected the consensus in the landed political class to which Lords of Session themselves belonged. Heritors gained absolute control over poor relief funds including very often substantial bequests in time past to kirk sessions 'for the poors behoof'. The General Assembly of the Kirk rightly protested against the gross erastianism implicit in the change, when the Crown Rights of the Redeemer had been weighed in the balance against those of Property, and found wanting, but elders who were landlords or judges, and Moderate clergy combined in future Assemblies to ensure that the issue was allowed to drop out of sight. The practical consequences, in terms of the working of the system, seem at first to have been small.

In the burghs the situation was fundamentally different. The incidence of urban destitution was greater and the failure to provide church accommodation to match the population ensured that voluntary collections were almost bound to fall short of the mark necessary to cope with the needs of the poor. Glasgow led the way in 1733 with the establishment of a Town's Hospital designed to house and employ the destitute. All the relevant bodies, the town council, the church, the Merchant's House, and the Incorporated Trades were involved in its foundation and administration. Very rapidly, it became clear that outdoor relief would have to be provided for those destitute persons who could not be housed in the new institution. Nevertheless similar workhouses were established in Aberdeen in 1739, Edinburgh proper in 1743, Paisley in 1752, Dumfries in 1753, in the parish of St Cuthbert's (part of Edinburgh plus a landward area) in 1759, and in the Canongate (physically the east end of the 'Royal Mile' of Edinburgh, but legally a separate jurisdiction) in 1762. In a sense these institutions were part of the price which the ruling oligarchies paid to ensure that the level of tension and resentment amongst the poorest indwellers of their burghs was kept below explosion point. Whereas the countryside never experienced peasant uprisings, the burghs were perpetually at risk of serious riot, especially when grain or meal prices rose. Despite its three workhouses, the biggest urban unit in Scotland, Edinburgh, was particularly susceptible to riot. Lord Provost James Stewart, who succeeded the greatest of Edinburgh Lord Provosts, George Drummond, after the latter's last term in office in 1764 promptly faced serious meal riots in 1764 and 1765.

One reason for the unusually volatile nature of Edinburgh society was that the city itself was changing rapidly. Like other Scottish burghs it had witnessed the atrophy of the ancient system whereby both merchants and craftsmen jealously guarded their virtually hereditary privileges and tried to exclude any outsider from participating in them. The Merchant Company of Edinburgh gave up trying to fine 'unfree' merchants (i.e. non-members of their company) after 1726. A spasmodic attempt to revive the exclusive system in 1736 had no life in it. The Merchant Company complained about hawkers, peddlers, and 'English riders' in the 1750s and 1760s, but to no effect. By then very serious plans were afoot vastly to expand Edinburgh by draining the marshes and Nor Loch to the north of the Castle Rock prior to building a bridge over the resulting dry valley in order to gain access to the empty acres of Bearford's Parks whereon was to be erected a New Town. *Proposals for carrying on certain Public Works in the City of Edinburgh* published in 1752 made it clear that the objective was the expansion and embellishment of Edinburgh as a capital city for Scotland capable of imparting to the Scottish economy at least some of the stimulus which it was widely realized the English economy derived from the pre-eminent vitality of London. Behind the drive to create a new Edinburgh stood the impressive figure of George Drummond, Presbyterian, Whig, and indeed for many years the leading agent of the Hanoverian régime in Edinburgh. He was Lord Provost in 1725–7, 1746–8, 1750–2, 1754–6, 1758–60, and 1762–4. In 1746 he succeeded the unfortunate Alexander Stewart, Lord Provost at the time of the seizure of the city by the Jacobite army of Prince Charles Edward. Resistance would simply have exposed the inhabitants to the dangers of storm and sack, but an angry London government prosecuted Stewart for complicity in the bloodless Jacobite occupation. Honourably acquitted in 1747 after a long trial, Stewart abandoned Edinburgh politics for banking in London. Drummond replaced him in 1746 after a poll of all burgesses, which was rendered necessary by the lapse of elections in 1745, and which showed that Drummond had support outside the magic circle of the town councillors.

Even so, it must be said that the only significant new scheme completed by 1760 was the Royal Exchange which formed a neo-classical square fronting on to the High Street of the old Edinburgh. Without support from the Bank of Scotland and the Royal Bank it would have been neither started nor finished. This was not inappropriate for the economic confidence underlying the attitudes of men like George Drummond was largely the product of successful mercantile capitalism and of the financial institutions created to sustain the operations of mercantile capital. Those financial institutions were in fact precociously developed in Scotland, given the relatively undeveloped nature of its economy as late as 1750. The Bank of Scotland, one of the earliest of European public banks, was established in 1695. It pursued in solitary state a profitable but hyper-conservative policy of lending almost exclusively on the security of heritable real-estate until in 1727 its chartered monopoly was breached by the establishment of the Royal Bank of Scotland. In 1727 it was alleged, with some truth but more exaggeration, that the Bank of Scotland was tainted with Jacobitism. The Royal Bank was certainly furiously Whig with close connections with the arch-Whig Clan Campbell and its High Chief, Argyll. It also pursued a much more flexible lending policy than the Bank of Scotland. By 1728 it was offering a cash credit facility or overdraft to any businessmen who could produce two adequate cautioners or guarantors. It had much closer London links than its older rival. Unlike the Bank of Scotland the Royal Bank rapidly established important connections with the rising tobacco trade of the west coast of Scotland, allowing importers significant cash credits and in exchange securing access to much of the liquidity, such as short-dated bills payable on London, which the tobacco merchants brought into Scotland. By 1741 Glasgow was importing 8 million pounds of tobacco. In 1743 the figure was 10 million, and by 1745 it was 13 million.

The Bank of Scotland was obliged to follow its rival into the field of cash credits, though its first venture into branch banking was brief. The so-called 'dual system' between 1727 and 1745 was therefore stimulating but limited in scope. It left the field open for other institutions, and above all for private banks. The latter developed fast. Between 1745 and 1772 Scotland evolved a complex, advanced 'multiple system' of banks. A new public bank emerged in an unusual way with the establishment in 1746 of the British Linen Company. Here the moving spirit was Andrew Fletcher, Lord Milton, Islay's right-hand man and from 1735 to 1766 a power in Scottish life. Islay himself had been first Governor of the Royal Bank. Milton co-operated with George Drummond, through whom Milton effectively controlled Edinburgh, in negotiations with the government on behalf of that bank, but Milton, through his interest in the Board of Trustees for Fisheries and Manufactures, became convinced that the linen trade was the key industry in the country and that a new institution was needed to provide working capital for that industry. Entitled both to trade and to bank the British Linen Company became increasingly a bank, though one with close links with the Royal. An attempt by the Royal and the Bank of Scotland in the early 1750s to crush the development of private banks outside Edinburgh fortunately failed in the vital case of Glasgow where the Ship Bank and the Arms Bank were sustained by the tobacco trade. By 1761 a third Glasgow bank, the Thistle Bank, was set up. There were 15 or so private banks in Edinburgh, all deferential to the public banks. An Aberdeen private bank had been crushed by the two old public banks in the 1750s, but by 1761 it was clear that future private banking developments outside Edinburgh could not be stopped. Already the banking system had largely overcome the old Scottish problem of a chronic shortage of metallic coin, especially gold and silver. Business in Scotland by the 1760s was conducted mainly in banknotes or commercial bills.

Several major trades were booming after 1750. The demographic surge in both Scotland and England helped to lift their economies out of a doldrums which had lasted for 30 or 40 years. Grain prices, low for nearly 40 years after the Union, at last became buoyant. It is no accident that the first private banker to become Lord Provost of Edinburgh was John Coutts in 1742–4. His family were originally grain merchants in Montrose. John Coutts appears to have abandoned their hereditary Jacobitism for tepid Whiggery. His own early grain-dealing clearly did him no harm socially. It was quite a good way of becoming acquainted with at least the agents of those 'People in Power' who, as the Bank of Scotland and the Royal knew to their cost, believed that 'the greater the Number of Banks so much the better for the country'. Easily available credit was most important to two other growing trades with an important bearing on rent rolls. One was linen. The export of Scottish yarns was sufficiently great for Scots weavers to complain that it raised the cost of yarn to them, but in 1748 the Board of Trustees in their annual 'State of the Linen Manufacture' noted the 'remarkable change' which had occurred in the shape of a great expansion in the export of coarse linen cloth, an expansion which it ascribed partly to the bounty on the export of coarse linens and partly to the establishment of the British Linen Company. By 1761 no less than 11,995,494 yards of linen were stamped for sale in Scotland, a quantity valued at £516,354. Black cattle flowed southwards either into expanding Scottish urban markets or, to a vastly greater extent, towards England. No two observers agreed as to the precise scale of the trade. All agreed that it grew steadily, funded mainly by cash credit from banks. When James Boswell and Dr Samuel Johnson reached the Isle of Skye in 1773, searching for an experience of a primitive patri-archal society, they found that the lairds' rents were mostly paid in bills which the tenants had acquired from drovers who moved into the Highlands armed with credit and emerged with cattle which they drove south. Falkirk Tryst was replacing Crieff as the great internal cattle market, so the Edinburgh banks were represented there after 1750 at all major cattle sales.

Dizzier still, though geographically exceptionally concentrated, was the rise of the Glasgow tobacco trade. Strictly speaking it was an Atlantic trade which involved trading in the cotton, coffee, sugar, and rum of the British West Indian islands, and in cargoes of goods out-wards from Scotland, as well as in the importation and re-export of the tobacco of the southern colonies of British North America. As such, it was well established, on a limited scale, in Restoration Scotland between 1660 and 1685. It was illegal under English law, but not under Scots law, and the English government was no more capable than any other early modern government of efficiently policing distant colonies. Expansion after 1707 was limited mainly by the inadequate financial resources of Glasgow merchants. However, the legal requirement under the English Old Colonial System that tobacco be first landed at a port in the mother-country before re-export to third countries placed the Clyde in a strong position as it was the handiest safe haven for ships traversing the North Atlantic from the tobacco colonies. Due to the unimproved nature of the upper reaches of the Clyde the minority of Glasgow merchants involved in the transatlantic trade were obliged to ship their goods through Greenock or Port Glasgow. However, the trade was a capital-hungry one, and the capitalists were Glasgow men. By concentrating their trade in relatively few hands these capitalists facilitated huge bulk deals with customers such as the 'Farmers General of the French Customs' who usually accounted for a third or so of tobacco re-exports from the Clyde in the 'Golden Age' of the Scottish tobacco trade between 1740 and 1775.

By the 1750s and 1760s Glasgow tobacco merchants were normally organized in groups incorporated in formal partnerships. They were dominated by a limited number of families, some of which like the Ritchies, Bogles, Dunlops, and Murdochs could trace their connections with the tobacco trade back before 1700. On the other hand, there were, in a trade which was always unpredictable, plenty of new dynasties like the Glassfords, the Speirs, and the Cunninghames. None of the latter three was even native to Glasgow. Nevertheless the tobacco merchants rapidly evolved into a closely-knit kinship group. Intermarriage was common and often crucially important due to the value of dowries. Alexander Speirs was only a man of modest fortune before marriage into the Buchanan dynasty of tobacco traders accelerated him to the higher reaches of the league. These merchants were often landed before 1750 and they all bought land or indeed more land as an investment and tangible sign of success as soon as they were in a position to do so. They did not retire from business. On the contrary, when they acquired land their landed respectability enabled them to tap by way of loans the accumulated savings of the upper and middling orders of society in the west of Scotland, savings which, due to lack of alternative outlets, were more than adequate for even the needs of transatlantic trade. Manufactures were secondary in significance. Indeed they were often financed by tobacco money and geared to the need for outward cargoes for the colonies.

Commercial development in this period therefore reinforced rather than undermined the hegemony of existing local élites. Central government in the eighteenth century was largely confined to war, diplomacy, and the raising of revenues. To the local élites local government was far more significant in their daily lives, and in this sphere the ascendancy of the local oligarchs was absolute. All sheriffdoms were Crown appointments after 1747, but the Sheriff-depute appointed in each Scottish county to exercise shrieval functions was invariably a leading member of the aristocracy. He was the principal executive officer of the Crown in the localities and usually appointed a Sheriff-substite or substitutes to help him with his work. Usually these were young Edinburgh advocates. Most future Lords of Session had served as a Sheriff-substitute. After the Sheriff-depute in importance came county Commissioners of Supply responsible for raising the land tax, roads and bridges, catching and holding criminals, and keeping the parishes up to the mark in education provision. Chosen from the ranks of Justices of the Peace, the Commissioners led the way after about 1756 in the development of county meetings as means of articulating upper-class opinion on political issues. Justices of the Peace never assumed the importance they had in contemporary England. The Commission of the Peace simply reflected the composition of existing county and burghal élites, to the point where known Jacobites managed to stay entrenched on many Commissions until just after the '45. The Sheriff Court left JPs only a minimal jurisdiction over oaths, licenses, and weights and measures, while the parish handled the problem of the poor, subject to the financial control of its landowners as heritors. A wise ruler like Islay used his powers of patronage, which included thousands of appointments from those under Commissions of the Peace to those under the Board of Customs, to reinforce local ruling groups, if they were generally amenable to the régime, rather than to challenge them.

This rock-like stability in both the social and the political structure of an increasingly prosperous land was the essential precondition for the continued flowering of Scottish intellectual and artistic life, and this for two reasons. Firstly, prosperity generated the revenues required for the enlightened patronage of the arts and learning. Secondly, the governing classes were not tempted by fear of social upheavel, into a blind opposition to any form of critical thought. This latter point is peculiarly important in view of the paradox that from 1739 or 1740 that intellectual phenomenon we call the Scottish Enlightenment of the eighteenth century had, ticking away underneath it, a time bomb capable of destroying some of its basic assumptions. This was David Hume's *A Treatise of Human Nature*. Reason lay at the heart of the Scottish Enlightenment, expressed as much in the balance and neo-classical form of its visual arts as in its reasonable religion, commonsense philosophy, and belles-lettres. Hume argued that the traditional analysis of cause and effect was indefensible. Causation, the basis of logical argument in all fields of human knowledge other than logic and mathematics, was, according to Hume, only 'a lively idea related to or associated with a present impression'. Certainty was therefore unattainable, as much in moral as in physical matters. Hume himself recorded that the *Treatise* 'fell dead-born from the press', and an attempt by the author to stir interest in it by publishing an *Abstract* of its main argument was even more unsuccessful.

Nevertheless, the Scottish Age of Reason could not ignore the fact that it had spawned a systematic anti-rationalist. Hume's *Treatise* was alive enough by 1745 to lose him the succession to the chair of Moral Philosophy in the University of Edinburgh. Hume was an agnostic to whom the dogmatic atheism of the contemporary French philosophers whom he knew so well was deeply distasteful, but he was palpably unfit to occupy a chair whose duties specifically implied a commitment to the validity of the Christian Revelation. His defeat was tied up with a struggle for power on the town council and William Cleghorn, the eventually successful candidate, was the candidate of the Tweeddale faction on the council. What is impressive is that the heretical Hume was seriously considered and indeed supported by several prominent Moderate clergymen such as Robert Wallace, Minister of the New North Church, Chaplain to the King, and Moderator of the General Assembly in 1743. Hume was an intellectual radical but not a social or political radical. Scion of a minor Berwickshire laird's family, he early sought a tutorship in a noble household and achieved it in 1745 with his attachment to the Marquess of Annandale, who most unfortunately turned out to be mentally deranged. Though well aware of the element of humbug in the Whig ideology of the Glorious Revolution, Hume was a firm anti-Jacobite and supporter of the established order as his *Three Essays, Moral and Political* published in 1748 made clear. After acting as secretary to his distant kinsman General St Clair on military and diplomatic missions in Europe Hume settled in Edinburgh in 1751, and in 1752, the year when he published his *Political Discourses*, he became Keeper of the Advocates Library, a job which underlined his acceptability to the Edinburgh social establishment.

Hume's predecessor as Keeper had been Thomas Ruddiman, a living demonstration that the intellectual roots of the Scottish Enlightenment ran back into the fertile soil of Restoration Scotland. Ruddiman was a conservative in all things, a great Latinist even by the exalted standards of Scottish Latinity, a printer with a patriotic anti-Union spirit, and a sentimental Jacobite. By the time of his death in 1752 intellectual fashion had turned strongly against men like

Ruddiman, or the much younger Jacobite poet William Hamilton of Bangor, who fought in the '45 and wrote verse which in some ways prefigured the literary triumphs of Scotsmen in the wider English-speaking world of the later eighteenth century. In culture as in politics the victory of Whiggism was inevitable. Philosophically, the foundations of that triumph had been laid by Francis Hutcheson, Professor of Moral Philosophy in the University of Glasgow from 1730 and one of the long succession of Ulster Presbyterians whose talents enhanced the quality of eighteenth — and nineteenth-century Scottish academic life. He taught and deeply influenced Adam Smith, a future holder of his own chair and the father of modern economics. Hutcheson's moral philosophy, summed up in two posthumous works, a *Short Introduction to Moral Philosophy* (1747) and a *System of Moral Philosophy* (1755), was set in a Christian context but assumed that man is endowed with an innate moral sense capable of indicating what is right, and that on the whole the sum of moral actions would tend to the progress of the welfare and happiness of mankind. A sense of original sin was not a prominent feature of Hutcheson's thought, but a self-consciously Whig approach to society and politics was. He was an upholder of a constitution formed of checks and balances and with a close relationship between the possession of property and the exercise of power. So far from hankering after royal absolutism was he that he regarded people in general as 'too tame and tractable'. David Hume was more of an establishment Whig. Though his secular vision of politics accepted the need to limit the power of arbitrary government, it also totally rejected the sovereignty of the people. Hume feared anarchy more than tyranny. Protection of property was for him the prime purpose of government. The *status quo* suited him very well.

It was, however, less by its technical moral and political philosophy, which comparatively few understood, than by its contribution to general literature that the Scottish Enlightenment impinged on the consciousness of the polite world in the 1750s. Hume's contemporary reputation rested on the six volumes of his *History of England* which appeared between 1754 and 1762. Significantly, in 1760 the Town Council of Edinburgh established a new chair of Rhetoric to which they appointed the Reverend Hugh Blair, a leading Moderate clergyman of the city. By 1762 a royal commission had turned Blair into a Regius Professor of Rhetoric and Belles Lettres in the University of Edinburgh. Already another Moderate clergyman, John Home, incumbent of Athelstaneford in East Lothian, had written a play, *Douglas*, successfully produced on the Edinburgh stage in 1756, and later in London, with acclaim well beyond its minimal merits. There had been uproar in the General Assembly of the Kirk on a scale greater than that accompanying an abortive attempt in the previous year, 1755, to arraign David Hume and the judge Henry Home Lord Kames, another prominent writer with discursive but vaguely disturbing interests, on charges of heresy. In 1757 the General Assembly passed an act forbidding clergy to attend the theatre. It proved unenforceable. John Home resigned his charge, went to London, and became personal secretary to Lord Bute and tutor to the Prince of Wales, soon to be George III.

The 'literati' were too well connected with decision-taking members of the political class to be crushed. In Edinburgh lairds, judges, politicians, artists, and writers mingled in such convivial clubs as the Select Society which David Hume helped to establish in 1752. William Cullen, Professor of Medicine at Glasgow and later holder of chairs of Chemistry and Medicine in Edinburgh was a fine physician, but his early career owed much to the patronage of the 'Argyll Interest'. Lord Kames had introduced him to the Earl of Islay in 1749. Islay, that canny Scots lawyer who dressed no better after he became Duke of Argyll than he had before, presided over a process whereby the leaders of Scottish intellectual life became spokesmen, overtly or tacitly, for that very conservative court or establishment Whiggism which was the prevailing ideology of Hanoverian Britain. Islay merited at least some of the respect in which even David Hume privately held him. This machine politician had created a system which gratified, at the price of continual shuffling, juggling, and adjustment, three major interests at the same time. Islay's interest lay in exploiting his grip on the Scottish constituencies to enhance his own social and political weight in London. The British government was interested in disposing of as large a bloc as possible of obedient North British votes at Westminster, preferably without having to pay the price of attending to specifically Scottish political problems. The Scottish ruling classes were obsessed with, rather than merely interested in, access to government patronage. When Ramsay of Ochtertyre described Islay as 'the most enlightened patriot Scotland has produced', he is best understood as saying that Islay secured more jobs for boys who mattered than anyone before him.

3
Growth, Enlightenment, and Integration 1760 – 1775

In its classical form, Islay's political system predeceased him, partly as a result of changes of personnel and power patterns in the highest circles of British politics and partly because of a more deep-seated long-term change in the general political atmosphere. The death of George II in the autumn of 1760 and the accession of the 22-year-old George III was bound to be followed by changes, for nobody questioned the right of a new king to appoint new ministers to conduct his business, if he so wished, though practical considerations usually ensured that the exercise resembled nothing so much as a shuffling of a well-worn pack of cards. What made the accession of the new sovereign so significant to the uncrowned king of Scotland was the fact that George III was very much under the influence of Islay's own nephew, John Stuart, 3rd Earl of Bute. Bute was an early example of the Anglo-Scot. Educated at Eton and in the Netherlands at Leiden, he did not actually live in Scotland before 1739 and he left the country again in 1745 for good. As a man he was proud, haughty in manner, and lacking in commonsense, but it mattered not, for by 1755 he had become confidential adviser to the widowed Princess of Wales as well as the beloved mentor of her son, the future George III. Born in 1713, Bute was 25 years older than the prince, to whom he undoubtedly became a sort of father figure. Bute was not at all wealthy but his association with the future ruler made him so obviously a coming man that by 1756 a small group of Scots MPs, led by Gilbert Elliot and by Bute's own brother James Stuart Mackenzie, had separated themselves out from the phalanx of Argathelians and were looking quite openly to Bute for leadership.

Seventeen fifty-six was also the year in which Britain became involved in the Seven Years War. This great struggle was, from the British point of view, a world war against the power of Bourbon France which was reinforced at a later stage by the power of Spain, on whose throne sat another branch of the Bourbon family. Under the charismatic leadership of Pitt the Elder, ably supported by the political talents of that arch-manager and compulsive fusspot the Duke of Newcastle, Hanoverian Britain recovered from early reverses to scale unprecedented heights of conquest and glory. Despite the fact that the new king of Britain and his principal adviser Lord Bute were anxious to bring about an early and moderate peace settlement, the Peace of Paris of 1763, which brought hostilities to an end, left Great Britain the dominant European power in both North America and in the sub-continent of India. From an early stage in the war it became clear that a new generation of articulate Scots had emerged which looked forward to a degree of integration with and participation in the British state well beyond that taken for granted by their elderly political leaders. Not that Islay himself was at all unenthusiastic about the war. On the contrary, his rock-like support for measures needed to raise more and more troops endeared him, for the first time, to the teutonic martinet who sat on the throne as George II. This new warmth of regard from the king even gave Islay the edge in his endless guerrilla warfare with the jealous and suspicious Duke of Newcastle who would dearly have liked to take Scottish patronage into his own hands and to reduce Islay's satrapacy to the status of one of the larger English counties like Yorkshire.

By 1760 Islay's position was so strong that he could use the support of the sovereign to make Newcastle swallow the to him unpalatable proposal of the Duke of Atholl that Atholl's nephew John Murray, son of the Jacobite general Lord George Murray, be allowed to stand for Perthshire at the next general election. Bute, who had started an extremely complex quarrel with Islay in 1759 over the representation of the Ayr district of burghs at the impending election, seemed poised for defeat when death handed him victory by striking down George II. Yet Bute undoubtedly represented more than the result of a toss of the dice of mortality. There had been widespread resentment in Scotland in 1757 when the Militia Act passed in that year specifically excluded Scotland on account of English distrust of the nation which had spawned the '45. One of the two most important Edinburgh social clubs in the late eighteenth century, the Poker Club, was so-named to commemorate the considerable agitation in Scotland over the need for a national militia, as much to underline the integration of Scotland into Great Britain as to defend the United Kingdom against its foes. The title of the club, which lasted from 1762 to 1784, was suggested by Adam Ferguson, one of the most interesting of the intellectuals of the great age of the Scottish Enlightenment. It referred to the need to 'poke-up' Scottish sentiment into a blaze on this issue. Ferguson was a Gael and a son of the manse from the parish of Logierait in Perthshire who had served as a chaplain in the Black Watch for 10 years, seeing active service on such bloody Flanders battlefields as Fontenoy. Chagrin at the failure of the Duke of Atholl to nominate him to a parish drove him out of the clerical profession and to Edinburgh, where in the Select Society and elsewhere he rapidly became a prominent figure in the social life of the more intellectual circles in the city. An appropriate chair not being available, he was in 1759 jobbed into the chair of Natural Philosophy (i.e. physics) in the University of E linburgh. To his friends such as David Hume and Adam Smith his known ignorance of the subject when appointed was a topic for amusement. Only in 1764 did he secure the infinitely more appropriate chair of Moral Philosophy. In the Poker Club he rubbed shoulders not only with fellow authors like Adam Smith and David Hume (whom he had succeeded as Keeper of the Advocates' Library in 1757), but also Moderate divines like 'Jupiter' Carlyle and Principal Robertson, as well as lawyers like Henry Dundas and peers such as the Earl of Haddington and the Duke of Buccleuch.

Islay had seen no point in becoming excited about Scotland's exclusion from the Militia Act. He pointed out that there was nothing to stop a Scots nobleman from taking advantage of still valid legislation of the seventeenth-century Scots Parliament to raise a fencible regiment in his own county, and this both he and the Earl of Sutherland did, as Lords Lieutenant of their respective counties. However Islay was nothing if not a realist and if the arrival of Bute in power was bound to restrict his previous freedom of action, his ability to accept this fact gracefully enabled him to escape total eclipse. Precisely because Bute, like George III, gloried in the name of Briton, he did not want to become immersed in the provincial complexities of Scottish politics. When it became clear that the former manager of Scotland was prepared to accept a more subordinate rôle, his expertise became too valuable to loose. Islay was reappointed Keeper of the Great Seal in Scotland as a sign that he was still in favour. The Ayr burghs quarrel was patched up by a compromise. Part of the problem had always been that Bute virtually owned one of the group, Rothesay, while Campbeltown and Inverary were equally subject to his uncle, and Ayr and Irvine, the remaining members of the group, belonged to neither party. Indeed Ayr town council became heartily sick of the antics of the rival noble lords and made them squirm at the end by being thoroughly obstructive towards the delicate process of setting up a satisfactory compromise. Nevertheless in the 1761 general election Islay, back in the subordinate rôle he had previously acted out under Walpole in the early 1740s, still had the details of Scottish politics in his hands to the point where he had the pleasure of ramming the odd unpalatable candidate down Newcastle's throat. An example was Lord Lovat's son Simon Fraser who had compensated for his father's well-merited execution for high treason by raising a regiment to fight for the house of Hanover from western Europe to the Plains of Abraham in Canada. Newcastle still found it difficult to forgive Fraser for his own youthful participation in the '45.

When Islay unexpectedly died in 1761, Bute had no desire to don his mantle. Rather did he try to find a replacement in the shape of his own brother James Stuart Mackenzie, who took his name from an estate he had inherited. Married to a daughter of the second Duke of Argyll and a former British envoy at Turin, he was as unacceptable as any other ex-Argathelian to English politicians like the Duke of Newcastle or the very influential Lord Chancellor Hardwicke. On an articulate plane Newcastle and Hardwicke denounced the Argyll interest and its heirs such as Bute and Stuart Mackenzie as a 'Highland' interest 'soft on Jacobitism', and argued that to counter this it was essential to support 'Lowland' influences and what was left of the old Squadrone Party. In reality the objection was to the placing of a ring fence round the daily workings of Scottish politics and the nomination of a specific Scottish manager to attend to what went on within it. Against this muttering in high circles must be set the plain fact that the Bute era of integration with general British affairs with a much reduced but still significant measure of autonomy in the management of Scottish politics does seem to have met the wishes of the more pushing Scots of the younger generation. Indeed Bute's dominant position in government must have struck many of them as too good to be true, which it certainly was.

Patronage by the powerful in London, the metropolitan centre of Hanoverian Britain, was the likeliest key to rapid advancement for an ambitious Scot in the decades before the tempo of industrialization in Scotland itself became so hectic as to offer an alternative series of routes for an assault on Olympus. Earlier in the eighteenth century individual Scots had managed to carve brilliant London careers for themselves, though they often had difficulty, however outstanding their talents, in maintaining a stable patronage base. The mathematician James Stirling (a cadet of the Stirlings of Garden), for example, was fatally hampered by his family's Jacobitism and by his own passionate High Tory principles when it came to capitalizing on the remarkable reputation he built up while yet an undergraduate at Oxford. Despite the friendship of Newton, he had to retire abroad whence he returned to become a leading light in the 1730s both at the Royal Society and in the circle of intellectuals around the fallen angel of Tory politics, Viscount Bolingbroke. However, in 1735 he returned to Scotland as manager of the Leadhill Mines. He corresponded with mathematicians of European repute, such as the Swiss Euler but in 1754 he resigned his membership of the Royal Society. He died in 1770 at the age of 78 after an outstandingly successful managerial career.

James Gibb or Gibbs, the Aberdonian architect who came from a Roman Catholic background and was trained in Rome under Carlo Fontana, the leading architect of Pope Clement XI (1700–21), was greatly helped when he returned to London in 1709 by the patronage of the Earl of Mar and later by the support of Robert Harley first Earl of Oxford. Both men were in total political eclipse by 1716 but Gibbs was fortunate in that his career had already taken off by then and in any case he continued to have the private patronage of the still wealthy Harley family. He died in 1754 after over a decade of retirement in London leaving behind writings and a remarkable range of buildings from the royal parish church of St Martin-in-the-Fields to the Senate House at Cambridge and the Radcliffe Library at Oxford. His late baroque style, influenced by the fashionable, lighter palladian or neo-classical school of eighteenth-century England had an enduring influence over his successors but by the early 1750s the man himself was an anachronism, a survival from the brief age of Tory ascendancy under Queen Anne. Even a solidly conformist Scots literary adventurer like the poet James Thomson could have problems connected with the rise and fall of his patrons. Thomson, an ex divinity student who went to London to seek his fortune in 1725 and against the odds succeeded in becoming a successful poet with his series of poems known as 'The Seasons', was patronized by Whig politicians such as Lord Chancellor Talbot and George Lyttleton. Lyttleton was a member of the group of men around Frederick Louis, Prince of Wales, and when he and the prince quarrelled Thomson's grip on a political pension became insecure. It was in fact withdrawn in 1748, the year of his death.

Such vicissitudes of fortune are no doubt rather typical of most patronage systems and it is a nice question whether the accession of Bute to power marked any fundamental shift in the scale on which pensions, places, contracts, and favours flowed towards Scotsmen, as distinct from Englishmen or Irishmen. However, the important point is not reality but contemporary perceptions of the situation. Scotsmen on the make were undoubtedly buoyed by the thought that a fellow

Scot stood near the pinnacle of the political system. The early life of the architect Robert Adam is illuminating on this, and other aspects of the relationship between art and patronage in Britain in the 1750s and 1760s, the more so as he returned to London from his 'Grand Tour' of the Continent full of hopes as to what Bute himself might do for his career.

Robert Adam was the son of William Adam, the outstanding Scottish architect of the first half of the eighteenth century. Though he was as much a building contractor as what the twentieth century would call an architect, William Adam was intellectually distinguished as well as financially successful. His business successes enabled him to turn himself into a laird in Kinross-shire by the 1730s. His distinction as an architect was embodied in his buildings rather than in the collection of designs of public buildings and country houses entitled *Vitruvius Scotticus* which he drew and had engraved for publication. In his civic buildings or his work on country houses such as Hopetoun House near Edinburgh, Duff House near Banff, or Dun House near Montrose, the elder Adam showed a robustly masculine style, neo-classical in vocabulary but with a dramatic swagger consciously borrowed from the theatrical baroque tradition as mediated through the English architect Vanbrugh. The consumingly ambitious Robert Adam had been working with his father for some years when in 1754 he committed a substantial part of the family wealth to funding an indefinitely prolonged Grand Tour of Europe for himself. The decision combined enthusiasm with the coldest of calculation. Snobbery was the bridge across which Robert Adam meant to cross from contracts on Highland forts for the Board of Ordnance and commissions to build or alter houses for Scottish lairds to the vastly more lucrative and prestigious metropolitan world of the British ruling class.

Robert Adam went on the Grand Tour as the companion of the Honourable Charles Hope, the younger brother of the Earl of Hopetoun. By this time it was very normal for Scottish aristocrats to participate in the extraordinary and expensive finishing school of the Grand Tour of Europe, devised originally for the scions of the English aristocracy. Variety was characteristic of the exercise but the itinerary of Robert Adam and Charles Hope gives a good idea of the elements which went into the Tour. From London they crossed the Channel to Calais, and after an excursion into the southern Netherlands they worked their way down from Paris to Marseilles and Nice whence they took ship for Genoa. Rome was the supreme treasure house of the artistic masterpieces on which the noble tourist was expected to form his taste, though there were usually plenty of Scots to be found enjoying the sights of the larger and livelier city of Naples further south. So numerous and well-organized was the Scottish element in upper-class tourism in Italy that in 1784 Mrs Thrale Piozzi could refer to them as 'the national Phalanx'.

Partly, this Caledonian phalanx was composed of men resident in Italy with a Jacobite background or ancestry. James Byres, a principal of the very Scottish trading house of Byres and Moir, which was one of the biggest firms dealing in antiquities and art objects in Rome, was an example of a man with a strongly Jacobite family, but no active Jacobite record. Others like Andrew Lumsden, guide and contact-man extraordinary, were deeply implicated with the exiled court. Lumsden had fought in the '45 and in 1762 succeeded James Edgar as secretary to James, the Old Pretender. However, Lumsden had no illusions by the 1760s about the viability of the cause he served. He avoided politics and was happy to oblige committed Hanoverians. Technically, the Abbé Peter Grant, a Gaelic-speaking native of Glenlivet, was primarily employed as Scots Agent in Rome, a post to which he was appointed in 1737. In practice his bishop was correct in suspecting that much of the time which Grant should have devoted to his agency for the proscribed Roman Catholic Church in Scotland was spent obliging well-off tourists in a fashion more shaped by national than by religious loyalties. Wholly a-political appear to have been the motives which led Gavin Hamilton, a student at Glasgow University, to settle in later life in Rome as an archaeologist, art-dealer, friend of artists, painter of historical themes, and theorist of the neo-classical style which he himself practised.

Neo-classicism was a most important vehicle for the talents of Scottish architects and artists. The interpretation and glorification of the heritage of ancient Greece and Rome came naturally to sophisticated Scots reared in a country where classical culture was deeply entrenched in the national consciousness. The great traditions of Scottish Latin scholarship from George Buchanan to Thomas Ruddiman still waxed potent. Indeed they were given fresh vigour and much needed lightness of touch by a cult of Greek sculpture and letters. Alexander Boswell, Lord Auchinleck, the distinguished judge and much-tried father of the diarist James Boswell, is a good illustration of this. He built for himself at his Ayrshire seat Auchinleck House, a gem of neo-classical taste completed in 1762. Speaking broad Scots from the bench of the Court of Session, he was also an accomplished master of both the classical tongues with a particular fondness for the studied felicities of Horace among Roman poets and for the elegant trifles of Anacreon among the Greeks. That his poker-faced brand of humour and ponderously bleak style as a father both proved more than his unstable son and heir could stomach was a personal tragedy.

Other Scots managed to express more consistently the lightness and elegance which it was fashionable to admire in the heritage of the ancients. A famous example is furnished by the brothers Robert and Andrew Foulis, printers in Glasgow where Robert was appointed printer to the university in 1743. With the aid of local professors they produced editions of the Latin and Greek classics notable for accuracy and scholarship. Men applied the adjective 'immaculate' to their Horace, but the typography and book production of their best work was as stylish as the scholarship it presented. In 1753−4 the brothers founded an Academy of Arts which gave instruction in drawing, painting, engraving, and sculpture. Though this academy had financial troubles and closed after the death of Andrew Foulis in 1775, it would be wrong to conclude that enthusiasm for the artistic expression of the classical tradition was not widespread in Scotland outside Edinburgh. A generation later one can find in the small county burgh of Fife, Cupar, something not wholly disimilar to the Foulis Press. This was the Tullis Press whose proprietor Robert Tullis was Printer to the University of St Andrews. He was a bookseller and paper-maker as well as a printer, and from about 1807 he was producing, in association with St Andrews professors, editions of the classics in the 'immaculate' tradition.

It was vitally important for the careers of many ambitious Scots in the eighteenth century that various forms of classicism constituted an international cultural vocabulary immediately accessible to, and therefore saleable to the ruling classes of what contemporaries called the polite nations. To describe this cultural community simply as 'European' is both glib and myopic. For all the cultivation of Greek learning by the eighteenth century, Ancient Rome was the rock on which its various forms of classicism ultimately stood and the heritage of Ancient Rome had been handed down to even the most secular-minded of eighteenth-century men through the influence, at once preservative and distorting, of medieval Latin Christendom. However, the states born from the matrix of Latin Christendom had by 1750 created world-systems of political power, trade, and culture which stretched well beyond a Europe whose limits they by no means covered. There was still a great Islamic empire, that of Turkey, in the Balkans, while across the thousands of miles of the Atlantic stretched a cultural continuum, full of strains and stresses, but impressively resilient. Imperial Spain created universities in Mexico City and in Lima in Peru as early as 1551. When in 1767 the young Virginian planter and future president of the United States Thomas Jefferson determined to build himself a new mansion, which he named Monticello, he buckled down to an intensive study of the works of James Gibbs, and of the sixteenth-century Italian architect Andrea Palladio.

It is significant that the cult of Palladio, whose restrained yet light classicism was to capture completely the eighteenth-century English country house, had been launched early in that century by a young Scottish architect Colen Campbell and his patron Richard Boyle, third Earl of Burlington. The relationship between the great Scottish artistic and literary careerists of this era and the cultural traditions within which they advanced themselves was complex: they exploited those traditions while in part creating and constantly modifying them. Most of them were to the last degree self-conscious about what they were doing. Indeed, some understood the rules of the game better than their patrons.

A case in point was that eminent Moderate divine William Robertson. Bute had displayed real anxiety to act as Robertson's patron as soon as the latter made his name by publishing two quarto volumes of *A History of Scotland* in 1759. The period covered by the work was that of the reigns of Mary Queen of Scots and of King James VI until his accession to the throne of England in 1603. Robertson therefore shrewdly exploited one of the most dramatic periods in Scottish history and one with an unusually wide emotional appeal. His efforts were crowned with great success, for the book sold extremely well and was widely admired in England. When, therefore, a vacancy in the principalship of the University of Edinburgh occurred early in 1762, Robertson rapidly emerged as an overwhelming candidate backed by the Moderate party in the Kirk and by the dominant political interest of the day, managed in Scotland for Bute by the faithful Lord Milton. Indeed it would be wrong to suggest that there was any very sharp distinction between the lay and the ecclesiastical interests. The principal wheeler-dealer in the city politics of university patronage in Edinburgh, and contact-man with Milton, was John Jardine the Moderate minister of the Tron kirk, who ran Robertson's campaign with an expertise first developed when as a young man he managed the burgh of Lochmaben for Charles Erskine of Tinwald. Robertson, as the author of an enormously successful book, deserved to become Principal Robertson, to which prize was soon added the sinecure of Historiographer Royal for Scotland with a salary of £200 a year. Yet the astute divine ignored Bute's strong advice that he provide a modern introduction to the whole of Scottish history.

Robertson wanted a topic with wider appeal. He considered writing a History of England but veered away from the idea because his friend David Hume was beginning to dominate that field. Instead Robertson turned to a sweeping European theme and repeated in 1769 his previous brilliant success when he published in three volumes quarto a *History of the Reign of Charles V, with a view of the Progress of Society from the Subversion of the Roman Empire to the Commencement of the Sixteenth Century*. Robertson's third great work, possibly his greatest single achievement, was the *History of America* which he published in London in two volumes in 1777. Starting as a by-product of his interest in Charles V, this history became a great survey of Spanish American history which had no rival in the English-speaking world until the rise to fame of the blind American historian William Hickling Prescott whose histories of the conquest of Mexico and of Peru were published 60 to 70 years later. By any standards Robertson is an extremely important figure in the history of historical writing. It has been argued that he and Hume, and he far more than Hume, represent the first emergence of recognizably modern historical scholarship, combining the use of narrative form, buttressed by careful citation of authorities, with a capacity for penetrating thematic analysis of major issues. In this connection Robertson's remarkable survey of European civilization prior to the age of Charles V is justly famous. Even more impressive is the way he sought out and mastered a great mass of material on Latin America and then summed it all up in an astonishing analytical survey of Spanish colonial policy from the sixteenth century to the Bourbon reforms of his own day. In the eighteenth century only the Englishman Edward Gibbon, with his immortal *Decline And Fall Of The Roman Empire*, can be said to have combined erudition and analysis in a fashion comparable to Robertson with a prose style ineffably superior, and he was deeply influenced, as he admitted in his *Autobiography*, by 'the philosophic Hume' as well as by 'the vigorous sense' of Robertson.

Robertson's works were translated into all major western European languages. He was known literally from Philadelphia to St Petersburg, where the Empress Catherine the Great, as her Scottish physician Dr Rogerson told Robertson, read and admired the *History of the Reign of Charles V*. Such fame no doubt fuelled the self-satisfaction and aimiable, if tedious, pomposity which characterized the Reverend Principal in his latter days, but fame alone was not the prize. Starving in a garret for the sake of Art or Truth was not a lifestyle admired by the Scottish intellectuals of this period. They all tried to make money. By his own standards Robertson made a great deal. The 'copy money' he was paid for the manuscript of *Charles V* was no less than £4,000, for its day an unheard of sum. Yet Robertson managed to have his cake as well as eat it. Latterly he eschewed the parochialism of Scottish themes, but when he went to London to find a publisher for *Charles V*, he settled so advantageously with William Strachan who had changed his name to Strahan after moving from Edinburgh to London. Strahan became King's Printer and an MP. It was a period when the distinction between printer and publisher hardly existed in its modern form. Strahan published Gibbon's *Decline and Fall*, as well as the works of the literary pontiff or mastiff of the age, Dr Samuel Johnson. He also printed and published a clutch of famous Scottish names including David Hume, Robertson himself, and in 1776 Adam Smith's *Wealth of Nations*. The Scots literati tended to operate on two different, but not contradictory levels. Their material they deliberately tried to make as universal as possible, but in the manoeuvres which presented them with the crucial opportunities to seize Fame and Fortune they took it for granted they would be supported by a phalanx of fellow-Scots.

The fact that ambitious Scots thought in this way was only too obvious to non-Scottish contemporaries and is one explanation of the strong currents of anti-Scottish feeling which were to be found in England and more especially in London during the political apogee of Lord Bute. They would never have received the encouragement they did in high places but for the bitter hostility with which Bute's administration was regarded by men such as William Pitt the Elder and his ally Richard Grenville-Temple, first Earl Temple, whom Bute had ousted from power. It was a client of Temple, John Wilkes, who raised Scotophobia to unparalleled heights in the columns of the paper which he started in 1762 and entitled derisively the *North Briton*. Exploiting anti-ministerial passions with verve, impudence, and total lack of scruple, Wilkes managed eventually to become the hero of a protracted struggle between the House of Commons and the electorate of Middlesex whose repeated endorsements of Wilkes as their MP, in the face of equally stubborn refusal by the House to admit him, rendered the life of His Majesty's Government hideous in the years 1768—70. Yet Wilkes was never a straightforward character. He had been educated at Leiden where Scotsmen, of whom there were many at that distinguished Dutch university, were his favoured companions. 'The Middlesex Patriot' himself denied that his animus against Scotsmen could be separated from the political circumstances which raised Bute to power. This particular assertion was uttered in the circle of the arch-Tory Dr Johnson, with whom Wilkes 'that blasphemer of his God and a libeller of his King' was eventually very friendly. There is no reason to doubt the truth of the statement. Scotophobia in London had a long history going back to at least the arrival of needy Scots gentlemen in the train of James VI and I in 1603, but its virulence in the 1760s was inextricably bound up with the almost hysterical hatred of Bute in opposition circles. In practice Bute was not an effective politician. His nerve was broken by a crescendo of abusive and violent opposition to the point where he resigned office in April 1763. Even then, he was repeatedly and quite unfairly denounced as the secret influence behind the throne.

It was only too true that Scottish MPs and peers, as compared with their English counterparts, showed a marked proclivity to support His Majesty's Government, provided the administration of the day had the wit and ability to meet their, relatively modest, demands. Furthermore the reign of George III did see another stage in the progressive integration of Scotsmen into the life of the English governing classes, and not just as purveyors of improving literature and fine buildings or pictures. In the diplomatic service, which was still in the eighteenth century very much subject to the royal discretion in appointments, one Scot in perhaps every 20 diplomatic posts under William and Mary eventually turned into a proportion of one in seven under George III. In between Walpole had virtually cleared Scots out of the service, but the crucial point is that they crept back in the later 1740s and were being appointed in very substantial numbers from the outbreak of the Seven Years War in 1756. This was a field reserved for the nobility and gentry, but here as elsewhere the odious Caledonians were clearly deeply entrenched before Bute and unshaken by the fall of the man denounced, absurdly, as the 'Northern Machiavel'. In 1789 Sir Robert Murray Keith had just completed 20 years as envoy to Vienna, while Sir William Hamilton had been 25 years in the Naples embassy. Hugh Elliot, another Scot, was British ambassador at Copenhagen in 1789, one of a series of ambassadorial positions he had held for the best part of 15 years. At Constantinople Sir Robert Ainslie had represented the British Crown for nearly as long. Nor was there any slacking-off of the rate of appointment of Scots to diplomatic positions.

In Scotland itself Bute never faced any serious challenge to his ascendancy. He was lucky in the fact that for one reason or another the heads of nearly all the great magnate houses were ineffective. The Dukes of Gordon, Buccleuch, and Hamilton just happened to be minors. The Duke of Argyll, the former Major General John Campbell of Mamore who had played such a staunch and honourable rôle on the Hanoverian side during the '45, was old and by the standards of his house not very bright. The Duke of Montrose was blind and the Marquess of Tweeddale a cripple. Other Scots peers and MPs, partly because of a basic lack of interest in the details of English politics and partly because of the workings of patronage, tended to be obsequiously loyal to Bute. It was therefore natural for Bute to assume that he could dispose of the satrapacy of Scotland at will. Indeed he owed it to his political friends to make arrangements to protect them after his own retiral from power. To this end he made his brother James Stuart Mackenzie Lord Privy Seal in Scotland in 1763 and informed Baron Mure in April of that year that 'Scotch affairs will go on under the care of my brother, as they did under my late uncle'. It was an unconscious insult to the memory of the subtly intelligent Islay. Mackenzie was not nearly so strongly placed as Islay in his hey-day, and he was devoid of tact.

The ministry which took the reins from the faltering hands of the Scottish favourite rapidly came to be dominated by George Grenville, younger brother of Lord Temple. Grenville, like all his family, was pathologically pleased with himself, he was to wit 'a crashing bore with a mind like a cash-register'. Obsessively anxious to be the sole channel of royal favour, Grenville was soon at loggerheads with Mackenzie about Scottish patronage. Grenville seems at heart to have classed the Scots with the American colonists as troublemaking wasters of the public revenue. Whilst reducing the army and navy with a zeal which commended him to tax-weary back benchers, Grenville busied himself with a series of measures which laid the foundations of a serious Anglo-American political crisis. As a good House of Commons man, he did grasp the need to extend patronage to Scots MPs, but he clashed sharply with Mackenzie over the flow of jobs and favours to the Scots nobility and gentry as a whole. Unable to secure patronage, sniped at from behind by disgruntled North Britons, and locked in combat with a man as abrasively conceited as himself, Mackenzie's lot was a miserable one. By 1764 Grenville was able to dispense with Mackenzie's services. The last pale shadow of a semi-autonomous manager for Scottish politics had vanished, banished by a parsimonious windbag whom the king detested and contrived to oust from power in 1765, with a massive dose of support from his uncle the Duke of Cumberland, and the co-operation of the group known as the Rockingham Whigs. Cumberland, whose hatred of Scots waxed rather than waned in the years after his victory at Culloden, died late in 1765, but his association with the new régime was a guarantee that integration was the watchword of policy, in so far as there was any, towards Scotland.

During the next 15 or so years no ministry needed, or had time to formulate a Scottish policy. Crises came not singly but in battalions as one group after another exploited the appalling gaps between theory and practice in the British constitution, if indeed it can be held that there was such a thing, as distinct from a rather misleading mythology and a set of working arrangements. Whooping in the van of the assault came 'that Devil Wilkes'. Between 1763 and 1774 John Wilkes stimulated and used London radicalism for his own personal ends. More serious were the confrontations which developed between Westminster and the American colonies, and between Westminster and the Irish parliament in Dublin. By comparison with other peripheral provinces of the British Crown Scotland was quiet. It was therefore ignored.

The simple truth was that nearly all Scots who mattered were content, and this for a mixture of reasons within and without Scotland. Domestically the 1760s and early 1770s were an era of considerable prosperity in Scotland, and that prosperity was closely tied to the structure of the British imperial state-system, as may most conveniently be demonstrated by an examination of the way in which the 'tobacco lords' of Glasgow rose to the peak of their greatness in the first half of the 1770s. Great they certainly were for in the 1760s and 70s tobacco accounted for just under 50 per cent in value of all Scottish imports from outwith Britain and all but 2 per cent of that tobacco was imported through the ports of Greenock and Port Glasgow which were controlled financially by the rich merchants in Glasgow further up the Clyde. The cornerstone of this commercial empire was the legislation which compelled American planters to export their tobacco to a British port before it could be transferred to the European markets which were always more important than the domestic British one. However, the rise of Glasgow to eminence as one of the metropolitan centres of the Chesapeake tobacco trade was a competitive business. As the importance of Glasgow in the trade rose, so did that of other British ports decline.

Originally the south-western parts of Britain, plus London, had been heavily dominant in importing tobacco. Not only Bristol but scores of quite small harbours in counties like Cornwall and Devon ranked as significant tobacco ports. Then came a shift to north-west during which the tobacco trade of London and Bristol tended to stagnate, while that of smaller southern harbours dropped away to nothing. Liverpool and Whitehaven south of the Anglo-Scottish

Border followed the example of Glasgow and surpassed Bristol. London never lost its individual preponderance, which was based on the domestic market, but London apart the significance of British tobacco ports declined from north to south. Glasgow was Scotland as far as tobacco was concerned and in the three years from 1768 to 1770 the Scottish trade reached its greatest relative importance. In 1769, with 51.8 per cent of total British imports, the Scots tobacco trade for the first and last time exceeded that of England.

Apart from a shorter, safer Atlantic voyage from the waters of Chesapeake Bay which washes the shores of both Virginia and Maryland, Glasgow enjoyed other comparative advantages. It benefitted from the changing nature of the ultimate market. As long as the bulk of the tobacco crop of the British colonies was reshipped for sale in Amsterdam, it hardly mattered where it was landed in Britain, but when French and German buyers began to buy directly in the British market, they preferred to deal with a limited number of large ports. Much of the prosperity of Glasgow in the 1760s and 70s hinged on bulk purchases by the Farmers General of the French state tobacco monopoly. Glasgow also enjoyed the advantages of unusually well-developed banking and commercial facilities, but above all it throve on low operating costs. On the Clyde ships and labour were cheaper than elsewhere, as were refitting charges, and more profitable outward cargoes to America could be obtained. However, it was the way in which Glasgow merchants combined low shipping costs with a network of factors and stores in the colonies which seems to have been decisive.

Though their financial resources allowed the Glasgow firms to buy or hire the bigger ships which were more economical on the Atlantic run, it seems that the crucial point in the whole operation was turn-round time in the Chesapeake. A quick turn-round saved vital running costs and other charges. All the big Glasgow tobacco firms operated a store system, particularly in the inland areas beyond the falls on the rivers flowing into Chesapeake bay where tobacco cultivation was expanding in the hands of less wealthy planters. These men could exchange their staple crop for cash, or more usually for a combination of goods and money. The factor in charge of the store tried to accumulate tobacco in time to ensure a quick turn-about for his firm's ships when they arrived. Bulk sales at the other end ensured a rapid turnover which, allied to profit on goods exported, gave the Glasgow merchants a vital margin over rivals. The price for steady expansion rooted in competitive offers of credit was mounting American indebtedness. John Glassford, a leading Glasgow 'tobacco lord', estimated that in the early 1760s he and his fellows were owed some £500,000 by planters. In 1778 the estimated planter debt to Glasgow was £1,306,000.

It was no recipe for popularity with the debtors, one of whom compared 'A North Briton' to a species of obnoxious plant, quick to root and multiply, hard to eradicate, and poisonous to the ground it afflicted. The tobacco ships nevertheless carried an important outward cargo of men and ideas which deeply affected the developing societies of colonial America. Scotland, like the American colonies, was essentially a cultural province of Hanoverian England. An acute sense of inferiority pervaded the conscious cultural life of both Scots and Americans, breeding inevitably a love-hate relationship with the metropolitan power. Robert Wodrow, that conservative Presbyterian divine, complained bitterly that 'all the villainous, profane, and obscene books and plays, as printed in London, are got down by Allan Ramsay, and lent out, for an easy price, to young boys, servant women of the better sort, and gentlemen'. One hears here an extreme form of that suspicion of London which can be found in the quintessentially English novels of Jane Austen at the very end of the eighteenth century, in which evil is so often something which comes down from London into the pastoral world of a provincial middle-class family. Very eminent Scots intellectuals of the eighteenth century could be extraordinarily apologetic about their own provincial setting, at least in letters to London correspondents. David Hume said to such a one in 1756 that in exchange for valued metropolitan information he could offer only 'provincial stories which are in no way interesting'. Adam Smith in 1759 obsequiously remarked that such was the tedium of life benorth Tweed that no Scots correspondent could hope to offer entertaining matter to a sophisticated southerner. All this is of a kind with the excitement with which the young American Benjamin Franklin read an issue of the London *Spectator* and resolved to mould his own prose style on its metropolitan rhythms.

However Scots society was closer to that of the south of England in most ways than was provincial American society. Scotland had a far more elaborate and old-established educational system, for example. Its social structure, so decisively dominated by aristocracy and gentry, was similar to that of contemporary England, whereas the social structure of the American colonies was significantly different. Scotland could therefore mediate metropolitan culture to America and that in various ways. Scottish teachers found their way to America in some numbers. James Blair, an alumnus of Marischal College Aberdeen and of Edinburgh University, had in 1693 been largely instrumental in the foundation of what was later to be the College of William and Mary in Virginia. William Smith, another man with an Aberdeen background, became the first provost of the new College of Philadelphia in 1755, and played an important rôle in the transformation of American colleges from schools for clergymen into institutions more like universities. By far the greatest of these figures was the Reverend John Witherspoon of the Laigh Kirk in Paisley, who was persuaded in 1766 to go out to be sixth president of the College of New Jersey which subsequently grew to be Princeton University. Trained in the philosophical and rhetorical traditions of the University of Edinburgh in the middle of the eighteenth century, Witherspoon undoubtedly gave a sharp impetus to a process of culture-transfer which was already active. Scottish 'rhetoric and belles lettres' was a subject designed to facilitate precisely that acquisition of sophisticated, upper-class tastes and values which was the ambition of so many Americans. Equally, Scottish philosophy of the commonsense school provided a body of generally acceptable intellectual positions compatible with orthodox Christianity and particularly important as cement in the theological life of American Presbyterianism.

Yet the fact remains that the American colonies were, to those Scotsmen wielding power and influence who were not tobacco merchants, a subordinate facet of contemporary life. Nor were they at all a focus of disaffection, as New England certainly was from the very first days of its effective settlement to certain elements within English society. A small but significant segment of Scottish society was being forced to emigrate to America in the decades before 1776, yet once in America these people were remarkable for their loyalty to the British connection rather than the reverse. The key group in this movement were Highland tacksmen, those Gaelic-speaking gentlemen to whom the landlord chief was wont to lease large areas at low rents in exchange for political and military service. The Dukes of Argyll were amongst the earliest Highland magnates to adopt a policy of squeezing tacksmen out on the grounds that they were useless mouths. That view was an over-simplified one and many tacksmen survived for a long time in parts of the Highlands. Nevertheless, after 1763 tacksmen left the Highlands in substantial numbers, selling up their stock and property and taking with them large numbers of their sub-tenants and other dependents. The experience of soldiers in Highland regiments who had served in North America during the Seven Years War between 1756 and 1763 helped to give direction to what became a steady flow of emigrants. Six vessels carrying 1,200 persons from the Highlands and Islands sailed in 1770. In 1771 500 people from Islay and 370 from Skye took ship for North Carolina. A year later 200 people from Sutherland sailed for the same place. In 1773 Dr Samuel Johnson and his friend James Boswell were touring the Highlands during a summer full of the bustle and talk of emigration. Neither man approved of it. On Skye Boswell deplored the forcing out of tacksmen on the grounds that men of substance could withstand bad years better than a poor rack-rented tenantry, while on Coll Dr Johnson remarked, crushingly, that 'the Lairds, instead of improving their country, diminished their people'. Contemporaries believed that 20,000 people in all emigrated. Modern estimates are of the order of 10,000 or more, but the impressive aspect of the emigration was that it was led by men who had refused to accept a reduction in social status at home and who saw in America an opportunity to recreate a hierarchical society with themselves in an enhanced rather than a reduced position within it.

Jacobite exiles and sympathizers had emigrated to America after 1746. James Burd was one who went to Pennsylvania, and Hugh Mercer, who settled in Virginia, another. The great heroine of the aftermath of Culloden, Flora MacDonald, no Jacobite despite her key rôle in preserving the fugitive Prince Charles, emigrated to North Carolina in 1774. She moved just in time. By 1775 a worried British government facing a mounting crisis in the American colonies had banned further emigration. Flora's husband, Allan MacDonald of Kingsburgh, was a tacksman from Trotternish in the north-east of Skye. No great businessman, he was forced into emigration by a combination of bad years and a grasping landlord chief, Sir Alexander MacDonald of Sleat, whose harsh rent demands compared shamefully with the rebates which helped to preserve the tenants of other Skye chiefs such as Macleod of Macleod and Macleod of Raasay. Nevertheless, when under pressure from rebel activists to join them in 1776, MacDonald of Kingsburgh never hesitated. Like most of the Highland gentlemen newly settled in North Carolina, he became a Loyalist and turned out to fight for King George III against the Patriot or Whig rebels.

In so doing they testified to the way in which the British Hanoverian state system seemed to offer to virtually all ambitious Scots opportunities for enrichment and advancement which, however often they proved illusory in the case of specific individuals, were real enough to head off any serious discontent. That state structure was complex and unstable, spanning as it did the North Sea, the Irish Sea, and the Atlantic. It stretched literally from the Elbe to the Mississippi. However, there is no doubt that it was the opportunities, political, economic, and social, offered by its core state, the United Kingdom of Great Britain, which primarily determined the attitudes of the important Scottish élites during the 1760s and 1770s. The tobacco trade, for example, was in absolute terms important in the Scottish economy, but its impact was highly regionalized. Trades operating primarily within a British framework had a far wider impact on Scottish fortunes.

A good example is the accelerated expansion in the cattle trade after 1750. In the immediate aftermath of the '45 the breakdown of traditional authority in the Highlands led to more rather than less cattle thieving and in 1747 Graham of Gartmore estimated the direct and indirect loss to farmers and landowners in the Highlands, through stealing and blackmail, at no less than £37,000 sterling per annum. Slowly but surely small military garrisons and regular patrols of key routes and passes reduced the level of theft while the state gradually extended effective control over such strategic thieves' kitchens as the Moor of Rannoch, though it had to wait for the death of the indomitable and much-forfeited Alexander Robertson 'Elector of Struan' to do so. It was recorded in an official report that 'It was a saying of the late Strouan's [sic] that be the roads never so bad, his friends would see him and he wanted no visits from his enemys'. By 1755 a military road was being built to link Rannoch with the outside world. The progress of agriculture in those parts of the Lowlands adjacent to the Highlands, especially in connection with the new cultivation of turnips and artificial grasses, imparted an even more important stimulus to the cattle trade than the pacification of the Highlands. It is important to recognize that these new crops could be introduced without a root and branch reconstruction of traditional agricultural practices. This was just as well, for when Andrew Wight, a progressive tenant farmer from East Lothian, was charged by the Commissioners of the Forfeited Estates with the task of surveying the progress of new agricultural methods in Scotland it was said when he departed on his tour in July 1773 that 'the bulk of our farmers are creeping in the beaten path of miserable husbandry, without knowing better or even wishing to know better'.

Counties like Berwickshire, East Lothian, and Ayrshire were gratifyingly 'progressive' by Wight's standards. That is to say they had abolished the distinction between an intensively cultivated infield and a less worked and less cared for outfield. They were expanding their arable acreage and were levelling and straightening the ridges which were typical of the old agricultural methods. New crops, breeds, and tools were being adopted. Elsewhere in the Lowlands it was a different story. Lanarkshire in the 1770s was 'so conservative as to distress Wight. He took it for granted that improved methods had to be imposed from above on a mean-spirited tenantry. 'It is in vain' he lamented 'to expect improvement from them, unless some public-spirited gentlemen would take the lead'. Longer leases and new methods might then become the order of the day. Perthshire in 1772 was remarkable for the variety of its agricultural methods. Large parts were totally traditional, but around the city of Perth and on the estates of enlightened landlords like Sir William Stirling and Lord Kames, great changes had occurred. Sir William was an enterprising laird who, shortly after the '45, brought English experts and tools to Drummond Castle, which became a centre of experimentation in fallowing methods and the sowing of artificial grasses.

Lord Kames was a much more complex character whose life and career tell us much about eighteenth-century Scotland. The son of an impoverished Berwickshire laird of Jacobite and Episcopalian stock, but who had the wit to join the Hanoverian forces in the '15, Henry Home Lord Kames was born at Kames in Berwickshire, a mere three miles from the English border. Educated at home and in Edinburgh, he made such a slow start to his legal career that he at one time thought of volunteering for the famous Giant Grenadier Regiment of very tall soldiers maintained by Frederick William I King of Prussia. However, he remained in Edinburgh pushing his name into prominence as much by his varied writings as by his hard work in the courts. He compiled a collection of precedental decisions by the Court of Session. He wrote on what we would call the philosophy of law. The fullest development of his legal thought is to be found in his *Principles of Equity* (1760) which shows his view of law as being rooted in human nature, defined as much by its emotions and drives as by its rational faculties. His writings on religion were not much favoured by the Kirk, but they were in fact conservative compared with those of his friend David Hume, refusing flatly to accept Hume's attempt to reduce belief to the status of a particularly lively sense-impression. Home's elevation to the bench owed much to the patronage of the ducal house of Argyll and was achieved in 1752 despite a last-minute hitch when the Duke of Newcastle was told of the Jacobite background of the Home family and had to have the Hanoverian volunteer of the '15 paraded before him to calm his fluttering nerves.

As a Lord of Session Lord Kames went on writing to the end of a very long life on topics ranging from law to history to education. With his *Elements of Criticism* published in 1762 he became a best-selling author within the English-speaking world, rather to the surprise of

David Hume who had loyally interested his own London publisher Andrew Millar in handling the London issue of the book but who suspected that it was 'too abstruse and crabbed ever to take with the Public'. It was certainly complex, yet it was rooted in principles which proved eminently acceptable. To Kames, human nature, rightly understood, was the basis of aesthetic theory, and human knowledge to him was a product of the senses, both external and internal. The latter was defined as the inbuilt capacity to apprehend abstract qualities like virtue and beauty. Kames contended that 'we are framed by nature to relish order and connection'. Nevertheless, operating as he did within a psychological and empirical framework, Kames was bound to regard the aesthetic response as more emotional than intellectual. It was eminently susceptible of analysis and categorization which Kames supplied with all the enthusiasm, humanist learning, and social awareness of the contemporary Scots legal intellectual. For all its ultimate naïvety and lack of real philosophic depth, the *Elements* sold well in the British Isles where half a dozen editions appeared in the author's life. It became a standard philosophic text in North America until the middle of the nineteenth century. In France its reception was blighted by the wrath of Voltaire, an admirer of the historical works of Hume and Robertson, but no friend of Kames, who was rash enough to criticize one of his poems in the *Elements*. The German translation first appeared in 1766, being re-issued in 1772, 1785, 1790, and 1791. Whilst the great contemporary German writers on aesthetics like Johann Friedrich Herder and Gotthold Ephraim Lessing necessarily changed and transcended the message of Kames, they knew their *Elements* and held it in high esteem.

Intellectual and professional success on this scale inevitably gave Kames access to power and to the supreme contemporary embodiment of power — land. He was a member of the Board of Trustees for Fisheries and Manufactures in Scotland, as well as a Commissioner for the Forfeited Annexed Estates. His literary and other extra-legal activities, allied to a decided eccentricity of manner, led latterly to a measure of criticism of his performance of his judicial duties. In 1766 his wife became heiress to the estate of Blair Drummond on the upper reaches of the Forth near Stirling, where her husband arguably made his most permanent mark on the Scottish heritage by embarking on a very large-scale project to clear the vast mosses or bogs which lay 6 to 12 feet above good alluvial land for 12 miles or so up the Forth valley between Stirling and the Menteith Hills. The mosses were cut up and floated down new-cut channels into the Forth by Highland peasants induced to settle by favourable terms offered by Kames. Financially rewarding in the shape of new rents, the enterprise was later said, on dubious grounds, to have had a very bad effect on the salmon population and oyster beds of the Forth. Yet it altered irreversibly the strategic geography of Scotland by creating a broad corridor of good dry land where in previous centuries had lain only a narrow passable track totally dominated by the soaring fastness of Stirling Castle Rock.

Andrew Wight found that agricultural methods were not necessarily more affected by innovation in counties close to Lothian. Fife, just across the Firth of Forth, disappointed him by the conservatism of its farming. There was excellent reason for this state of affairs. Available drainage techniques were quite incapable of dealing with the mosses, moors, and myriad small lochs of central Fife at an economic cost. In any case such operations could hardly be justified except as the prelude to a substantial increase in arable farming, but the buoyant demand in the agricultural markets of Fife was that of English drovers for black cattle, which could be produced within the context of existing agricultural patterns. Forfarshire or Angus, on the northern shore of the Tay, was a much more progressive county, from Wight's point of view, than Fife. Partly this was because it was larger. Dundee, the largest urban unit, was cut off from the rest of the county by the Sidlaw Hills immediately behind it. In the vicinity of Dundee potato husbandry was notably advanced, while the export-oriented production of grain on the light soils of the southern slopes of the Sidlaws continued to flourish. Beyond the Sidlaws the county of Angus embraced both a great Lowland area in the shape of the Vale of Strathmore and a large Highland area linked to Strathmore by five great glens running like the thumb and fingers from a palm into the massif of the southern Grampians. Lowland Angus was famous for its oats and cattle. One of the earliest improving lairds had been the Honorable James Stuart Mackenzie, Lord Privy Seal, who had brought experts from England to instruct his tenantry, but Wight reported that zeal for improvement 'has now laid hold of almost every person who hath a bit of ground to cultivate'. From its own Highland area, and from further afield Lowland Angus received cattle for fattening on its pastures before they were sold to English drovers.

It is true that in the county of Kincardine north of Angus Wight was depressed by the fact 'that agriculture in this county makes little figure, except among a few patriotic gentlemen' such as Barclay of Ury, while in Aberdeenshire improvement as he understood it was confined to the vicinity of the city of Aberdeen and to the home farms of the landowners, but agriculture was only one facet of a general current of expansion. Textile production grew and diversified, albeit at a price. The long-established woollen industry was of purely regional importance by the 1760s. Stirling, with 160 woollen looms at work in 1771, was a centre for the production of cheap woollens such as serges, plaids, and carpetings. In Aberdeen in the same year no less than 22 business houses were engaged in exporting woollen stockings hand-knitted by the country folk of Aberdeenshire and Kincardine, though the development of a more mechanized industry on the Borders using stocking frames posed a challenge to the Aberdeen firms. Linen continued to be the outstanding growth sector of Scottish textiles. Its main centres were the counties of Forfar (or Angus), Fife, Perth, Lanark, and Renfrew. Increasingly, all but the last two of these produced more and more coarse linen, much of it for export. Lanark and Renfrew in 1768 produced together 23 per cent in volume and 40 per cent in value of Scottish linen production by specializing in fine goods such as lawns and cambrics which replaced imports in the British market after legislation of 1748 prohibited the importation of French lawns and cambrics. However, change and instability were the price of progress.

Change was most significant in the increasing use of cotton wool in the western Lowlands, where a new cotton industry, based on the Clyde's extensive trade with the West Indies, was growing out of the linen industry. Cotton wool imports rose from 105,831 lb. in 1755 to 157,127 lb. in 1767, to a peak (not surpassed until after 1785) in 1770 of 466,589 lb. Some pure cotton cloth was being made but the bulk was used in hybrids with linen warps and cotton wefts. Naturally, the credit facilities required by so buoyant a textile trade had expanded well beyond those originally supplied by the older chartered banks like the Bank of Scotland and the Royal Bank, with their conservative lending policies and suspicion of branch banking. The British Linen Company, sponsored by Lord Milton, the Argathelian branch manager for Scottish politics, and chartered in 1746, had originally intended to enter the mercantile side of the linen trade, which indeed it did, but by 1747 it had taken the first steps towards the banking business which came to engross more and more of its efforts. It began to issue notes to weavers and manufacturers. Unlike normal banknotes, these were effectively receipts for goods and originally the lowest denomination was for £5, but very quickly notes for £1 and indeed 10 shillings were issued and became acceptable as currency all over the country. Despite hostility from the older banks the British Linen Company persisted in what it found to be a very profitable line, though up to the 1770s it still specialized in cash credits to linen manufacturers, linen merchants, or to the relatively heavily capitalized bleachers, who not only bleached but also carried out other finishing operations which often required substantial machinery. Smaller local banks sprang up in various towns. On the 1 August 1763, for example, 36 persons signed a contract of co-partnery to trade as The Dundee Banking Company in a town where previously there had only been a few shopkeepers willing to give cash for bills on London or to sell bills on London to those wishing to make remittances to elsewhere. The nominal capital of the new bank was £12,600. No less than six new banks were founded in Perth in 1763. In 1766 they fused into the Perth United Company.

Such vigorous growth was bound to involve dangers and tensions. Credit extension is always hazardous if done with more panache than judgement. Large-scale manufacture oriented towards external markets is always susceptible to occasional slumps in demand. In 1769 Douglas Heron and Company, better known as the Ayr Bank, was established with the admitted aim of increasing the supply of finance for industry and agriculture. Its chairman was the wealthy Duke of Queensberry, noted agricultural improver and chairman of the newly established Forth and Clyde Navigation Company which was trying to link the Firths of Forth and Clyde by canal. With a nominal capital of £150,000, of which £96,000 was subscribed, and the backing of many wealthy landlords in the western Lowlands of Scotland, the bank embarked on an aggressive lending policy which stretched its own resources to the limit leading it into devious paths such as excessive note issue and raising credit by chains of bills on London. The bank's misfortune was that it commenced business towards the end of a long period of rising economic activity and had barely time to over-commit itself before the peak of the economic boom was past in 1771. By 1772 all the indices of production turned down. It is true that there was virtually no fall off in the linen trade, for the period 1769–72 inclusive saw over 13 million yards stamped annually in Scotland, but the total for 1773 fell sharply to 10,750,000, which suggests that very large stocks proved unsaleable in 1772. General contraction proved fatal to the Ayr Bank, which failed on 25 June 1772. By August 1775, no less than 114 out of 226 partners in the Ayr Bank were insolvent, so the repayment of creditors inevitably involved the sale of estates. It was estimated that no less than £750,000 of landed property changed hands as a result.

Scotland also saw serious food riots in 1772–3, which was hardly surprising. A survey of Britain between 1735 and 1800 revealed that roughly two-thirds of all popular disturbances seem to have been triggered off by absolute shortage or high prices of food. Since the end of the '45 Scotland had enjoyed an exceptional run of average or better than average harvests with occasional bumper years such as 1759—60 when fine harvests brought good, cheap living to working people whose diet was dominated by a few staple items. Demand for these items was, however, notably inelastic so when, as in 1772, basic food prices soared at a time when real earnings were in decline, the resulting tension could become explosive. From 1764 the weather had become more unpredictable and in 1772—3 the poor harvest in the European grain zone was so general that foreign supplies were not available to alleviate internal shortages. Rioting broke out in Dumfries in 1771. It spread to Tayside in 1772—3, mainly as a form of direct action against shipment of grain out of the region to more lucrative internal markets. The riots assumed the form of an urban — rural confrontation with mobs from the burghs of Tayside like Perth, Newburgh, Cupar, and Dundee trying to seize grain stored in the warehouses or barns of corn merchants or farmers. They were resisted by not only the gentry of the region, but also by the bulk of the country folk in the affected areas.

Episodes like the Ayr Bank failure or these grain riots neither threatened the ascendancy nor sapped the morale of the Scottish ruling élites as a whole. There was no reason why they should. The Ayr Bank collapse only struck hard at the pockets of a particular regional group. It bore none of the moral stigma that surrounded similar occurrences in the Victorian era, when the middle-class cult of respectability reigned supreme. The gambling instinct was built into the life-style of the aristocracy which gave its own tone to the rest of eighteenth-century society. Some men had played for high stakes and lost. Others would win. Whereas in England the market for estates may well have gradually narrowed as oligarchic tendencies grew stronger amongst the eighteenth-century aristocracy, in Scotland this was not so. Bankruptcies such as that of the Ayr Bank or of the York Buildings Company, which bought huge tracts of confiscated Scottish Jacobite estates after the '15 and finally lurched into admitted bankruptcy in the early 1770s, simply made available to rising mercantile interests, like the tobacco lords of Glasgow, many attractive estates. The tobacco lords, by and large, were able to restrict their purchases of land to counties adjacent to Glasgow. Around Perth it was a different story. The stability of the local aristocracy was such that merchants anxious to purchase estates had to go far afield. It was unusual in the county of Angus or Forfarshire for a merchant to become a substantial landowner, outwith the immediate neighbourhood of Dundee.

Nevertheless, it was possible, however difficult, for rising men of business to buy estates in Scotland, and that fact could but cement their loyalty to the political and social order.

Though judges waxed eloquent against 'the licentious practice of mobbing', it was not, in the form of a traditional grain riot, a threat to the established social order. Rather was it an attempt to assert a traditional moral economy which did not allow men to exploit market mechanisms to the full in pursuit of profit when such behaviour was hazarding their neighbours' lives. It did not set rich against poor, so much as town against country, and Westminster had the wit to liberalize the protective Corn Laws so as to ease tensions by facilitating the import of foreign corn in times of internal dearth or high prices. Confidence among the possessing classes in Scotland was profound and reflected in their very high propensity to invest with a view to future profit. That was one reason why they enthusiastically supported new banks with a liberal lending policy which, in a country chronically short of specie, inevitably meant a credit structure based on various forms of paper. Scotland had an endemic balance of payments problem which, when outside funds were withdrawn, could create grave internal crises as in 1762−3. The older banks had then insisted on a deflationary policy, but the bulk of those who mattered in Scotland in the 1760s and 70s seem to have been more than ready to gamble on growth despite unmistakeable evidence that they lived in an economy increasingly characterized by alternating spasms of expansion and deflation.

This aggressive optimism was not confined to the neighbourhoods of Glasgow or Edinburgh. It was diffused over the face of the Kingdom. Work on the Forth and Clyde canal linking the two most important Scottish regions began in 1768, but by 1773 the great engineer James Watt was surveying for the line of the Caledonian canal which was to run through the very heart of the Highlands to join Inverness with Fort William by continuous water communication. In 1770 Watt spent several weeks in Strathmore, the great Lowland valley between the Sidlaw Hills north of Dundee and the Highland boundary fault, surveying for a canal linking Perth with Forfar. The idea was sponsored by a leading Coupar Angus linen merchant, George Young, and by the sixth Earl of Findlater, a nobleman notable for his zeal for improvement. The plan proved abortive, yet its very existence is a measure of the vigorous ambition of Perth which had opened its new bridge across the Tay in 1771, and which was expanding in area and in its manufacturing sector, especially linen. Nor was

Perth alone among provincial burghs in its zest for improvement. Between 1758 and 1764 Aberdeen nourished in the venerable cradle of Old Aberdeen, a still distinct but unmistakeably suburban community clustered around St Machar's Cathedral north of the main city, the Gordon's Mill Farming Club. There progressive landed gentlemen such as Sir Archibald Grant of Monymusk, or Mr Silver, a successful Jamaica tea-planter who had purchased estates when he returned home, discussed recent advances in agriculture along with professional people including members of staff form the two Aberdeen universities, Marischal College and King's College in Old Aberdeen. There was also an active Aberdeen Literary and Philosophical Society in which Dr Thomas Reid, the father of the Scots 'Common Sense' school of philosophy, was prominent before his translation to Glasgow. Another member of this society Dr David Skene, a local physician, was a natural scientist of international repute, an esteemed correspondent of the great Swedish botanist Linnaeus, and a man whose interest in applied geology led him to visit coalmines both in Fife and in northern England.

Recovery from the severe but temporary cyclical depression of 1772–3 was inevitable in a buoyant society confident of its potential for growth and automatic in its deference to the prevailing social and political systems. However, the British world, of which Scotland was so very consciously a part, was an Atlantic phenomenon and in the mainland colonies in British North America a grave crisis had been building up, certainly since the end of the Great War for the Empire in 1763. In 1776 that crisis came to a head and burst into the central experience of the English-speaking peoples – the break-up of the Hanoverian state complex. Scotland, itself a classic illustration of internal Hanoverian colonialism in the daunting of the Highlands after 1745, could not but be deeply affected.

4

A Loyal Province and the Crisis of the State 1775 – 1784

That the second half of the eighteenth century saw a crisis of cohesion in the British Atlantic community and state system was hardly surprising. The British Empire was the first of the great European-based Atlantic empires to crumble from within, but it had always been the most ramshackle of such empires, having neither the logical structure and institutional framework of the Spanish imperial system, nor any intention of forging a systematic and more radical alternative rooted in the Whigs' much-vaunted 'Revolution Principles'. In England itself Tory exaltation of central authority was by no means destroyed by the Glorious Revolution of 1688. On the contrary, it survived to become a potent element in that very complicated structure of views, prejudices, and practices which was the working creed of the eighteenth-century British ruling class and which can only at the cost of some misunderstanding be described by the adjective 'Whig', to which some residual radicalism in the last analysis must always adhere. Concern for liberty, however defined, was always to be found in the best circles in eighteenth-century Britain, but concern for order and above all for the security of property were usually much stronger.

It was a chronic problem for the integrity of the British state-structure that peripheral parts of the English-speaking world had an irritating habit of taking Whig and Revolution Principles much more seriously than the sophisticated and wordly-wise men who presided over the political organs of the core state in that structure — England. At the time of the debates over the incorporating parliamentary union with England in early-eighteenth-century Scotland the most articulate opposition to the form of union proposed had come from that archetypal Scots Whig Andrew Fletcher of Saltoun, and the Irish Protestant and Whig William Molyneux had as early as 1698 in his *Case of Ireland being bound by Acts of Parliament in England* protested passionately against the way in which the English Parliament, with absolutely no legal let alone moral justification, was blandly taking over the arbitrary and absolute sovereignty claimed by the later Stewart monarchs.

The American colonies, which of course stretched from Canada to the southern Caribbean, were particularly sensitive to the ideological contradictions at the heart of the British imperial system. The New England colonies in particular had a long history of barely nominal allegiance to the Crown. Virtually autonomous, usually disobedient, and ideologically deviant, they had felt the justified wrath of James VII and II who had revoked their charters and pulled them into a unified Dominion of New England under a royal governor. Balanced perhaps by a southern dominion, New England, like Scotland, was meant by James to be one of the component parts of his British Atlantic world organized rather like the Spanish empire into a series of at least nominally equal kingdoms held together by royal authority reinforced by bureaucracy and naval and military power. In practice, this vision crumbled in 1688—9. The individual colonies reasserted their identity as the Dominion of New England sank, but the Crown's rôle in imperial matters. was not officially altered. An uncontrolled prerogative in the hands of the English parliament was taken for granted by English statesmen as the ultimate imperial authority.

The vague possibility that the overseas plantations might revolt was alluded to by such late-seventeenth — and early-eighteenth-century English political economists as Sir Josiah Child, Charles Davenant, William Wood, and John Trenchard, but none of these specifically admits a right to rebel on the part of colonists. The first influential statement of that right can be found in the teaching of a Scottish professor of moral philosophy, Francis Hutcheson. Holder of a Glasgow chair from 1730 to his death in 1746, Hutcheson published only a short summary of his teaching materials in his lifetime, and that appeared due to the initiative of the printer Robert Foulis, one of his former students. However a complete *System of Moral Philosophy* was published from his manuscripts nine years after his death. It contains a lengthy argument to the effect that if

> oppressive laws are made with respect to the colonies or provinces;
> and any colony is so increased in numbers and strength that they
> are sufficient by themselves, for all the good ends of a political
> union; they are not bound to continue in their subjection, when
> it is grown so much more burdensome than was expected.

Their   consent to be subject to a safe and gentle plan of power or laws, imposes no subjection to the dangerous and oppressive ones.

Like other professors in the Scottish universities of his time, Hutcheson regarded moral philosophy as including a discussion of natural law, the nature of civil society, and the concepts of contract and rights. However, it must be stressed that his application of radical Whig doctrines to imperial matters was in no way typical of Scottish opinion in his own time, let alone a generation later. Hutcheson was an Ulsterman. He never lost contact with radical Protestant circles in the Dublin where he originally made his name and in particular with Robert Molesworth, the 'Commonwealthman', a very radical, indeed a thinly-veiled republican Whig who was himself a friend of Molyneux. By the time the American crisis came to a head in the 1770s, it had been clear for decades that neither in theory nor in practice was Scotland likely to endorse demands for a reconstruction of British central government in a way calculated to render it more responsive to the governed.

In practice Scotland had become the most undemanding and subservient of British provinces, partly because of repeated purges of recalcitrant members of her ruling classes after the Jacobite rebellions of 1715, 1719, and 1745. The great bulk of the nobility had effectively abandoned the country to pursue social, political, military, or naval careers which required the systematic cultivation of metropolitan society in the south of England. Representation in the House of Lords gave some Scots peers vital political leverage, provided they were generally reliable from the point of view of the administration of the day. The second Duke of Argyll became Commander-in-Chief of the British Army in 1742 after helping to drive Walpole from power and he was succeeded by another Scots peer and field marshal (the rank was created in 1736), the second Earl of Stair, another staunch ally of the new administration. The Royal Navy was less popular as a career for Scots noblemen. Lord Duffus was prominent in it under Queen Anne, but he proved a Jacobite in 1715 and subsequently fled into the Russian service, with a significant number of sea officers of the same persuasion, thereby making British governments hyper-sensitive to reports of Russian ships off the Scottish coast. By the time the seventh Lord Colville of Culross achieved the rank of a rear admiral in 1762 the Jacobite scare was dying and it was quite dead when another Scots peer, the sixth Earl of Northesk, became Admiral of the White in 1778 at the height of the American war. As we have seen, in politics and diplomacy the Scottish nobility and gentry did very well for themselves in a British context after 1750.

Apart from anything else, the monetary rewards for success in London-centred careers were vastly in excess of anything which could be picked up in Scotland. Ordinary Lords of Session, amongst the most prestigious of resident Scots, had their annual salaries raised from £500 to £700 in 1759 and again to £1,000 in 1766. At the same times the salary of the Lord President went up from £1,000 to £1,300 and then to £2,000. In London a Lordship of the Treasury such as a Scot like Gilbert Elliot of Minto obtained was worth £2,500 per year. Even a Lordship of Police, of which there were nine and they all pure sinecures held with other jobs, ranged from £400 to £1,200 per annum. A mere handful of spectacularly successful Edinburgh advocates may have contrived to earn over £1,000 a year at the Scottish bar in the eighteenth century, most earned far less. Other professional careers were paid pittances by English standards. The Principal of Glasgow University was paid £150 in 1753, a year when the Professor of Divinity at Edinburgh had emoluments of £160 as well as his free house. The 900 or so livings in the Church of Scotland ranged from about £140 annual value down to £30 in 1751, with the great bulk being at the lower end of the scale. A not very bright but astutely obsequious minor politician in Westminster could easily pick up much more than a resident Scot at the top of his profession.

Not much wonder that capable adult members of the highest social class in eighteenth-century Scotland were nearly all absentees. They looked after their Scottish interests through resident agents, of whom it has become fashionable to argue that a large proportion were Edinburgh lawyers and to whom it is equally fashionable to ascribe a fair measure of autonomous initiative. Neither view seems wholly tenable. Scotland was and is more than Edinburgh, though the brilliance of certain aspects of life in the Scottish capital between 1750 and 1832 always tempts intellectual historians to think otherwise. Agents of various kinds were required all over Scotland for the purpose of political or property management and they were drawn from several social groups including merchants and lairds as well as practising lawyers. Nor had these agents any very significant capacity for innovative initiative. They were normally totally subservient, in all but the most routine of dealings, to the will of their ultimate masters. Only when those power-holders were themselves susceptible to an ideology of change could their agents hope to give shape to major policies, and such a time had hardly come by the 1770s. At a political level only Andrew Fletcher Lord Milton (1692—1766), the Argyll man of business in Scotland, appears to have been able to have a significant, if very limited, ability to influence major policies. The last thing which most Scots peers and MPs at Westminster wanted to do was to represent the political views of their constituents. They were out for their own interests, eager for jobs and advancement. Advocating Scottish causes embarrassing to government was no highway to success. Only Edmund Burke, an Irishman and a Whig of the Rockingham group, managed to give lapidary expression to the view that his first duty was to his Westminster faction and not to his Bristol constituents, crowning it with the statement that if his constituency dared reject him, he would think the more of himself. Such public arrogance was ill-judged, but not untypical of many of his discreeter Westminster colleagues' thoughts.

Few parts of the English-speaking world were less likely to offer constructive sympathy to the troubled American colonies than Scotland. That is not to say that Scotsmen were not interested in America. The reverse was the case. In the period when the American crisis was at its most acute — from the early 1760s to the Peace of Paris in 1783 — a total of 50 or so newspapers and periodicals circulated in Scotland at one time or another. Their proprietors had to cater for a very strong interest in American news. Indeed, the proprietor of the *Caledonian Mercury*, when about to turn his thrice-weekly paper into a daily, appealed to the appetite for trans-Atlantic information by saying he would 'omit no American information that he can procure and depend upon as authentic'. In most other Scottish periodicals the American section was often the largest one. When *Ruddiman's Weekly Mercury* received information of the disastrous British defeat at Saratoga in 1777, it turned over the entire contents of one issue to American affairs. It was very common for American intelligence to take precedence of major domestic news items. In 1775 the *Caledonian Mercury* delayed printing its report on the General Assembly of the Kirk By Law Established in order to publish accounts of the outbreak of the first serious fighting between British regulars and American rebels. Nor was significant Scottish opinion hawk-like during the train of crises which led to the musket-shots at Concord and Lexington in 1775. The Glasgow merchants were vocally in favour of conciliation with America during the crisis sparked off by the passing of the Stamp Act by the British legislature in 1765. A petition and deputation from Glasgow helped secure the repeal of that legislation in 1766, and in 1775 Glasgow merchants again co-operated with London interests in pressing for conciliatory measures, to secure trade. The Glaswegians specifically denounced 'the unnecessary and oppressive acts passed last session'.

When, however, it became clear that conciliation had either failed, or had ceased to be a short-term option from the British point of view, Scottish opinion was overwhelmingly behind the efforts of His Majesty's Government to bring the disloyal to heel. Active sympathy for the rebellious Whig element in the American colonies there could hardly be in Scotland on any scale, for the Scots were emphatically on the Westminster side of the great ideological fissure which disrupted the British world of the eighteenth century. It was essentially a divide between those who were convinced that the liberties secured by the Glorious Revolution were meaningful and were threatened by the growth of executive tyranny and corruption, and those who simply did not share this obsession. The latter could be divided into two groups: the so-called 'vulgar Whigs', who were happy to parrot the slogans used by the régime to justify itself, and the very much more sophisticated thinkers like David Hume, who were totally committed to the political status-quo without accepting much of its crude, contradictory, and obscure public self-justification. Such categorization is itself excessively crude. What existed amongst that section of the British peoples resident in Great Britain when they thought, if they thought, about their system of government was a spectrum of opinion, not a polarization. What was lacking on that spectrum was any significant segment of opinion dedicated to clarifying the avowed 'Revolution Principles' on which government rested, and if necessary to restructuring the machinery of state power to ensure that it reflected them. Earlier in the century with an unpopular one-party Whig ascendancy and episodes like the South Sea Bubble when the government, almost certainly including the royal family, could be seen as trying to swindle the general public out of its money, total disillusionment had been not uncommon. With the accession of the palpably well-meaning George III in 1760 and the end of discrimination against what was left of the Tories, general satisfaction with a 'mild and regular government' was much commoner.

In David Hume the Scots even produced a man who understood the danger to the system of over-enthusiastic support. In the first volume of his *History of England* he deprecated excessive emphasis on the pedigree of English liberties:

> Above all, a civilized nation, like the English, who have happily established the most perfect and most accurate system of liberty, that ever was found compatible with government, ought to be cautious of appealing to the practice of their ancestors, or regarding

the maxims of uncultivated ages as certain rules for their present conduct.

Hume was anxious to see his fellow subjects 'cherish their present constitution' rather than be snared into the dangers of adjusting it because it did not live up to the full promise of its supposed historical antecedents. What little chance there was of long-term harmony between the British peoples on both sides of the Atlantic really hinged on a willingness to recognize that the absolutist claims and the unrepresentative nature of the Westminster legislature constituted problems in their own right. Hume was unusually sophisticated in his refusal to contemplate serious political adjustment, but not a-typical of the very self-satisfied Scottish élite of his day in his immobilism. His response to the American crisis was logically consistent with the conservatism of the views he shared with so many others, but again unusual in its precise form. His 'sceptical Whiggism' led him to declare before his death in 1776 that he was 'American in my principles', which in terms of daily politics he was certainly not. What he meant was that he would prefer to be rid of an insoluble problem which might also act as a catalyst of political change in Britain. He wished to see the American colonies 'revolted totally and finally'. The colonies, 'no longer in their Infancy', could not be crushed. 'Let us therefore', he wrote, 'lay aside all Anger; shake hands, and part Friends'. The emotional context was wildly unrealistic, but the basic gambit of conserving the existing order at the core of the power-structure by sacrificing exposed positions on the periphery was to be of enormous future significance.

Most contemporary Scottish intellectuals, when the crunch came, were for repressing rebellion by force. Lord Kames was sympathetic to American problems and corresponded with Benjamin Franklin about some form of federal union with American representatives in the British parliament, but by 1774 he was denouncing colonial claims that they could not be taxed if not politically represented. Principal Robertson was vaguely benign about American aspirations but clear by 1775 that independence was unacceptable and that dependence was to be maintained if necessary by force. These were mild positions compared with, say, the views of the painter Allan Ramsay. From 1775 Ramsay had favoured the public with his opinions under the pseudonym 'Britannicus'. In 1778 he published *A Plan of Re-Union between Great Britain and her Colonies*, and his last effusion on the American question was called, appropriately, *On The Right of Conquest*. Despite a systematic use of various *noms de plume* Ramsay's authorship was well-known and his views at one stage denounced by a London critic as 'Scotch mists'. They were perhaps unrealistic by 1778 but there was nothing soft or wet in their nature. Ramsay may or may not have been to the right of Attilla the Hun, but he certainly believed in the same tactics as that distinguished monarch, preaching a systematic devastation of property and if necessary life in the revolting colonies in order to bring them back to their correct position, unequivocal subjection. Though the drastic nature of Ramsay's proposals shook some contemporaries, his general position was hardly surprising. In his book on the *State of the Arts in England*, whose English version appeared in 1755, the Frenchman Jean André Rouquet had remarked on the need for political patronage there for any artist who wished for advancement. Not for nothing was Ramsay Principal Painter to the King.

Both at home and abroad articulate Scots opinion was overwhelmingly behind the British war effort. For example, at the start of the war cities like Edinburgh and Dundee and smaller burghs like Arbroath produced loyal addresses calling for the firmest measures against the rebels. The Scottish press was enthusiastically in favour of recruiting, particularly after the rebels allied with the Popish despotism of France in 1778. General conservatism seems to have been an important constituent in this consensus, for the American cause was often identified with that of levelling republicanism; factious opposition to His Majesty's Government in Westminster; or even with individual British radicals from Lord Chatham to John Wilkes. More justifiable was a general revulsion from the savagery with which the American Whig or Patriot rebels habitually dealt with the substantial pro-British Loyalist element in their society. Anxious to uphold British ascendancy, and exclusive trading rights under the Acts of Navigation, Scottish opinion adjusted itself only slowly and reluctantly to the possibility of defeat. Nor was this reluctance solely the reflection of vulgar jingoism. The philosopher Adam Ferguson shared it in full measure. He had been liberal in his attitude as the American crisis came to a head and had early doubts as to whether the war could be won, but he had no doubts at all about the rightness of the British case, to the point where his public defence of it helped secure for him the secretaryship of the peace commission sent to the colonies in 1778 with a view to negotiations with the rebels. He returned from this unsuccessful mission a hard-liner, arguing in 1779 that Britain must not lose the will to fight on, for half the population of the colonies was loyal and vigorous action would isolate a rebel leadership full of 'the most abandoned Villains in the World'.

The Scottish community with the most intimate connections with the American colonies, the city of Glasgow, evinced resolute optimism about the colonial crisis until 1777−8. Most major tobacco merchants in early 1775 believed, as John Herries the Scottish agent for the farmers-general of the French customs reported to his employers, that differences between mother country and colonies would soon be settled and tobacco prices would then return to former levels. In Glasgow uniquely high tobacco stocks were on hand in 1775−6, mainly due to vicissitudes of harvests and prices, and credit eased rather than froze after the outbreak of war, so the giant firms run by the Glassfords, Cunninghames, and Speirs weathered the initial shock of war easily. The greatest bankruptcy of the period, that of Buchanan, Hastie and Company, with allied firms like Bogle, Jamieson and Company, and James Jamieson and Company, seems to be explicable in terms of long-standing financial and management problems rather than in terms of comparatively moderate American losses. Of course, there were very substantial losses for many Glaswegians, as defaulting debtors were prominent in the rebel leadership. William Woodford who commanded the rebel forces which burned Norfolk, Virginia, and with it the property of several Glasgow merchants, was quite open about the fact that he owed Scots merchants more than he was worth or ever intended to pay. He and his kind reinforced pro-government sentiment, in so far as it needed reinforcing, in Glasgow.

What is clear is that the Glaswegians consistently underestimated the gravity of the war. At the start they had no conception of the capacity of the colonists to resist firm action by regular troops. They did not understand the sheer scale of the logistical problems involved in supplying a large army on the other side of the North Atlantic. In 1775 French intervention was hardly recognized as a possibility. Only after defeat at Saratoga and the French declaration of war did Glasgow appreciate the grim nature of its situation. Then indeed credit tightened, the Glasgow Regiment was raised, and merchants began to seek the classic compensation for depressed trade due to war, by investing in privateering. However, it must be said that the Glasgow merchants throughout assumed a degree of resolution, firmness, and commonsense on the part of the British government which proved sorely wanting. George III by 'abolishing party' had opened the gates to 'an orgy of faction'. Even if these phrases exaggerate, the way in which politics permeated the British high command proved catastrophic in the all-important early stages of the war. Lord Amherst the outstanding British general of the day refused to serve, as did Lord

Cavendish. Admiral Keppel, a member of the Rockingham faction amongst the opposition, refused to serve until the war became a war with France. Indeed Admiral Lord Howe and his brother General Sir William, who were given the supreme naval and military commands at the start of the war, had both expressed opposition to ministerial policy in America and insisted on very generous powers to negotiate a settlement as an integral part of their authority. The upshot was an early demonstration of the effect of aimiable half-measures which fail to conciliate the disaffected, and give them time to rally their strength, while eroding the morale both of the government forces and of the crucial Loyalist element.

The war provided the Scottish aristocracy and gentry with a splendid opportunity to show their talents as military entrepreneurs, for the government had great difficulty securing troops. Only in August 1775 was an increase in the establishment from 33,000 to 55,000 men authorized. Attempts at virtual conscription of the 'idle and able-bodied' proved ineffectual save in the rather specialized instance of reprieved criminals who in 1776 made up three whole regiments of the British forces in America. Yet as late as 1781 34,000 troops were available to British commanders in America. Some were German mercenaries. The Hanoverian state-system was partly German so there was no rational argument against the use of Hessians and other German-speaking professional soldiers by what was, ultimately, a north German dynasty. However the great bulk of at least nominally voluntary recruiting drew on two other traditional reservoirs of military manpower – Ireland and Scotland.

Proposals for raising troops for the British service in the Highlands had been advanced as early as 1738 by Duncan Forbes of Culloden, the great Whig lawyer and laird. After the '45 suggestions from the Duke of Argyll that regiments be raised amongst the disaffected clans were considered and rejected. Government policy, as Lord Findlater reminded the Duke of Newcastle in July 1748, was to root out the military spirit in the Highlands, not to sustain it by extensive recruiting, and Westminster tended to draw no fine distinctions between loyal and disloyal Highlanders. With the outbreak of the Seven Years War in 1756 Newcastle did tentatively suggest the raising of regular regiments in the Highlands, only to see George II veto the scheme. Defeats in that year, allied to a serious manpower crisis in the British Army produced a reassessment of the situation. Late in 1756 the Duke of Cumberland recommended the raising of Highland regiments and the idea was enthusiastically adopted by his former protegé, the Elder Pitt, who persuaded King George and his ministers to swallow it. The avowed objective was to transport potential Jacobites to foreign battle-fields where they could be slaughtered fighting the French, rather than leave them to plot subversion at home. The first regiment, the 77th or Montgomery's Highlanders, was commanded by Colonel Archibald Montgomery, a son of the Earl of Eglinton, but it was deliberately recruited in areas with a Jacobite past, while the second Highland regiment embodied in 1757 was the 78th regiment or Fraser's Highlanders, raised by its future commander, Simon Fraser, son of the executed Jacobite Lord Lovat. Young Simon was busy working his passage back into Hanoverian favour.

The success of this particular experiment in the 1750s naturally led to offers to raise units from Highland landowners in the 1770s. Though there was a significant outlay involved in raising a corps of any size, there were government grants which covered most of the costs, such as clothing and bounty money to encourage recruits, while any loss made by an aspiring colonel was obviously more than compensated for by political and patronage gains. Such gestures of loyal enthusiasm were nicely calculated to assist a gentleman's career in arms or politics or both. At the same time, the commissions in his regiment gave the colonel a formidable instrument of patronage amongst the local gentry. Six new Highland regiments were raised for the war in America in 1777–8. They fought alongside older Highland regiments with their usual courage and dash. They certainly did not find their duties contrary to the spirit of the bulk of their fellow-countrymen in the colonies. On the contrary, Scottish emigrants tended to be staunchly loyal to the British cause. Even former Jacobites exiled for their convictions were far more likely to turn up under the banner of King George than in the rebel ranks. The Highlanders of North Carolina formed a small Loyalist army in which Flora Macdonald's husband held a brigadier's commission before the battle of Moor's Creek in 1776, when they were caught and shattered by a superior force of rebel Whigs. In the southern colonies Scottish emigrants were divided in their response to the heightening of military activity which followed the large-scale British invasion of the region in 1780 under Lord Cornwallis. Scots could be found both in the ranks of Loyalist units and in those of the Whig or Patriot forces which won major victories at King's Mountain and Cowpens. Nevertheless, it is clear that the Scots displayed nothing like the solidarity of the Scotch-Irish, those embattled settlers from Protestant Ulster, who when the die was cast formed perhaps the toughest ethnic phalanx in the rebel line of battle.

Protestant Ireland distrusted and disliked the British government which it saw, not without reason, as only too ready to discriminate against and betray the Protestant interest in Ireland. By the end of the American war Irish politicians were using the lever provided by the rise of the Irish Volunteers to prize Westminster's controlling fingers away from key levers of power within the Irish political system. Despite their own overwhelming Protestantism, the response of the Scots to the American crisis most closely resembled that of the Roman Catholic Irish. Both communities had a long history of armed resistance to English power. Both by 1776 were anxious to win the favour of Westminster by a display of enthusiastic loyalty to the British cause. To the Catholic Irish the objective was help in breaking the discriminatory system operated against them by their fellow Irishmen. The Scottish objective, to be attained by a similar cultivation of English good will, was political and material advancement for the ruling groups in North Britain. Not much wonder that 'a free exportation to Scotchmen and Tories' became a common toast in Patriot circles in America. It is even less surprising that the minutes of the New York Saint Andrew's Society, established in 1756 to provide relief for Scotsmen in distress in New York State and modelled on a similar society already in existence in Philadelphia, are discreetly missing for the years 1775 to 1784. No doubt if extant they would reveal just how Loyalist was the tone of an organization whose seat was New York City, itself occupied by British forces for most of the war.

Exceptions in the shape of prominent home-domiciled Scotsmen consistently sympathetic to the American cause tend merely to prove the rule that most Scots of consequence were not so disposed. The one outstanding Scots parliamentarian who systematically opposed the government's American policy was George Dempster, MP for the Perth Burghs between 1761 and 1790. Apart from Dempster, who by 1778 was convinced that American independence should be granted, Scots MPs and peers richly merited the taunt hurled at them by, among others, the relentless Wilkes that no body in parliament was a more reliable supporter of the royal government and its American policy. Significantly, Dempster, an outstandingly independent man, was a vocal critic of the arbitrary and unrepresentative nature of the contemporary Scots parliamentary franchise and a champion of demands for its radical reform. In this, too, he was a-typical of the leading Scotsmen of his day. The great English county of Yorkshire showed more critical and independent spirits active in politics in the latter part of the American crisis than all Scotland put together. The Reverend Christopher Wyvill was the moving spirit in the Yorkshire Association which was widely supported by men of substance and which agitated for a reduction in government influence in parliament, an increase in the number of independent county members, and triennial elections. Admittedly only half a dozen other English counties had associations pledged to the full Yorkshire programme, but in Scotland a man like Professor Adam Ferguson could regard the activities of the Yorkshire reformers with real alarm. In 1780 Christopher Wyvill addressed a circular appeal to the Scots. Ferguson hoped for early military successes to silence such subversion on the home front. Ferguson did accept that the rulers of Ireland would have to be appeased in the short run, though he hoped to draw their fangs, in the long run, by an incorporating union.

Only in the field of religion were emotions strong enough to mobilize a vocal opposition to government policy roused during the American crisis. That party in the Church of Scotland known as the Evangelicals showed signs of sympathy with the American rebels, partly no doubt by way of reaction to the unswervingly pro-government line of the ascendant Moderates, but partly because of genuine sympathy with a cause itself deeply influenced by radical American Presbyterianism. The best-known example of this sympathy was the Reverend John Erskine who published a pamphlet *Shall I go to war with my American Brethren* in 1769 and again in 1776. Both in the General Assembly of the Kirk and at the level of local synods, there was considerable tension over the American issue during the war years. The government's system of management proved adequate to head off the Evangelical's challenge, but that challenge was itself part of a rising current of opposition to a stranglehold from which the Kirk had benefitted only to a limited degree. Islay had early on built up a structure of control in the General Assembly, based on the extensive ecclesiastical patronage of the Crown, and employing after 1736 the Reverend Patrick Cumming of the Old Kirk of Edinburgh as his principal mananger. Islay set a firm example of using Crown patronage with no respect for or consultation with parishioners. Other lay patrons, previously often conciliatory towards the views of congregations, tended to follow suit. Cumming and others of his kidney argued that by being conciliatory to Islay, a man of little religion and less respect for the cloth, they could secure practical concessions. In fact an attempt by the General Assembly in 1749–51 to secure augmentation of ministerial stipends, many of which had become with time miserably inadequate, elicited no support whatever from the civil power, and provoked a quite remarkable display of belligerent mean-mindedness from the landed gentry of virtually every Scottish county.

By 1761 Cumming's leadership of the church was at an end and his successor in that capacity, Principal William Robertson of Edinburgh University, was a more independent figure than he, though a militant champion of patronage. He and his supporters believed that by co-operating with the state on equal terms and by interpenetrating the influential levels of contemporary secular society it was possible for the Church of Scotland to resist 'a slavish corrupting dependance' on the political boss of the moment in Scotland. However, even Robertson's talents, eminence, and commitment to conciliatory and reasonable policies could not stop the process whereby Moderatism was placed on the defensive after 1776. His own resignation from leadership in the Assembly in 1780 was not unconnected with the American crisis, though the linkage was such that he could regard the gesture as an expression of his belief in religious toleration. Government attempts to cope with its need for troops by encouraging recruiting among British Roman Catholics had led logically to a very mild proposal to relieve Roman Catholics of a few of their many legal disabilities. Dissenters and Evangelicals of the established churches at once reacted with a fit of suspicious No-Popery agitation expressed institutionally in Protestant Associations which found a charismatic leader in a young Scots MP, Lord George Gordon, a brother of the Duke of Gordon and the bore, despair, and scourge of the House of Commons.

Lord North had already tried to buy him out of politics with the lucrative Vice-Admiralty of Scotland, so when he became a key figure in a frightening mass agitation North's offers went up. Lord George was mentally unstable, but he was impervious to bribery as well as a sympathizer with 'the worthy patriots of our injured colonies'. The culmination of his career came in a week in early July 1780 when, after the House of Commons had refused to take seriously the petition of the Protestant Association, London was dominated by a reckless, drunken, and radical mob acknowledging the somewhat nominal leadership of 'the mad Scotchman', Lord George. Eventually the rioters were crushed and dispersed by regular troops, militia, and middle-class volunteer units, directed to act by an unlikely combination of George III and John Wilkes. The latter, always a calculating as well as an impudent egotist, was not prepared by 1780 to see popular agitation divide the ruling class, of which he was a member, and threaten the social order.

Lord George, a constitutionally religious man who later converted to Judaism, had become a symbol of the half-articulate resentments of the lower orders. The London riots were parallelled by less extensive disturbances in Glasgow and Edinburgh. The thinly-veiled secularism of the ruling cliques at Westminster was bound to be a source of weakness to governments chosen on an arbitrary and unrepresentative basis which was justified at least to some extent by official propaganda on the grounds that the régime operated a 'Protestant Constitution'. However, with Lord George in hiding and later firmly in Newgate jail, it was possible to defuse the crisis simply by withdrawing the relief bill. Principal Robertson, like his hero the Emperor Charles V, chose to retire from the public stage before his time, ostensibly to devote more effort to historical studies. Privately, he deplored the revival of religious bigotry. At a deeper level he, who had like many self-conscious liberals progressively lost interest in conciliating those who differed from him, may have sensed the tide was turning against his own Moderate ascendancy.

The London government genuinely expected Scottish Presbyterians to be more responsive to radical American principles than most Britons, but its fears were misplaced. The ruling groups in Scotland were behind the war which, throughout Britain, was a popular war until after the defeat of Cornwallis at Yorktown in 1781 when it became increasingly clear that it could not be won. Heavy Scottish losses were incurred from start to finish, and not purely by rebel action. The pattern of Atlantic summer gales in the 1770s and 1780s differed from what it is in the twentieth century. Cyclones came roaring across the 3,000 miles of sea between Scotland and America with much greater frequency then rather than sweeping eastward in the latitudes of Iceland and Norway as today. The convoy which set out from the Clyde late in April 1776 carrying the Highland Brigade to reinforce General Howe in his Manhattan campaign was so battered and scattered by the fury of the elements that it eventually lost seven ships and 800 men, nearly as many as the British had lost at the bloody engagement at Bunker's Hill. However, their superiors could stomach such losses with equanimity.

Perhaps there would have been more of an outcry if the Scottish economy had seen its steady recovery from the depression of 1772–3 seriously interrupted by the war, but this did not happen before 1780. Capital was abundantly available in 1775 and 1776, at rates as low as 3 per cent. A series of good harvests kept grain prices low and breweries and distilleries busy. The construction industry was eventually affected by diversion of funds into government loans, but not before 1779–80. After 1780 there was a deficit on the visible balance of trade. War with two big naval powers such as France and Spain was bound to affect overseas trade. Re-exports of colonial produce naturally declined, but internal British markets seem actually to have expanded. Scottish ironworks profited from war demand as did

Scottish producers of leatherware such as boots and saddles. Only at the very end of the war can it be shown to have been holding back expansion in the growing Scots linen and cotton manufactures. The disastrous harvest of 1782 was a more alarming crisis than any purely commercial downturn in the wartime Scottish economy. So grave was the situation that the landlords and the government had to combine to avert the threat of famine. The Royal Navy shipped grain and peas to the worst affected parts of the Highlands and Islands. Peace in 1783 came timely to the shaken economy of North Britain.

The rising figure in Scottish politics, such as they were, at this time was undoubtedly Henry Dundas of Arniston, a half-brother of Robert, second Lord Arniston, President of the Court of Session. Henry Dundas sat as MP for Midlothian and became Lord Advocate in 1775. At the start of the war he was trying to expand his electoral influence in Scotland, to increase his bargaining power at Westminster. To curry favour in London he made such exaggerated objections to the odd groups of religious Seceders who passed motions in favour of conciliating the American colonies that George III found his boot-licking egregious and described him in 1778 as a pest. Dundas duly toned down his style and did what Lord North told him to do, albeit grudgingly since North did not heap favours on him. Dundas resented not being made Keeper of the Scottish Signet for life and by 1780 was beginning to realize, with many others, that America was lost. Nevertheless, in a snap election called in 1780 to try to strengthen North's ministry Dundas did his electoral duty. Out of 45 MPs from Scotland 41 reliable supporters of government were returned, and of these Dundas personally controlled 12. The Scots votes were increasingly important after war-weariness forced North to resign in 1782, and Westminster descended into extreme instability. Rockingham, the leading opposition peer, formed a ministry. Dundas blandly served him as he had North. When Rockingham suddenly died and the much-distrusted Lord Shelburne took over, Lord Advocate Dundas sat tight reaping rich rewards as Shelburne drifted towards the political rocks. With the life Keepership of the Signet under his belt Dundas, leading his file of wonderfully reliable Scots MPs towards whichever lobby suited those in power, survived and prospered in the midst of political hurricanes. He himself was full of ideas for opportunist coalitions to replace the sinking Shelburne.

By sheer accident the coalition which came, the Fox – North coalition, was about the only one Dundas could not live with. Charles Fox simply could not abide the Scotch 'Sycophant-Fiscal' to George III and replaced him as Lord Advocate in 1783 with Henry Erskine. Dundas

had no option except the one he cheerfully embraced of aligning himself with the King's 'only resource', William Pitt the Younger, who
along with his cousin and political ally Lord Temple was manoeuvring
to use two parts of the sovereign body, monarch and House of Lords,
to strike down party bosses trying to rule from a secure base only in the
House of Commons. It happened that from 1781 or so Dundas had
made rather a speciality of the complex problems of the East India
Company, the very issue on which Fox and North fell because it was
feared that they were trying by proposed regulatory legislation to lay
hands on enormous Indian patronage. There was undoubtedly a
steady swing of opinion towards the 24-year-old Pitt after George III
named him First Lord of the Treasury and Chancellor of the
Exchequer in December 1783. The opposition politicians, ever since
Rockingham achieved office, had made it clear that they were not
interested in reform, only power. The voice of Edmund Burke, principal apologist for Rockingham and Fox, had risen to a shrill 'scream
of passion' at the mere suggestion of parliamentary reform. Opinion at
large in the political nation deplored the bullying of George III, especially by Charles Fox who was no very attractive alternative to his royal
enemy. Pitt actually managed to win over the existing House of
Commons, after a desperate early struggle, and in a general election in
1784 a sustained surge of support in the electorate, aided but not
created by Crown and East India Company influence, saw him
through to a famous victory.

Dundas was a rock of dependability, producing the usual phalanx
of pro-government MPs from Scotland. Even at the height of George
III's troubles only seven Scots MPs had dared vote against his influence
in 1780 when John Dunning's famous motion that 'the influence of the
Crown has increased, is increasing, and ought to be diminished' was
carried by 233 to 215. Twenty-three Scots MPs opposed the motion
while 15 others were absent. By 1784 any competent manager could
have returned the usual block of pro-administration North Britons.
What was more significant was the fact that out of the 45 Scottish seats
Dundas had some sort of grip over 22 of them. Nor was his political
power anywhere near its zenith. Islay was come again, but if anything
the new colossus was to surpass the stature of his sole predecessor.

5

Patronage and Enlightenment during the Consolidation of the Dundas Ascendancy 1784 – 1793

The American War had proved to the hilt the loyalty of the Scottish political nation to the political and social system centred on London. A few radicals had protested, predictably, against ministerial policy, but they had awakened gratifyingly little response in the masses of the Scottish people. The upper classes of North Britain had behaved impeccably from the point of view of Westminster. There were one or two exceptions to this last statement, but they were such that they could be dismissed as cranks or eccentrics. James Boswell, who succeeded his father as Laird of Auchinleck in 1782, had always rejected the violently anti-American views of his hero and mentor Dr Johnson. By February 1780 Boswell had reached the opinion that the Americans were 'in the right to insist on independence'. However, he was in other respects conservative to the point of absurdity and his American views could easily be dismissed as a product of that inner frenzy which, despite his amiable social qualities, was driving him into a self-destructive downward spiral compounded of manic depression, alcoholism, and venereal disease.

In much the same way, David Steuart Erskine, eleventh Earl of Buchan, could be dismissed as an unbalanced, whimsical fellow whose support for the American rebels was marred by the same note of egregious self-advertisement which had been prominent in the support Boswell had offered to the cause of Corsican independence and its embodiment General Pascal Paoli in the late 1760s. The Earl saw some of his best ideas such as a plan for a parochial survey of Scotland, executed by others. Buchan also had the great misfortune in advanced old age to earn the dislike of Sir Walter Scott and of Scott's son-in-law and biographer John Gibson Lockhart and the acid comments of that formidable pair were until recently the last nails in the coffin of Buchan's reputation. Buchan was in fact a man of ability and public spirit whose ideas were often far in advance of his time. Educated at

St Andrews, Glasgow, and Edinburgh Universities, he was the moving spirit behind the foundation of the Society of Antiquaries of Scotland, a body for which he helped obtain a royal charter. His vision for that society was remarkable for, from its foundation in 1780 to his own disillusioned resignation from its ranks in 1790, he tried to make it not only the custodian of an important national museum but also a general clearing house for a revitalized school of Scottish history. Buchan studied source material for Scottish medieval history in Paris and Rome. No great *Monasticon Scotiae* ever emerged, but unlike Boswell, all of whose patriotically Scottish publishing projects[1] proved abortive, Buchan did write several works of Scottish history.

One of them was a life of Andrew Fletcher of Saltoun. Buchan, essentially a radical Whig, naturally admired the principles expounded by that patriot laird. He believed that American politicians like Benjamin Franklin or the future President of the United States Thomas Jefferson represented the living embodiment of Fletcher's tradition of thought. There is certainly no reason to doubt that Jefferson's approach to politics grew out of the same radical Whig principles which Fletcher embraced. Buchan admired George Washington, corresponded with him at length, and toyed with the idea of migrating to America after the war. He was already too old for this to be practical. Instead he settled down in Dryburgh Abbey where he indulged in his literary enthusiasms. He did much to build up the cult of James Thomson, the author of 'The Seasons', 'The Castle of Indolence', and other poems. Activities of this kind, along with the advocacy of such patently absurd and wrongheaded causes as female education and emancipation, enabled the sensible men of his time to write him off as an elderly buffoon long before his death in 1829.

With pro-American views so despised by those who mattered it was scarcely surprising that the decision to return the Forfeited Annexed Estates to the descendants of the Jacobites from whom they had been confiscated after the '45 was put into effect by what was known as 'The Disannexing Act' of 1784. The writing had been on the wall for the Commissioners of the Forfeited Estates since about 1774. Henry Dundas had begun to agitate seriously for the return of the estates in 1775 and when he himself was appointed a Commissioner in 1783 it was clear that state control of these properties was about to be aban-

---

[1] They ranged from a Scots dictionary to rival the English dictionary of Johnson to a biography of James IV of Scotland and a history of the '45.

doned. The heirs were not always pleased to find that they inherited not only the property but also any accumulated debts connected with it. However, the return of the estates was more significant as a piece of political symbolism than as a transfer of property. It set the final seal on the total reconciliation between the Scottish aristocracy and a British government which as late as 1746 had harboured doubts as to whether there was such an animal as a reliable Scotsman. The gentlemen of Scotland, with rare exceptions, had proved in the American War that they could be relied upon to support even disastrously unsuccessful policies. Westminster could ask no more.

The Younger Pitt always talked of himself as a national British leader, but quite clearly he ruled as man of business to the possessing classes. Pitt had a reputation as something of a reformer and the wit to see that few things tarnish a political reputation so badly as an over-hasty jettisoning in office of the principles on which a man has ostensibly risen to power. Not without skill, he contrived both to express limited support for a few reforming causes such as the reform of parliamentary representation, and to preside blandly over their progressive decay as serious issues. Concessions to reforming agitation which threatened to dismantle the existing social and political hierarchies were never part of the new régime's programme. In Scotland such agitation was hardly prominent but the discomfiture and discrediting of government in the latter stages of the American War had helped to provoke a movement for reform in that most indefensible and corrupt part of the Scottish political power structure – burghal government.

The agitation was launched by a rich Edinburgh merchant and burgess, Thomas McGrugar, who in late 1782 and early 1783 published so-called 'Letters of Zeno' in the Edinburgh newspaper the *Caledonian Mercury*. The self-perpetuating cliques which formed the town councils of Scotland were wildly unrepresentative even of the wealthier classes in their communities, so the fact that only the town council had the vote in parliamentary elections was particularly offensive. Nor was 1782–3 a good time for the doctrine of 'virtual representation' whereby Westminster habitually tried to persuade those who were not represented there that in some mystic way they really were. McGrugar was no popular demagogue. He resented the fact that only 25 men chose Edinburgh's MP, but he argued only for the granting of the franchise to the propertied middle class, not to the swinish and uneducated dregs or bulk of the urban population. His writings had by 1783 stimulated the creation of a central committee dedicated to Scottish burghal reform. It demanded changes both in the parliamentary franchise and in the notoriously corrupt and inefficient internal government of the burghs. By March 1784 the movement could assemble delegates from half the 66 royal burghs in a convention in Edinburgh.

At local level the agitation was carried on mainly by merchants consumed by a social, moral, and financial contempt for what they saw as a disreputable and incompetent gaggle of rentiers who monopolized municipal government. The Edinburgh committee which tried to co-ordinate and lead the movement was, like so many Edinburgh committees, dominated by lawyers. Prominent were younger members of the Society of Advocates such as Archibald Fletcher and Henry Erskine, the brother of the Earl of Buchan and a man who shared most of Buchan's radical enthusiasms though not his eccentricity. John Clerk of Eldin was another lawyer active on the committee which in Lord Gardenstone even boasted a Lord of Session. Despite the respectability of those involved, it rapidly became clear that the legislature would entertain no proposals for parliamentary reform. By 1785 the Scottish burgh reformers had accepted this and abandoned hope for all but internal burgh reform.

Their proposals were for the enfranchisement of all burgesses and an end to self-selected councils. Instead it was proposed that on the same day all over Scotland there should be an annual election of councillors. The voters were also to select seven auditors of accounts to oversee the traditionally crooked ways of the council with burgh revenues and the 'common good' or burgh assets. Test cases in 1784 and 1787 underlined the urgent need for reform, for they confirmed that there was no legal sanction against absentee councillors and no survival of the power wielded by the old pre-union exchequer of Scotland which entitled it to audit burgh accounts. The British state simply washed its hands of the matter and every single Scots MP, including some self-styled reformers, refused to introduce the reform proposals to the House of Commons. Only the gallant and public-spirited advocacy of the playwright-MP Richard Sheridan gave them a hearing there, but Henry Dundas was too busy exploiting old abuses to support new reforms. He opposed and crushed the proposals.

Dundas did not particularly want to change anything. His political power was based on existing social structures. In 1784 his influence was still centred on the Lothians where he was hand in glove with Henry, third Duke of Buccleuch, a nobleman with no taste for high office but with the closest of ties with governing circles in London.

Buccleuch's mother, Lady Caroline Campbell Scott, was a daughter of the second Duke of Argyll and widow of the heir to the dukedom of Buccleuch. Her second marriage was to 'that splendid shuttle-cock' Charles Townshend who was a notably kind stepfather to the Buccleuch children, but died in 1767 after making a major contribution in office to the coming of the American Revolution. His stepson Henry lived until 1812, managing the ducal estates and Scottish elections in the Dundas interest. Withall he was a man of culture tutored by Adam Smith in France between 1764 and 1766. Smith was subsequently a frequent visitor at Dalkeith Palace, the principal Buccleuch residence, as was Sir Walter Scott. In 1783 when the Royal Society of Edinburgh was established to further the study of physical science and by implication to do down Buchan's Society of Antiquaries with its faint radical tinge, Buccleuch became its first president.

The world of the regional magnates was one which Dundas knew and understood. He was not one of their number, though his membership of the family of the Dundases of Arniston gave him the necessary standing for familiar access to and intercourse with the greatest in the land. Henry Dundas was the son of a Lord President of the Court of Session and Anne, daughter of Sir William Gordon of Invergordon. In 1760, as he grew to manhood, his older half-brother, Robert, became Lord President. The Arniston family was undoubtedly at the very pinnacle of the *noblesse de robe* of Scotland. The fact did not guarantee any solidarity with them on the part of other members of that order. The other branches of the Dundas family were remarkable for their sustained hostility towards what they saw as the upstart house of Arniston. Until his death in September 1781 Sir Lawrence Dundas of an elder branch of the family controlled and represented the city of Edinburgh in a spirit of virulent hostility to Henry Dundas. The latter moved in on Edinburgh over the grave of his kinsman and in the closest possible alliance with the Duke of Buccleuch. Even so, there were plenty of relatives left to oppose the rising Arniston ascendancy. Until he became a peer in 1794, Sir Thomas Dundas, head of the Dundas of Dundas family, repulsed all attempts, fair and foul, by Henry Dundas to unseat him as representative of Stirlingshire. Some small consolation was available to Henry in 1790 when he did unseat another hostile relative, Colonel Thomas Dundas of Fingask, in the remote Orkney constituency.

Hardly surprisingly, Dundas expanded his empire of electoral influence not through collateral branches of his own family, most of whom loathed him, but by tactical alliances with local magnates. His 'conquest' of the north-east, that shoulder of Scotland whose regional capital is Aberdeen, was a classic illustration of his technique, and of its subtlety. The foundation of Dundas's campaign was an alliance with Alexander, fourth Duke of Gordon, the head of a once mighty family long in decline. His Grace was afflicted with such staggering debts that he could hardly show his face in the metropolis during a London season. All this was hard on a man who had tried to purge any trace of Jacobite connections in his family by recruiting a fencible regiment (the first of four he raised altogether) in 1759 when he was aged only 17. The congenial obscurity of Gordon Castle was even less attractive to his eccentric and tempestuous wife, Jane Maxwell. Late in 1783 the Duke of Gordon embraced Henry Dundas as his political guide, philosopher, and friend, mentioning only an English peerage as an appropriately modest object of his ambition. Financial embarrassment amongst Scots peers was, incidentally, always a great help to Dundas. About the same time that the Duke of Gordon moved into the Dundas orbit, Lord Napier, another impoverished North Briton burdened with debts incurred to purchase a company commander's commission in the era of the American war, wrote to Dundas successfully soliciting an increased pension from the state in exchange for stolid support for the official line in such matters as Scots peerage elections.

Yet the Dundas – Gordon axis rapidly proved inadequate in the face of the rival electoral interest of the Earl of Fife, to which was allied men of local substance like Lord Findlater and Sir James Grant. Dundas had no real reason to quarrel with the Earl of Fife, a man interested in improved farming methods but otherwise fanatically conservative and a sincere admirer of William Pitt. By September 1787 Dundas was engaged in ramming a compromise with Lord Fife down the reluctant ducal throat. His Grace eventually swallowed hard. The enlarged alliance by 1790 swept the north-east as far indeed as Inverness, where Dundas successfully negotiated with Sir James Grant and the Frasers of Lovat for the return of a suitably 'reliable' candidate, Norman Macleod. Dundas was ever a man who respected strength. Faced with opposition from an MP whom he thought he could safely isolate and crush, he was ruthless. His normal technique was to seek to deprive that MP of even the most minimal and routine patronage without which it was difficult for the unfortunate man to retain any standing in his own constituency. Faced with a vested territorial interest backed by hard cash, Dundas usually tested its strength and if the opposition failed to crumple under his assault, he tried to come to terms with it. For example, it was a pact with the Earl of Eglinton, finalized about 1789, which gave Dundas control of Ayrshire.

It was a measure of the lack of common sense of the diarist James Boswell that he tried, with of course absolutely no success, to insert himself as a candidate for Ayrshire in defiance of these arrangements. It was typical of the generosity Dundas could show to a fallen opponent who did not threaten his power that in 1791 he gave Boswell's brother David a job in the Navy Office worth £100 a year which Boswell had been seeking for his sibling for years. Fully to secure the Dundas grip on a complex county political scene could be the work of many years. Thus, in the county of Fife Dundas discovered by the educative experience of losing elections that he needed the support of both the Wemyss family and that of the Earl of Fife. The Wemyss interest he had bought by 1788 with British and West Indian appointments. Lord Fife, as has been demonstrated, was the subject of elaborate negotiations covering his interest in the north-east as well as in Fife before he could be safely gathered into the Dundas camp. Those who played along with Dundas seldom violated their basic conservative instincts and all derived benefits from access to central political power. The Duke of Gordon achieved a hereditary seat in the Lords in 1784 when he was made Baron Gordon of Huntly and Earl of Norwich in the United Kingdom peerage. He was able once more to hold court in his London house in St James's Square during 'the Season', or rather his wife did, marrying off three of her five daughters to dukes and one to a marquis (the fifth had to settle for a mere baronet).

Viewed from the top downwards the Dundas ascendancy was therefore little more than a larger around William Pitt into which the ruling class in Scotland progressively moved, partly out of conviction and partly as the result of systematic pressure and cajolery from Dundas, who happened to be Pitt's personal friend and drinking companion as well as an important minister and the acknowledged manager of Scotland. The only change most of these people wanted was change in the economy in order to make them richer. Yet the Dundas era was more than just a period of political and social immobilism. The régime of the Younger Pitt, of which Dundas was so devoted a servant, was rooted in change as well as stability. At the general election of 1790 dynamism was not the keynote of the political process in Scotland. Only nine counties and seven brughs were contested. Imprecise though any figure was bound to be, it was reckoned that 34 out of 45 MPs were of the Dundas interest. Yet Dundas owed this measure of success to some extent to the fact that he represented the internal and external expansion of the British state.

India is a good example of the way in which Dundas embodied long-standing trends in British policy, and Indian patronage was very important indeed in binding together his domestic political empire. Despite the failure of the proposals put forward by Fox and North, it was clear that the British state would have to assume a much larger measure of responsibility for the territorial empire established in the Indian subcontinent by the Honourable East India Company, so in August 1784 Pitt's India Bill was passed into law. It established a joint régime of Company and Crown for British India. The Directors of the Company retained control of commerce and patronage but a new Board of Control consisting of six unpaid privy councillors was entitled 'to superintend, direct and control all acts, operations and concerns which in anywise relate to the civil or military government or the revenues of the British territorial possessions in the East Indies'. Dundas was one of the leading members of the Board from 1784 to 1801 and in 1793 the salaried office of President of the Board of Control was created for him. He might just as well have been called Secretary of State for India, since he presided over a full department complete with secretaries and clerks. One of the biographers of Dundas (C. Matheson) is at pains to depict his hero as both a stoutly patriotic Scot and a good British imperialist. Neither description wholly fits the realities of eighteenth-century politics, but if Scotland to Dundas was, at the height of his career, a home province to which he retired occasionally to slaughter game and fix elections, India was undoubtedly something of an intellectual passion to him, though of course he never went there. He worked regularly at the offices of the Board; read every scrap of information he could obtain on India from a wide range of sources; and dominated his colleagues to the point where membership of the Board in his day was poor training for independent office in India. George Canning, a member between 1799 and 1801, agreed that Dundas was active and diligent but added that he was also 'selfish and Scotch' and that his policy was 'pillage and patronage : pillage by conquest and patronage at home'.

It is important to be clear about the parameters of the possible in 'Dundas's India'. The great age of unbridled profiteering in Bengal by Company servants was over before 1784. It hinged on the right of those servants to participate privately in internal trade and in the so-called 'country trade' from India to South-East Asia. The Bengal over which the Company exercised effective control after Clive's victory at Plassey in 1757 was described by a Scot (A. Dow) who had served there as one of 'the richest, most populous and best cultivated kingdoms of the world'. It was also until about 1760 a country where desirable goods were relatively cheap as well as abundant. Exemption from taxation, political pressure, and brute force enabled Company men to become extremely rich remarkably fast. When the unscrupulous John Johnstone retired back to Scotland in the 1760s he was worth £300,000 and could buy three estates and establish a parliamentary interest. 'Nabobs' like Johnstone were a fact of life in Scotland in the 1780s. One of them, Alexander Brodie, was so powerful in the north-east that Dundas had to come to terms, which included Brodie's unanimous election for the Elgin District of Burghs in 1790. Reforming Governors, inflation, and a sense of moral outrage in Britain epito-mized by the eventually unsuccessful trial of the great Governor General Warren Hastings in the years 1787–95, had put an end to the worst excesses in India. Sir John Macpherson, a Scot who arrived in India in 1767 as a ship's purser, and contrived to end up Governor General for a year and a bit (1785–6) when Warren Hastings returned to England, was one of the last of the old-style officials, and his nick-name 'Johnny McShuffle', showed he had outlived his time. Dundas knew, and made sure that friends such as the Duchess of Buccleuch were cognisant of his conviction, that he had to use his influence in India with reasonable moderation, lest he hazard it altogether.

He still had enormous influence. Appointment to a good position in the 'covenanted' or established and exclusively British branch of the Company service was by nomination of a Director. The Directors were elected by the Court of Proprietors of the Company and could in theory be dismissed but in practice were life-tenants of positions which were expensive to gain and gave them a vested interest in enjoying favour with Dundas who in any case set about building his own reliable power-base in the Directorate. The rate of commercial profit in Britain in 1700 seems to have normally ranged from 6 to 12 per cent. In 1776 Adam Smith thought 8 to 10 per cent a good profit. In Bengal in 1767 normal profit in internal trade reputedly ranged from 20 to 30 per cent and access to this world for a Scot was usually by nomination. Inevitably many Scots had bought East India stock for the sake of influence in the Court of Proprietors and what Adam Smith grimly described as a share 'if not in the plunder, yet in the appointment of the plunderers'. Dundas represented after 1784 a cleaned-up, to some extent centralized, and almost respectable version of what could be saved from the old rackets.

He did help to export his countrymen in large numbers to India, though he was pilloried by English cartoonists like Gillray for this propensity. Dundas knew full well that there were limits beyond which he must not go for fear of giving some unscrupulous demagogue like Wilkes the chance to whip up a violently anti-Scottish agitation. In 1787 Dundas warned the new Governor of Madras, Sir Archibald Campbell, that:

> It is said with a Scotchman at the head of the Board of Control and a Scotchman at the Government of Madras, all India will soon be in their hands, and that the County of Argyle will be depopulated by the emigration of Campbells to be provided for by you at Madras.

Nevertheless, Dundas undoubtedly in his Indian appointments favoured his fellow Scotsmen and looked after his relatives. In 1821 Sir Walter Scott referred to the Board of Control as 'the corn chest for Scotland'. Part of the explanation for this was simply the enormous expansion of British India in the Dundas era, which created many opportunities for civil and military appointments and for the lucky survivors (the death rate was always high) opportunities for spectacular careers. Colonel Colin Mackenzie, for example, the son of a Stornoway merchant, rose to be first Surveyor-General of India in 1815. He owed his initial appointment to the Madras Engineers in 1782 to the patronage of the Seaforth family, the once Jacobite Mackenzie chieftains. The Earl of Seaforth actually died at sea on his way to India with a regiment in 1781, while his heir died in India in 1783 of wounds received in battle with Maratha pirates. Colin Mackenzie went on to campaign against Tipu Sultan, ruler of the south Indian state of Mysore, in the army of Arthur Wellesley, the future Duke of Wellington. Surveys of conquered territory in India interspersed with service in the Dutch East Indies against a Dutch régime allied to Revolutionary France were the background to his final elevation in 1815 to a post he held until he died at Calcutta in 1821. Mackenzie was an immensely professional surveyor and a man with a deep scholarly interest in Indian culture, but patronage and aggressive war lay at the base of his career.

Expansion on the scale that happened in India was hardly envisaged by anybody in 1784. The debacle in America had coincided with a debacle in British India. British territory was organized in three presidencies; Bombay, Madras, and Calcutta. Only the last-named had anything like a territorial empire. Madras controlled an area known as the Northern Circars from which, as Dundas was only too aware, it drew depressingly little revenue. An attempt by the Bombay presidency to seize an enlarged territorial base on the Malabar or western coast of India led to humiliating defeat at the hands of Tipu of Mysore and the Treaty of Mangalore of 1784, whereby Bombay surrendered rather than gained territory. The Company debt stood at £8,000,000. Pitt's India Bill specifically renounced war and annexation. Yet expansion came, partly at any rate because Dundas was open to arguments ultimately rooted in the conviction of the Bombay presidency officials (most of whom were also private traders on a large scale) that force must be used to secure control of products necessary for the booming China trade. Here rather than in India did the Company make its money, by importing ever-increasing amounts of China tea into Britain where a mass market was being created by Pitt's policy of drastically cutting the duty on tea to discourage smuggling. In the absence of any profitable large-scale European export to China tea was paid for by the despatch of Indian goods to China by private traders. The west coast of India produced pepper and other spices, sandalwood, and above all the raw cotton on whose export was built the original greatness of Bombay. Two Mysore wars, the first of which ended in 1792 with defeat for Tipu and the loss of half his territory, and the second in 1799 with his complete overthrow and death, were not unconnected with British determination to control the sources of exports to China.

Pressure on Dundas for a more forward policy for the sake of the China trade ultimately derived from an interest in penetrating Far Eastern markets which had waxed strong long before the American war. One leading figure in this school of thought was Alexander Dalrymple, navigator, explorer, publicist, and hydrographer. He came from a distinguished Scots family. Amongst his elder brothers were the judge and writer Lord Hailes; James who commanded a regiment in the conquest of French Canada; Hugh who was a Captain in the Royal Navy and a friend of the Pacific explorer Captain Cook; and James, Lord Provost of Edinburgh. Alexander Dalrymple, who died in 1808, rose to be hydrographer to first the East India Company and then the Royal Navy. His professional standards were such as to give Britain a world lead in a field in which she had previously lagged. He was an omen of a most significant change. The day of the rascally adventurer was drawing to a close. Some survived well into the Dundas era in India. Murdoch Brown, who left Scotland for Lisbon in 1750, is a good example. He somehow appeared on the Malabar or western coast of India as a consul for Maria Theresa, Empress of Austria, and later changed from Austrian nationality to French. At one stage he was Danish. After the tide of British conquest swept over the scene he emerged from the wreckage as Police Commissioner in Mahé. Always he looked after his pocket, whether as Scot, Dane, Austrian, Frenchman, or North Briton. His like could not come again. Nor, blessedly, could the career of a predator like Lauchlin Macleane, a Maclean of Coll born in Ulster, who in 20 years between 1757 and 1777 campaigned as an army doctor in Canada, speculated dishonesty in captured West Indian land, intrigued in India, and operated as a totally corrupt and ruthless MP and stock-speculator in London.

The second great wave of conquest which occurred in India during the Dundas era owed little to the muddy self-seeking of sharks like Lauchlin Macleane. It was basically premeditated aggression by the Marquis Wellesley, Governor General 1798–1805, which Wellesley justified largely in terms of anticipating French intrigues in India, in which he does not seem truly to have believed. Fortunately for him, Dundas was more inclined to take such threats seriously. Scots were prominent in the conquest and organization of continental power in the Mysore and Maratha wars, but as devoted soldiers like Sir David Baird, or deeply conscientious administrators like Mountstuart Elphinstone, or that grandson of the manse Sir John Malcolm, not as self-seeking opportunists like Murdoch Brown.

Scotsmen were in fact very significant in that general overhauling and professionalization of British government which was perhaps the greatest single achievement of the Pitt-Dundas axis, or rather the price they and the ruling groups they served had to pay to restore the moral authority of the state after the American catastrophe. It is no accident that Scottish intellectuals and the products of Dissenting academies in England played a disproportionately important rôle in re-structuring the prevailing concepts of the appropriate rôle of the state in society. The Scots combined a precocious educational establishment with a strong tradition of socially relevant analytical thought. Scottish thinkers like Lord Kames or Adam Smith regarded civilization as synonymous with a highly organized political society whose workings were susceptible to the processes of reason. Edward Gibbon's *Autobiography* may have given an unfair picture of port and prejudice as the prevailing attributes of eighteenth-century Oxford, but certainly the two ancient English universities simply did not produce articulate thinkers on major issues of public policy to match the much-distrusted Dissenters and North Britons who clustered around Lord Shelburne, George III's first post-war premier, and later around the Younger Pitt, who appropriated without much acknowledgement many aspects of Shelburne's style and policy.

Scottish contributions to discussions on the theory of economic policy predated the Union of 1707. John Law of Lauriston, Controller General of Finances in France in 1720, came from an Edinburgh banking family and published his first tract on political economy, his *Money and Trade considered*, in 1705 as a contribution to the debate on the revitalization of the Scottish economy. The tradition of the faintly Jacobite Law can be seen as reaching its peak in the work of the erstwhile active Jacobite Sir James Steuart (1713—80), who expiated his sins of commission during the '45 with a very lengthy exile in France, Germany, and Holland. Returning to Scotland in 1763 he showed total loyalty to the Hanoverian dynasty and published early in 1767, with encouragement from friends such as the philosophic Hume, the two imposing octavo volumes of his *An Inquiry into the Principles of Political Oeconomy*. It is a pioneering work by a man with a very real grasp of the mechanism of the market, but who also accepted the need for constant readiness on the part of the state to intervene to protect major interests. Sir James deals exclusively with economic rather than political problems. His interest is directed towards prosperity, not power, but he stressed that

> In treating every question of political oeconomy, I constantly suppose a statesman at the head of government, systematically conducting every part of it, so as to prevent the vicissitudes of manners and innovations, by their natural and immediate effects or consequences, from hurting any interest within the commonwealth.

Seventeen years of exile on the Continent of Europe had undoubtedly attuned Steuart's mind more to Continental than to British realities. Nevertheless, after his full pardon was underlined by his presentation at court in 1772, he tentatively embarked on the rôle of adviser to government. On behalf of the East India Company, he investigated the currency problems of Bengal, publishing his results in an essay entitled *Principles of Money Applied to the State of the Coin in Bengal*. In 1776 Adam Smith's *An Inquiry Into The Nature And Causes Of The Wealth Of Nations* struck a mortal blow at Steuart's reputation by quite deliberately making no reference whatsoever to his work, despite its abundance and its at times very high quality. Smith's book was, as an intellectual artefact, vastly superior to anything

Steuart wrote, for it possessed an elegance and rigour of construction allied to a persuasive lucidity of style which had never been seen before in this field of English letters, and which was seldom to be seen again.

Adam Smith was accorded quite extraordinary status by the leading politicians of his day after 1776. When it was reported in 1787 that 'Dr Smith was much with the ministry', one of the friends of the resentful and superannuated Shelburne (now Marquis of Lansdowne) remarked that he was 'vexed that Pitt should have done so right a thing as to consult Smith'. At a famous dinner party in the house of Henry Dundas at Wimbledon, William Pitt gave Adam Smith the ultimate accolade by bidding him be seated first because 'We are all your scholars'. It was partly a tribute to sheer intellectual brilliance. It was also, of course, a testimonial to the effect that Adam Smith was telling the political leaders at Westminster roughly what they wanted to hear anyway. Smith's message was acceptable as Steuart's had not been.

Because Adam Smith stands at the origins of a line of economic thinkers which can conveniently be described as the English School of Classical Economists (many of the most prominent of whom were Scotch), it was his fate to become a cult-figure for middle-class, liberal industrialists and bankers of the nineteenth and twentieth centuries. They read and misread him in the light of their own circumstances. He knew only his own. Of mechanized industrial production, be it said, he knew virtually nothing. Linen production, or nail-making were both to him essentially handcraft industries. The great engine of economic growth to Smith is therefore not mechanization, nor more surprisingly that rapid population growth which so obsessed another eighteenth-century writer, the Reverend Thomas Malthus, but the rational division and organization of labour. Though *The Wealth Of Nations* is a doric temple hewn out of the granite of self-interest, two qualifications, both of which sharply reduce the distance between it and other contemporary intellectual structures, are essential. First, like all contemporary Scottish thinkers of any consequence, Smith utterly rejected the idea associated with the writings of Bernard de Mandeville (?1670–1733) that naked self-seeking and the social good were ultimately compatible. Enlightened self-interest was Smith's theme. Secondly, *The Wealth Of Nations* was only part of the grand design for a general survey of man in society which began with the publication of *The Theory of Moral Sentiments* in 1759, and whose uncompleted sections have left traces in the shape of students' notes, such as those made in Glasgow at his lectures in 1763 and finally published in 1896 as *Lectures on Justice, Police, Revenue and Arms*.

Smith was pre-industrial, to some extent pre-commercial, and totally pre-democratic in his assumptions. Not for him the vague cosmopolitanism sometimes ascribed to him. His central criterion of policy was national advantage and, as one would expect from a keen North British admirer of the Union of 1707, he defined the national unit as the area over which the Westminster legislature could effectively assert its authority. He did not damn himself in the eyes of those who mattered by an unseemly zeal for American independence. He rejected the proposals put forward by the English clergyman Dean Josiah Tucker for voluntary separation by Britain from the 'ungrateful, ungovernable, and rebellious' Americans. Indeed in 1777 Smith was urging on Wedderburn, Lord North's Solicitor-General, a type of Anglo-American union based on the precedent of 1707. On the other hand, he regarded the loss of the colonies as no economic disaster, and rightly saw that their autonomous status reinforced his arguments for a vast simplification of existing trade regulations to give more scope for market forces and regional specialization. Britain, because of the advanced nature of her economy, still had a great future as a market and supplier of goods to the United States after 1783.

Adam Smith was clear that defence was more important than opulence. He distrusted merchants, being convinced that they seldom met even for conviviality without conspiring against the public. He hated chartered monopoly. Free Trade in the Victorian sense of no discriminatory duties at all, he never thought feasible. Like many contemporaries he hoped for the abolition or lowering of unnecessary or unprofitable restraints on trade. The rambling structure of British protectionism, much of it pure hand-to-mouth expedients introduced to raise vital cash during war, presented an easy target, fossilized and inefficient. By christening his Aunty Sally the 'Mercantile System' Smith may well have bestowed on it more brains than it ever possessed, but he remained firm in his view that by creating distortions leading to misallocation of scarce resources it had lowered economic achievement below that attainable by 'the obvious and simple system of natural liberty'. He never regarded his favourite system as an absolute. There were occasional justifiable exceptions of which he thought the restrictive Navigation Acts were a good example, being essential to the naval supremacy of Britain. His Majesty's Government could clasp the bachelor Scots professor from Kirkcaldy to its bosom with no fear at all that he would turn into an academic asp. He not only did not want the political ascendancy which made him a Commissioner of Customs in

Edinburgh in 1778 to fall, but was also convinced that it would not. Removal of distortions would in·his view lead to more, not less, emphasis on and investment in what he regarded as the only really permanent form of wealth — improved land. His contacts with French thinkers known as the Physiocrats no doubt reinforced his emphasis on the transience of commercial as distinct from landed wealth. Nevertheless, in practical British terms he was right, in his lifetime. Elected Lord Rector of Glasgow University in 1787, he died in 1790, when Pitt and Dundas, those rationalizing men of business to what was still basically The Landed Interest, were riding a high wave of electoral success.

It was not only in fiscal reform that Scots intellectuals played a prominent rôle. They were to the fore in most areas where state power was being consolidated, rationalized, or rendered more morally defensible. Patrick Colquhoun, for example, a former Glasgow merchant who became a London magistrate, was a leading figure in the debate on law and order in the 1790s. He championed the development of the penitentiary partly as an answer to a crisis in the prisons due to the loss of transportation facilities to America. He strongly urged the creation of a salaried police force for the metropolis, where London docks alone sustained a huge and minutely sub-divided community of thieves. The tone of his writings was so authoritarian that it is easy to understand the dislike of the Tory back-benchers for such eager Scotch busybodies earnestly occupied in the great task of undermining the liberties of free-born Englishmen. It is just as well that the British police tradition with its emphasis on disarmed, decentralized forces was deeply influenced by the revulsion raised by some of Colquhoun's proposals.

Even more striking was the rôle of Scottish intellectuals in the single most dramatic gesture of moral validation undertaken by the pre-1832 British social and political system — the campaign against negro slavery. Despite occasional individual protests down the centuries, it is quite clear that the main cultural currents of Christian civilization were not inherently incompatible with the concept of chattel slavery until a surprisingly late stage in history. It was therefore of immense significance when the great French thinker Montesquieu, in book XV, chapter V of *L'Esprit des Lois* published in 1748 attacked the principle of slavery. Francis Hutcheson stood at the head of the increasingly articulate Scottish intellectual opposition to slavery in the eighteenth century. To him the structure of morality was based on the twin principles of utility and benevolence, and neither was compatible with the classical arguments for slavery. Adam Smith, his successor as Professor of Moral Philosophy at Glasgow, adopted a broadly similar stance underlining the inexpediency of slavery with the passage in *The Wealth of Nations* in which he said 'The experience of all ages and nations demonstrates that the work done by slaves, though it appears to cost only their maintenance, is in the end dearest of all'.

David Hume, though sympathetic to anti-slavery, hazarded in a famous footnote to his essay 'Of National Character' published in 1754 the conjecture that negroes were naturally inferior in capacity to whites. Henry Home, Lord Kames, developed this in his *Sketches in the History of Man* (1774) into the theory that negroes were totally inferior and indeed close to the apes. Another Lord of Session, James Burnett Lord Monboddo, was totally opposed to such views, buttressing his own pleas for the abolition of slavery with a passionate statement of the unity of all races of man and indeed of all primates. Far more important than the bickerings of these learned gentlemen was the testimony of Scots whose opposition to slavery was rooted in their strong Evangelical Christianity. The Reverend James Ramsay, an Episcopalian born in Fraserburgh in 1733, spent 18 years as a clergyman in the West Indies before returning to England where he became Vicar of Teston in Kent by the patronage of the great naval administrator Sir Charles Middleton, later Lord Barham. Educated at King's College Aberdeen, where he made a lifelong friend of his teacher the philosopher Thomas Reid, Ramsay leapt to fame late with the publication in 1784 of *An Essay on the Treatment and Conversion of African Slaves in the British Sugar Colonies*. Before he died in 1789 Ramsay had provided leading figures in the emancipation struggle, such as William Wilberforce and Thomas Clarkson, with invaluable material full of his own passionate rejection of both the slave trade and slavery.

There is no doubt that by the last decades of the eighteenth century the Scottish thinker who was most successfully publicizing anti-slavery sentiment on an international basis was Dr James Beattie, born in Laurencekirk in Kincardineshire in 1735, and appointed Professor of Moral Philosophy and Logic in Marischal College Aberdeen in 1760. Beattie was one of those literary North Britons who attained eminence by providing the English-speaking world with exactly what it wanted. He was a voluminous, influential, and vapid poet, but the foundation of his enormous contemporary reputation was the publication in 1769 of the bombastically entitled *Essay on the Nature and Immutability of Truth, in Opposition to Sophistry and Scepticism*. The book was supposed to demolish the 'infidel fallacies' of Hume and Voltaire and was widely read in France and America, where Beattie was made a member of the American Philosophical Society. In fact Beattie was quite incompetent in the subject he professed and so far from demolishing Hume this shoddily self-satisfied book simply failed to understand him. Yet Beattie's advocacy of anti-slavery, especially in the lectures which he published so successfully in 1790 as *Elements of Moral Science*, was of great significance. The twin strands of Enlightenment thought and Evangelical fervour gave him unique access to the mind of his age. Not for nothing did Sir Josuah Reynolds depict Beattie smugly banishing daemonic influences with a languid wave of his *Essay on Truth*. The revulsion from any proposed changes which followed the outbreak of the French Revolutionary wars delayed the abolition of the British slave trade until 1807, and the abolition of slavery itself in the British Empire until 1834, but there is a sense in which the vital intellectual battles had all been won by the 1780s and 90s, in large measure thanks to the labours and talents of men like Beattie and Ramsay.

What rendered the integration of the educated classes of Scotland into the British state system so complete in the late eighteenth century was the way in which the intellectual and spiritual influence of a limited number of outstanding Scottish publicists was supplemented by solid career opportunities for many more North Britons. To the bachelor Adam Smith his access to the great and powerful such as Dundas was clearly useful mainly as a means of securing small favours, often for colleagues or acquaintances or indeed for their wives and families after the decease of their breadwinner. To many Scottish graduates who were never likely to hob-nob with Pitt or Dundas, the British realms still offered very great opportunities for personal advancement, and of no group was this more true than the medical graduates. Equally, the existence of such opportunities was bound to affect the structure of Scottish educational provision, and of this the development of the Edinburgh medical school is an outstanding example.

There had long existed in Glasgow a chartered Faculty of Physicians and Surgeons and in Edinburgh a College of Physicians and an Incorporation of Surgeons. Medical qualification was usually achieved by an apprenticeship of some years to a practitioner, though the corporate bodies of physicians and surgeons (to whom apothecaries and barbers remained attached until the late eighteenth or early nineteenth centuries) normally provided some measure of academic instruction. Those Scots who sought formal university courses in medicine had long gone abroad to French or German universities and latterly to those of the United Netherlands. However, the eighteenth century saw the rapid creation of substantial schools of medicine in Scottish universities. No less than 11 medical chairs were established in the University of Edinburgh between 1685 and 1807, but the decisive moment was probably the appointment in 1720 of Alexander Monro (1697–1767) as Professor of Anatomy. Alexander Monro had studied medicine in Edinburgh, London, Paris, and Leiden. The solid support of Edinburgh Town Council, which ruled over the town's college it had founded, secured him against damaging demarcation disputes with the Faculty of Surgeons. It also helped to provide vital facilities such as a new anatomical lecture theatre and access to the infirmary which was established in 1738. Thereafter the build-up of staff and facilities was supported by manifest success in attracting students. Between 1720 and 1790 roughly 12,800 men passed through the Edinburgh medical school.

Edinburgh could expand its university teaching of medicine much faster than Glasgow, where an effective medical school only began to function from about 1750. Dr William Cullen, who moved from Hamilton to Glasgow in 1744 and began to lecture on medicine outside the university, was the key figure in Glasgow. By 1746 he was lecturing within the university. By 1747 he had persuaded the university to fit up a chemical laboratory where he taught chemistry with the aid of John Carrick, assistant to the Professor of Anatomy. In 1748 Cullen also began to teach *materia medica* and botany and in January 1751 he was appointed Professor of Medicine. One of the problems facing medical education in Glasgow was the continuing conflict between the Faculty of Physicians and Surgeons and the university. It was gradually overcome and with the opening of Glasgow Royal Infirmary in 1794, where classes in clinical medicine and clinical surgery were being held under university auspices by the end of the century, Glasgow built up individual medical classes of 200 students. Few of these graduated. Most were qualifying by apprenticeship. The improving facilities of the university were being used by them to supplement a more traditional training. Crown initiative led to the creation of no less than five regius chairs (in natural history, surgery, midwifery, botany, and chemistry) between 1807 and 1818, but these underlined another peculiarly Glaswegian problem. Decisions of the Court of Session in 1771–2 had confirmed that the government of the University of Glasgow was a closed corporation consisting of the Faculty or the holders of the 13 then established chairs plus the principal of the university. Regius professors were excluded from not only the governance of the institution, but also from examining.

Nevertheless, Glasgow's medical school was the second most important in Scotland. The two Aberdeen universities had no systematic teaching of medicine, though each maintained on its staff a mediciner, and each exercised the right to award the degree of MD, after due payment of fees. A conjoint medical school was to have been one result of a proposed union of the universities in 1786, but that union aborted. From 1818 a joint supervisory committee from Marischal College and King's did successfully manage a programme of medical instruction, but between 1826 and 1839 King's awarded only 4 degrees in medicine, and Marischal 25. St Andrews had from 1722 a Chandos Professor of Medicine and Anatomy whose main function was to vet candidates for MD degrees. He had no other significant function for he had no medical colleagues and the shoals of St Andrews MDs evoked bitter criticism from Edinburgh, though they were all in theory established medical men and included leading Edinburgh medical figures as well as such exotics as Jean Paul Marat, the future French revolutionary.

Careers lay at the base of rapid expansion of medical education in Edinburgh and to a lesser extent Glasgow. Scotsmen were already outstanding figures in the medical world of London around 1750. Three Lanarkshire men in particular stand out. The first to make his name was Dr William Smellie, the leading London obstetrician of his day and author of a celebrated textbook on midwifery which was revised by another Glasgow medical man, the novelist Tobias Smollett (1721–71), who went to London in 1739 and discovered that his vocation lay in the picaresque novel rather than the medical scene. The two other Lanarkshire doctors were William and John Hunter. William had worked with William Cullen in a country practice near Hamilton but his ambition led him to London, where he stayed first with the hospitable Smellie and then established himself as a private teacher of anatomy. His brother John joined him in that most competitive field in which he rose to astonishing eminence. The last 25 years of John Hunter's life were spent as surgeon to St George's Hospital. He died in 1793, loaded with honours: Surgeon-General to the Army, Inspector-General of Hospitals, and Surgeon-Extraordinary to the King. William Hunter had already perpetuated their joint names in 1781 with the princely bequest of collections and cash to the University of Glasgow which led to the creation of the Hunterian Museum.

Such careers were not without precedent. Dr John Arbuthnot (1667–1735), a graduate of Marischal College in arts and a St Andrews MD, had been physician to Queen Anne and an intimate friend of Pope and Swift two generations before. What the later eighteenth century offered to the medical entrepreneur from Scotland was unprecedented scope. Dr James Graham, born in Edinburgh in 1745, can serve as an (extreme) example for many. After studying medicine in Edinburgh, he made a fortune by practice in England and America. Returning to Edinburgh in 1783 he delivered public discourses on health illustrated by the nubile charms of 'Vestina' his female assistant who posed on a pillar and later became Admiral Nelson's Lady Hamilton. Sadly, Dr Graham did not live to see 'Vestina's' later triumphs. He died in 1794, after being declared mad in 1788.

Medicine was unusual in being a profession with a very buoyant demand for its services. There were comparatively few such professions in eighteenth-century Scotland. The Kirk was chronically over-subscribed, partly because access to its divinity schools cost little or nothing, apart from a frugal subsistence during academic terms. Would-be incumbents could, of course, eke out a living as tutors or schoolmasters whilst they waited for a favourable conjunction of parish and patron. Nevertheless, the 'stickit minister' who never was able to call a pulpit his own, was already a problem in the eighteenth century, long before he became a stock figure in the prose of the sentimental 'kailyard' writers of the nineteenth century. Law, as we have seen, involved an expensive training and was dominated by the upper classes who tended to view the Scottish legal system as virtually their own private domain. This did not prevent individuals from amongst the upper echelons of Scottish society from carving out highly successful legal careers for themselves in England. The best example is William Murray, the fourth son of David, fifth Viscount Stormont. Educated at Westminster School and Christ Church Oxford, Murray made much of his Scottish connections to gain his first briefs at the English bar. Once established, his intellectual capacity and silver tongue carried him upwards in a dazzling legal-political career which culminated in the achievement of the position of Lord Chief Justice of the King's Bench in 1756 and the English Earldom of Mansfield in 1776. Notably liberal on Roman Catholic emancipation, Mansfield struck a great blow for negro emancipation by his judgement in

Somersett's case in 1771, a judgement which freed any slave in Britain. Yet on central political issues like the Jacobite threat, the American Revolution, or the French Revolution Mansfield was 'sound'. He detested them all.

Scottish universities were themselves a buoyant field of professional enterprise. There was plenty of nepotism in them. Alexander Monro *primus* (1697–1767) was succeeded in the Edinburgh Chair of Anatomy by his son Alexander Monro *secundus* (1733–1817), who was duly succeeded by his son Alexander Monro *tertius* (1773–1859). St Andrews, which was not particularly distinguished in this era, was at least outstanding in the scale of the nepotism sponsored by its dominant figure, George Hill, Professor of Greek from 1772 and Principal of St Mary's College between 1791 and 1819. As the acknowledged leader of the Moderate party in the General Assembly after the retiral of Principal Robertson, Hill necessarily worked hand-in-glove with Henry Dundas, who served as Chancellor of the University from 1788 to 1811. Though such a chancellor was of some assistance to the institution and its students, particularly when they were looking for jobs, Dundas did not fail also to advance his own interests and those of his ally Hill, whose relatives at one stage held 6 out of 13 places on the St Andrews Senate. In all Scottish universities professors tended to view their chairs as life freeholds and failure to perform the most minimal of teaching duties was quite common. Adam Smith's view that the system of class fees as a major element in professorial incomes in Scotland was a guarantee of application to teaching duties was obviously an oversimplification, but one which contained a large element of truth.

Class fees were never very high. Most divinity courses were free. Even as late as 1826 three to four guineas was about as much as anyone expected to pay for a university class in Scotland. Just how much it cost a student to survive the six-month academic term from autumn to early summer is not easy to say, for it varied from institution to institution and from person to person, but £14 to £20 was a range which would include most careful if not penurious students. Professors whose subjects were compulsory, such as moral philosophy in the Arts Faculty, and professors whose subjects were popular, could and did make a lot of money from their large classes. Dugald Stewart, Professor of Moral Philosophy in the University of Edinburgh from 1785 to 1811, was fortunate both in the status of his subject and in his talents as 'one of the greatest didactic orators'. A pupil of Thomas Reid, he actually succeeded his own father as Professor of

Mathematics in Edinburgh a decade before he moved to the vastly more appropriate philosophical chair. Though no original thinker, he popularized the philosophical tradition of Reid, both by lectures and by writings such as the *Elements of the Philosophy of the Human Mind*, whose first volume appeared in 1792, to become at once a standard text in the colleges of the United States, as well as influential in Britain. In lectures on political economy Stewart popularized the main conclusions of Adam Smith. When the French war drove young English aristocrats such as the future Lords Lansdowne, Palmerston, and John Russell off the Grand Tour and into his lecture theatre, Stewart improved the shining hour by boarding them at £400 a boarder per session. Stewart was an academic entrepreneur behind a lectern.

To some extent this was what would now be called extra-mural lecturing: instructive entertainment which made major academic developments available to non-specialist audiences in very simplified form. Indeed Thomas Charles Hope, Professor of Chemistry in Edinburgh for over 40 years from 1799, abandoned pure research to polish the demonstration techniques which kept numbers in his spectacular and popular regular class as high as 500. Extra-mural lectures to a wide variety of audiences ranging from the Faculty of Advocates to fashionable ladies yielded him annual fees for a single class as high as £700. Edinburgh University regularly tried to poach outstanding staff from other Scottish universities. Prominent Glasgow professors such as William Cullen and his successor Joseph Black, for example, moved across to Edinburgh chairs and one of the incentives was undoubtedly the attraction of fees from large classes.

In a more profound sense the Scottish university system in this era happened to be in a phase of rapid expansion at the very end of a long phase of contraction in the universities of most of western Europe. The late sixteenth and early seventeenth centuries had seen a huge expansion in matriculations at Oxford and Cambridge. Imperial Spain, at the height of its Golden Age, had no less than 40 universities within its world empire. By the end of the seventeenth century this 'education revolution' had run its course. Everywhere in the western world student numbers tended to decline for about a century or more. England shared this experience, but not Scotland where a unique if fading cultural heritage, and the profit motive, moved a minority of professors to generate a unique dynamism which was further fuelled by the relatively favourable opportunities offered by an expanding British political and economic system to educated men. The frustrated and therefore alienated intellectual was unimportant in eighteenth-century Scotland. This was a most significant fact, for student numbers increased steadily in every university except St Andrews where there were some 150 students in 1730 and not many more in 1824. Edinburgh, however, had 400 students around 1700, about 1,300 in 1800, and 2,300 in 1824. Glasgow rose from 400 in 1702 to 1,240 by 1824. The two Aberdeen universities had a combined total of 257 students in 1776 and about 730 by 1824.

On the other hand, cultural shock and identity crises were prominent features of the late-eighteenth-century Scottish literary landscape. This was hardly surprising when the leading Scottish intellectuals were so obviously bent on joining the headlong movement towards a profitable and anglicized integration into the British world ruled from Westminster. The slow rhythms of agricultural life in a still predominantly pre-industrial society and the ingrained, if waning, cultural heritage of an older, independent Scotland inevitably resisted the gadarene rush spearheaded by the nobility and so well supported by the professors. The central figure in the early revival of Scots vernacular poetry was the elder Allan Ramsay who came to Edinburgh from Leadhills in Lanarkshire around 1700 and who died in 1758. His life and work underline the paradoxes and tensions of his mental world. Co-founder of the Easy-Club in 1712, he aped the manner of the Augustan wits of the court of Queen Anne, adopting the soubriquet of 'Isaac Bickerstaff' which he exchanged for the very Scottish 'Gavin Douglas' in 1713. Always capable of Augustan English verse of little merit, which he could even use for strongly patriotic Scottish themes, Ramsay is important for his use of the contemporary vernacular and for his editing of selections of Scottish songs and ballads, and of the great poetry of late medieval Scotland. His collection of Scots songs for *The Tea-Table Miscellany* was part of a patriotic cult which culminated in the remarkable achievement of Robert Burns in this field. His cavalier editorship of poets like Dunbar and Henryson in *The Ever Green* was as significant for the survival of a distinct Scots literary tradition as it is infuriating to modern scholars. At his best, he could use the vernacular in poems about Edinburgh characters in a way which fixed people like Maggy Johnston, John Cowper, and Lucky Wood like flies in amber. At his worst, he displayed an uncertain, arch, and even patronizing attitude towards the Scots tongue which underlined its ambiguous and confused literary status.

Incomparably greater as a poet of the vernacular revival, despite his

short life, was Robert Fergusson (1750–74). Born in Edinburgh and .
possessed of a brilliant mind, Fergusson was educated at the High
School of Edinburgh, Dundee, and at the University of St Andrews,
which he left with no degree because his father died and an attempt to
secure vital financial support from a landed branch of his family
proved abortive. A life of quill-pushing drudgery as a Commissary
Clerk was diversified by the social revels of the Cape Club, a typical
Edinburgh drinking club with intellectual as well as alcoholic
interests. Fergusson always had a streak of unreconstructed Scottish
nationalism in him, as his lines indicate:

> Black be the day that e're to England's ground
> Scotland was eikit by the Union's bond

This did not prevent him from writing indifferent verse in Augustan
English, but his use of Scots to reflect the teeming urban life of the
Edinburgh he knew so well was far more assured as well as more skilful
than the similar exercises of Ramsay. It is appropriate that Fergusson's
masterpiece is generally considered to be his substantial poem on
Edinburgh entitled 'Auld Reekie'. Fergusson published a single
volume of verse in 1773, from which he seems financially to have
reaped about twice what Robert Burns made out of his own
Kilmarnock edition. Yet in a deeper sense the publication failed, for it
attracted no flattering reviews, no upper-class patronage. By 18
October 1774 Fergusson was dead of a complex mixture of alcoholism,
depressive mania, and physical trauma, yet it is important to
remember Burns's comment on this tragedy. Burns always revered the
memory of Fergusson; indeed it was he who placed the headstone on
Fergusson's grave, and Burns was clear that it was lack of patronage
which drove a great poet to an early grave:

> My curse upon your Whunstane hearts
> Ye Enbrugh gentry!
> The tythe o'what ye waste at Cartes
> Wad stow'd his pantry!

The great figure of Burns himself never lacked patronage of a sort
after the publication of his first collection of verse, but his career illustrates fully the multiple crises of identity which haunted the Scottish
literary scene of his day. He was the son of an Ayrshire tenant farmer
who haled, like Fergusson's father, from the north-east of Scotland.

Despite inadequate fare, frugality, and cripplingly hard work which probably permanently undermined the constitution of the young Robert Burns, the family never managed to make an economic success of its tenancies. The rents demanded by some Ayrshire landlords in the two decades after the birth of Burns in 1759 clearly outran prospects of practical improvement, especially on poor soil. Robert Burns even entered into partnership with a rascally flax-dresser in the Ayrshire port of Irvine, in the hopes that the growing and preparing of flax might offer a chance of prosperity, but the episode ended in farce and frustration. However, it must be said that Burns was well schooled and quite prodigiously well read. He could write correct standard English, and apparently speak it with less of a Scottish accent than the philosopher Hume. After toying with the idea of emigration, Burns launched upon the world in 1786 the famous Kilmarnock edition of *Poems, Chiefly in the Scottish Dialect, by Robert Burns*. The Reverend George Lawrie, minister of Loudon, sent a copy to Edinburgh, and Burns was famous overnight.

He was lionized and patronized by the *literati*, the self-appointed arbiters of literary merit in Edinburgh, of whom perhaps the most dominant in 1786 when Burns came to the city in person was Henry Mackenzie (1745–1831), the master of the sentimental novel. Mackenzie made his name in 1771 by the publication (originally anonymously) of *The Man of Feeling* which went through 9 editions by 1800 and 30 more by 1824. So successful was it that an unhappy English clergyman, Mr Eccles of Bath, tried to exploit the work's original anonymity by claiming to have written it. Burns read two copies of the book, claiming to revere it next to the Bible. To modern taste it is a depressingly humourless collection of stock situations designed to elicit pathos and pity. Yet Mackenzie was a central figure in Edinburgh intellectual life to the end of his days, which came the year before the demise of his close friend Walter Scott. In a periodical called *The Lounger* in December 1786 Mackenzie wrote the first important criticism of Burns, praising his 'unimitable delicacy' and 'rapt and inspired melancholy'. Though the *literati*, including Hugh Blair, the Reverend Professor of Rhetoric, and Dugald Stewart, the philosopher, responded enthusiastically to the very misleading image of Burns as 'the unlettered ploughman' (which he was not despite his own and Mackenzie's publicity on this theme) they were hostile to the Scots tongue and would have turned Burns into a sentimental spouter of neo-classical English. James Beattie produced in 1787, when Burns was in Edinburgh, a list of Scotticisms to be avoided.

It is the measure of the genius of Burns that though he did write undistinguished English verse, he continued to use Scots in a sophisticated range of density which made him the first and last man in the eighteenth and nineteenth centuries to apparently surmount the two great linguistic crises facing Lowlanders. One was the disintegration of standard court Scots into a series of regional dialects after 1603. The other was the divorce between the language of the head, English, and that of the heart, Scots. His vast range of styles is all the more impressive in a man whose last years of creative activity were largely given up to a tremendous work on Scottish songs. Through much of his work runs a strain of iconoclastic radicalism. His own ambiguous and fragile rôle in the company of his betters gave an edge to his social satire no less keen than that on his biting Juvenal-like attacks against the more hypocritical and illiberal side of the Kirk. For politicians there is nearly always a note of contempt. Burns was an open admirer of the French Revolution, being cut by upper-class friends for his pains. Yet even Burns represented no real threat to the social order or Dundas ascendancy. Security for Burns and for the large legitimate and illegitimate brood he loved was his job as an Excise Officer in Dumfries, a job which he openly acknowledged he owed to the benign patronage of James, Earl of Glencairn and patron of Kilmarnock parish. Before he died of rheumatic heart disease in 1796 he had recanted his pro-Revolutionary views to keep his Excise job. After 1793 he penned patriotic anti-French verse. His eldest son attended both Edinburgh and Glasgow Universities before embarking on a distinguished civil service career. His second and third sons William Nicol Burns and James Glencairn Burns were to be colonels in the Indian Army.

6

Political Attitudes during the French Revolutionary and Napoleonic Wars 1793–1815

Arguably the outbreak of war with Revolutionary France simply consolidated the grip of the Dundas system on Scottish political life. By 1793 it was already formidable and much of what appeared on the surface as spontaneous expression of opinion by the county élites was probably studied sycophancy with ulterior motives in view. When, for example, late in 1793 it became clear that Dundas was not prepared to promote the son of Sir Robert Anstruther from a lieutenancy to a captaincy in the Royal Navy the indignant father, who carried much electoral weight in the Anstruther Easter District of Burghs, claimed of himself that 'no one has been more ready in promoting every address, subscription, and other county measure which was supposed acceptable to the ministry'. Certainly, Dundas was fierce and vigilant in protecting and expanding what he saw as his electoral interest at by-elections, crushing ruthlessly signs of disaffection by the Marquis of Tweeddale in Haddingtonshire in 1795 and wresting Kirkcudbrightshire from the control of the Earl of Galloway, with the aid of a flood of patronage in the same year. However, it was really the declaration of war by the French Convention early in 1793 on Great Britain and Holland that opened the way to the apogee of the Dundas ascendancy in North Britain.

Though clear that the Glorious Revolution of 1688 was the last British revolution he wanted to hear about, and that in terms only of vague panegyric, Dundas hardly welcomed the war. Nevertheless he more than any other individual ran it at the administrative level, first as Home Secretary and then as Secretary of State for War until Pitt's government resigned in March 1801. Control over the vastly expanded armed forces could only massively enhance the patronage at his disposal. Pressure of business at the War, Home, and India Offices compelled Dundas to transfer the detailed management of Scotland to his nephew, Robert Dundas of Arniston, a tactful, aimiable mediocrity who served as Lord Advocate. His task was easy, for virtually the entire membership of the ruling classes of Scotland rallied to the régime under the twin pressures of patriotism and social panic. Writers like Thomas Paine, the English champion of both the French and American Revolutions, were indeed advocating very radical social and political change. His *Rights of Man* (1792) was widely read in Scotland.

In retrospect it is clear that the activities of radical activists were a great help to the Dundases. The French Revolution certainly helped to stimulate political awareness in Scotland. In 1782 there were 8 Scottish newspapers. By 1790 there were 27 and more were established in 1791−2. In July 1792 the first society of Friends of the People in Scotland met in Edinburgh. By 1792 similar societies were spreading all over Scotland. In September 1792 the Dundee Friends of the Constitution constituted themselves. The Glasgow Associated Friends of the Constitution and of the People came into existence about the same time. Though led by radical lairds and lawyers these Scottish societies had low subscriptions and had more in common with the populist London corresponding Society than with the London Friends of the People, which had a high subscription and consisted of very upper-class men bent mainly on emasculating any popular political movement by appropriating its leadership. Dundas himself seems to have shared the general alarm amongst the possessing classes in Scotland that a movement which encouraged political mobilization amongst the lower orders might lead on to effective demands for political and social reform. Spies were employed to infiltrate radical organizations. Money was disbursed to writers on papers like the *Edinburgh Herald* and *Caledonian Mercury*, and the official government line rapidly hardened into denouncing anyone who wanted any reform at all as a 'Leveller', 'Republican', or 'French Democrat'. Moderate clergyman like the Reverend Dr Hardy who had earned his spurs writing in defence of ecclesiastical patronage now denounced in print the 'system of pillage' advocated by Thomas Paine.

Seventeen ninety-two saw the first General Convention of the Friends of the People in Scotland. Thomas Muir, the son of a Glasgow merchant who had become an Edinburgh advocate, was prominent at it and insisted on reading an address from the society of United Irishmen which many delegates regarded as far too violent. The Convention itself, despite the backing of a movement full of radical shopkeepers and artisans, was extremely traditional in demanding equal representation in frequent parliaments. This had been a platitude of reform politics for generations. The Septennial Act had rendered elections offensively infrequent and the franchise was so irrational as to raise doubts as to whether it made any sense at all. From January 1793 the Crown law officers embarked on a series of sedition trials designed to discredit and intimidate the reform movement. Muir did not help his cause by visiting Paris and Dublin before his trial on exceedingly dubious charges of sedition. With the Lord Justice Clerk, Robert MacQueen Lord Braxfield openly baying for his blood he was sentenced to 14 years transportation. Next month Thomas Fysche Palmer, the Englishman who ministered to a small Unitarian congregation in Dundee, was condemned to seven years transportation on charges of writing an address against the war. In fact he probably only helped revise it, but a career which for him began as a schoolboy at Eton ended in Australia at Botany Bay.

Undaunted by such trials, which continued intermittently until 1820, and secured the transportation of, amongst others, William Skirving the moving spirit in the third and last General Convention of the Friends of People in Edinburgh in 1793, the tiny minority of active radicals continued along increasingly desperate paths. Their programme of annual parliaments, universal male suffrage, and an end to the war had virtually no support in the country at large. The French government persistently deluded itself that Scotland, like Ireland, was panting to throw off the English yoke. It was not true. There was no equivalent in Scotland of the political mobilization in Ireland which in 1798 produced a radical Presbyterian rising in Ulster and a Roman Catholic peasant rising in the south. Even on Ireland, the French were misled, because they wanted to believe him, by the optimistic tongue of Wolfe Tone.

Nevertheless, what made the response to the French Revolution in Scotland so alarming to the authorities in kirk and state was the way in which it involved groups well below those social levels which were traditionally expected to take an interest in politics. Weavers rioted quite seriously in many Scottish towns in 1773–4, threatening to emigrate 'to the colonies' unless they gained the points they were fighting for, but these were essentially traditional, acceptable riots concerned with material issues. Political militancy on such subjects as burghal and parliamentary reform was almost entirely confined to quite small groups composed of lawyers, merchants, and the odd disgruntled landowner. The Incorporated Trades of the Scottish burghs also tended to support agitation for parliamentary and municipal reform in the 1780s, thereby expressing an hostility to the town councils which ran back into the medieval period, when the merchant oligarchs first established a stranglehold on municipal government. Events in France in the early 1790s certainly interested these groups. The Friends of the People societies set up after 1792 tended to be led by merchants, lawyers, manufacturers, and teachers, but as the French Revolution became bloodier and more aggressive externally, the original leadership in the Scottish societies shrank back. From an early stage they had appealed for support from the skilled working class prepared to pay 3d. a quarter subscription. Now the lower middle class and these same skilled craftsmen, above all weavers, moved to the forefront.

Alienation amongst the traditional élites was instant and total. The Conveners' Courts which were the normal spokesmen for the political views of the Incorporated Trades in Dundee and St Andrews, for example, simply dropped their previously active support for reform until after 1815. As the government systematically persecuted the Friends of the People out of sight, governmental warnings of social subversion became a self-fulfilling prophecy. In industrial towns in the west of Scotland and in commercial towns in the east it was the skilled working class which resisted the government's political offensive and formed the much more militant United Scotsmen. Immigrant weavers from Ulster were active in this body. Indeed almost everyone accused of sedition in Scotland between 1797 and 1803 was a weaver. Only in textile counties with a high proportion of Seceders was there serious support for the United Scotsmen. By 1803 it was clear that this second radical wave had failed as completely as the first. It never had the least chance of success. Given the social and power structures of the time, radical weavers were about the last group capable of seizing power, and these precociously literate and articulate men merely reinforced the iniquities they denounced by helping to frighten everyone else into the conservative patriotic camp. Radical demands seldom went beyond the purely political, but invariably raised the spectre of social levelling.

The great bulk of the active males in the better-off classes rushed to display their military zeal by joining the numerous Volunteer Corps which sprang up all over Scotland to resist a French invasion. Robert Burns was a Royal Dumfries Volunteer while the young Walter Scott was Quartermaster, Secretary, and briefly Paymaster of the Royal Edinburgh Light Dragoons. It is true that a measure for embodying a militia of 6,000 men in Scotland in 1797 was only enforced after severe rioting in several places, rioting which cost lives before being crushed by Volunteers and regular troops. However, this was a perfectly reasonable act of resistance by the poorer classes (who alone were likely to be affected) against a system of conscription organized by the schoolmasters, who drew up the basic lists, and providing the government with a force only too likely to be drafted for regular service abroad.

The new radical group provided a continuing *bête noire* for the well-affected. George Mealmaker, the best-known United Scotsman martyr, was transported to Botany Bay in 1798. In 1799 the United Scotsmen were finally banned by name. They were never significant either in numbers or in personnel, being but a pathetic shadow of the United Irishmen they were so clearly influenced by. The simple fact is that Scotland was in no way remarkable for politically-motivated opposition to the government at this period. The Royal Navy, with its fleet mutinies at Spithead and the Nore in 1797, posed for graver problems for the politicians and put far more effective pressure on them to treat at least one section of the underprivileged with common decency. Characteristically, when the sailors returned to their duty it was a Scottish admiral, Adam Duncan, second son of Duncan of Lundie near Dundee, who led them to victory over the French-controlled Dutch fleet, at the battle from which he took his title of Viscount Camperdown.

Dundas himself approached the general election of 1796 in a spirit of near euphoria. His megalomania was that of the pure machine politician – he dreamed of a monopoly of power in his defined precinct: Scotland. In June 1796 he told Lord Hobart, Governor of Madras that he had been convinced 'that if I came to Scotland and exerted myself thoroughly, I might be able to prevent the return of any one Member for Scotland hostile to Government'. Sir David Carnegie MP for Forfarshire succeeded in defeating that ambition. He hated Dundas. About eight other Scots MPs were not quite totally in the Dundas interest. Otherwise '96 was a Roman Triumph for 'Harry the Ninth', the 'Scotch Dictator', the 'Satrap of Scotland', or as others put it 'the slee Dundas'. Socially conservative, but not averse to change if it made government easier or the executive more powerful without making it more responsible, the flexible Dundas had exploited the winds of change abroad in his world to create a unique position for himself. For the future his recipe was more of the lines of development he saw as wise. He supported Pitt's Union of Ireland and Great Britain in 1800 not just as necessary for the war effort, but as a further beneficient extension of the Union of Scotland and England in 1707, the foundation stone of his political universe. Scots MPs and peers were notably enthusiastic about the Union of 1800, holding before Irish eyes the vision of that wider stage of profit and honour, on which they themselves had acted so successfully.

Yet by 1800 the self-confidence of the ruling groups was shaken. The war which had so decimated the political opposition at first had dragged on too long. Over Roman Catholic emancipation the general sense of the ruling classes, on which Pitt and Dundas were ultimately so dependent, was against them. Pitt wanted it to rally Irish Catholics to the Union and the war effort. Dundas supported him but could not take religion seriously and was an appallingly bad guide to its future significance in nineteenth-century British politics. George III, much clearer than either Pitt or Dundas about the essentially confessional basis of the political structure inherited from the English past, dismissed the 'damned Scotch metaphysics' with which Dundas plied him on the Catholic question. A government originally established to vindicate the rôle of the Crown as a vital element in the sovereign body had no option. In 1801 Pitt resigned. With him went Dundas. War weariness was interlocked with resistance to Catholic emancipation, and Dundas was on both counts no longer acceptable in office. It was ironic that he who had by no means rejoiced at the outbreak of war should suffer when a long succession of military reverses allied to heavy war taxation punctured the inflated bellicosity of the ruling classes.

That the Scottish aristocracy, with its well-established tradition of political advancement by troop raising, was originally as bellicose as any other section of the British aristocracy is clear. It is equally clear that even within the landed classes there was always in Scotland a small and increasingly abused minority which stood outside the consensus for war and paid the penalty for presenting a rationally-argued alternative to one of those dramatic swings of mental fashion which in times of stress tend to be the characteristic reaction of the British Establishment. A Stirlingshire laird, Robert Haldane of Airthrey, illustrates neatly the strengths and weaknesses of these upper-class dissenters. He was an ex-officer of the Royal Navy and like his former commander Admiral Lord St Vincent he regarded the war with France as 'unnecessary, impolitic, and lamentable'. At first his views were treated as a permissible eccentricity. Socially he remained on good terms with Mr Secretary Dundas and other Scotch Pittites such as the gallant Sir Ralph Abercromby and the local magnate, the Duke of Montrose, who condescended to visit Airthrey as late as the summer of 1794.

However, party spirit mounted as Revolutionary France became to the Stirlingshire gentry a symbol of Godlessness and Democracy. Robert Haldane had the great moral courage to stand up at a county meeting presided over by the Duke of Montrose and oppose a proposal to raise a Volunteer Corps on the grounds that it was unnecessary for internal security and would inevitably be used to feed the war machine. He added, with dignity and insight, that the fanatical opposition to all change whatsoever characteristic of the supporters of the war struck him as singularly injudicious, and contrary to the basic principles of the Reformation. Evangelical religion as well as the rational analysis of the Enlightenment combined to form Robert Haldane's mind. Radical he was not. When in 1800 he published an 'Address on Politics' to vindicate his record he insisted that as soon as political societies embracing the lower orders were formed he opposed them as likely to inflame rather than inform the public. In any case, by 1795 he had abandoned politics for missionary religion, feeling called to witness in Bengal. East India Company hostility to missionaries blocked that scheme, so he and his brother James were diverted into evangelization at home. Nevertheless, men like Robert Haldane and the Earl of Lauderdale upheld an alternative policy of seeking peace which events made respectable again to all but a few unbalanced ideological warriors.

Specific individuals, faced with the dual challenge of external war and internal unrest rushed to the paranoid conclusion that there was a vast and active plot to subvert the entire social order. John Robison, who held the chair of Natural Philosophy in Edinburgh for 30 years, published in 1798 his *Proofs of a Conspiracy against all the Religions and Governments of Europe* in which he claimed that he had first obtained hints of this devilish conspiracy by mixing in Masonic circles in St Petersburg in the 1770s when, like not a few Scottish professional men, he had sought advancement and profit in the service of the westernizing government of the Russian Empire. Fear of social revolution had sent virtually all British politicians, including the weightier part of the former parliamentary opposition led by the Duke of Portland, into a tight phalanx around Pitt by 1794. From that date alone can the largely meaningless term Tory be applied without confusion to the party of government and the name Whig be reserved to the rump opposition led by C.J. Fox. The great majority of Scottish members of the ruling classes rushed into the Tory camp if they were not there already, but by 1802 neither the confidence nor the solidarity of that camp was quite what it had once been.

The resignation of Henry Dundas with that of the Pitt government in 1801 caused a spasm of consternation amongst his well-drilled Scottish supporters, who had come to assume that office and Dundas were synonymous terms. However, it soon became clear that there was an uneasy, tacit deal between Dundas and Pitt's successor Henry Addington. At the general election in 1802 Dundas supported the administration and secured the return of a squad of 31 MPs – 22 from the counties and 9 from districts of burghs. This represented a marginal but unmistakeable erosion of the Dundas interest. It is difficult to be precise, but Dundas definitely lost control in Fife and Stirling, and his decline was further underlined by the election for representative peers, where 5 out of the 16 chosen were his known enemies. In a by-election caused by the death of the Earl of Dumfries in 1803, Dundas even failed to return his man, Lord Kellie. Elevated to the peerage as Viscount Melville by Addington, Dundas came back into office as First Lord of the Admiralty in 1804 in Pitt's new administration formed after the renewal of war with France. He at once threw the weight of government patronage behind a counter-offensive in Fife, and by similar means ensured that Lord Kellie entered the House of Lords. Then in April 1805, as the result of revelations (in the 10th Report of the Commissioners of Naval Enquiry) about massive use of public funds passing through the Navy Pay Office for the purpose of private speculation by Alexander Trotter of Dreghorn, a Scots laird who was Paymaster of the Navy, Dundas was condemned by a vote of the House of Commons, forced to resign from the cabinet, and impeached. Money had never greatly interested the careless and generous Dundas, whose obsession was power, so his eventual acquittal was probably right as well as deeply gratifying to such supporters of the fallen minister as the future Sir Walter Scott, but the death of Pitt in January 1806 finished Dundas as an active politician.

He had never been able totally to crush resistance to his power in Scotland, though he tried hard enough. Indeed the treasurer and party manager of the opposition group centred on Fox and the Duke of Portland was, after 1789, a Scots laird from Fife, William Adam of Blair Adam, a lawyer who was a member of the great architectural family. William Adam had little time in the end for his architect uncles whose megalomania and lack of financial sense had brought the family fortunes to the brink of total disaster with their grandiose Adelphi building scheme off the Strand in London in 1768–74. William was a cautious politician, a supporter of Lord North, who even fought a duel with C.J. Fox before succumbing to the compelling charm of that wayward man. Thereafter he was the anchorman of the Foxite Whigs, protected to some extent from the wrath and fury of Pitt and Dundas by the reversionary interest and patronage of the Prince of Wales. He was appointed 'Solicitor-General to the Prince and endeared himself to the self-indulgent heir to the throne by his sustained efforts to redeem the usually dismal and scandalous state of 'Prinny's' finances. Long after 1800 Prinny and his equally scapegrace brothers, the Dukes of York and Clarence, were recurring themes in William Adam's correspondence, almost always with reference to their financial straits. After the split between Fox and Portland in 1792–4, William Adam, who had tried very hard to avert it, stubbornly and skilfully managed the business of the Foxite Whigs, especially in Scotland. There had always been an element amongst the nobility and gentry that could not stomach the subservience demanded by Dundas. On this rock Adam could build a small but vocal opposition. Nor should the issue be seen as purely one of personalities. In the eighteenth century it was a commonplace that it mattered less how a member reached the legislature than that he should there represent with manly independence the varied interests of the localities.

James Maitland, 8th Earl of Lauderdale, a violent-tempered, clever nobleman with a strong Scotch accent and a taste for political economy, was typical of the conservative wing of the Foxites. A representative peer who strongly opposed the war with France and the restrictions on personal liberty in Britain which accompanied it, he was excluded from the Lords by Dundas in 1796 and 1802 for his pains. Even an arch-conservative (though he called himself a Whig) like the 2nd Earl of Fife, who died in 1809 at the age of 80, was at times very unhappy about the dictatorial strain in Dundas, despite the fact that he supported most of his policies, including the French war. Fife was a most conscientious supporter of his own region's interests and he remarked in 1794 that:

> I wonder the Country does not see how much it is in their interest to support independency, you know what trouble and expense it cost me to support this principle. Mr Dundas wants to put down every independent man, and to annihilate that character as much as possible.

'Independency' against the odds seemed to reap its reward early in 1806 when the death of Pitt compelled George III to accept a 'Ministry of all the Talents' with Fox prominent in its ranks. Lauderdale was made a peer of the United Kingdom. His nomination as Governor-General of India was virtually black-balled by the Honourable East India Company, but he became Keeper of the Great Seal of Scotland and was sworn of the Privy Council. Henry Erskine, the brilliant Whig lawyer who had been removed from his position as Dean of the Faculty of Advocates on 12 January 1796 by a notable display of partisan rancour on the part of the Tory majority in that body, was appointed Lord Advocate for Scotland for the second time in his career. The 'manly patriots', numbering 38 in all, who had voted for him in January 1796, and who had been toasted at Whig social gatherings ever since, seemed vindicated. Henry's facile but absurdly vain youngest brother Thomas, who had not seen Scotland since 1764 when he left it to join, briefly, the Royal Navy, even achieved the gown of Lord Chancellor on the strength of his career at the English bar. Alas, in April 1807, with little positive achievement in Scotland, the government fell.

The Whigs had already experienced the fickle nature of Prinny's friendship. Thomas Erskine, having been dismissed as Attorney General to the Prince of Wales in 1792 for characteristically reckless support for the radical publicist Tom Paine, who was accused of slandering the Royal Family, should have been less crushed than he was when the Prince ratted decisively on his Whig friends once he became Prince Regent with full powers in February 1812. After April 1807 the Dundas régime was to all intents and purposes restored in Scotland. Now led by Robert Saunders Dundas, Melville's only son, it emerged from the 1807 general election rather battered with only 24 MPs, but its grip on the peerage election was impressive. Their Lordships only dared return one name not on the list of Dundas candidates hawked round by the Duke of Buccleuch. Henry Dundas died in 1811 after an extraordinary career based ultimately on his ability to manipulate the admittedly inadequate representation of Scotland at Westminster and to ensure that it raised no serious demands for attention from His Majesty's Government. His early zeal of administrative reform had long preceded him to the grave. Robert, 2nd Viscount Melville, had already succeeded smoothly to his regional political empire, and now succeeded to many of his offices, down to the Chancellorship of the University of St Andrews.

William Adam, like many prominent Scots Whigs, reached parliament by means of an English constituency. The only chancellorship he ever held was that of the Duchy of Cornwall, in the gift of the Prince of

Wales. Nevertheless, he believed his own political cause would triumph over a long haul, by making itself the spokesman for the ever more important commercial and manufacturing middle classes. Like so many theories, this one contained a vein of shrewd insight but was overall too simple by half. James Loch, the brains behind the Sutherland clearances, who was one of Adam's regular correspondents when 'hunting Dundas' was the favourite Whig sport in 1805−6, was a living illustration of the interconnections between land and industry, and between the middle classes and the ruling aristocracy. The Sutherlands and Adams tended to be Whigs. Most Scots landed and political dynasts were Tory. The Tory ascendancy ultimately fell more from internal fission than from external assault, and that more in England than in Scotland.

That is why the intellectual climate amongst the educated classes was so vital. Dugald Stewart, who succeeded Adam Ferguson as Professor of Moral Philosophy in Edinburgh in 1785 was, despite his lack of philosophical originality, therefore a very important figure, for this eloquent, charismatic teacher was not only the supreme exponent of the Scots 'Common Sense' school of philosophy stretching back in impeccable social respectability to Thomas Reid, but also a convinced Whig. If he was the most cautious of Whigs, capable of cringing apology to a Noble Lord for having inadvertently mentioned an infidel French philosopher like Condorcet in one of his writings without explicitly condemning him, that too merely enhanced the influence of a man whose books were accepted at once, in the United States of America as much as in Britain, as an authoritative summary of the philosophical school which had given the lie to the atheistical Hume. Certainly Dugald Stewart's class in Political Economy was a common bond between the four young men behind the *Edinburgh Review* whose first number appeared in October 1802. The four were Sidney Smith, an English parson serving as a tutor in Edinburgh; Francis Jeffrey, son of a Deputy Clerk to the Court of Session; Francis Horner, son of a merchant and grandson of a Writer to the Signet; and Henry Brougham, son of an English squire and a Scottish lady who was the niece of Principal Robertson. Both Horner and Brougham were called to the Scottish Bar. Both rapidly abandoned it for lusher pastures in London. Horner died prematurely in 1817. Brougham rose from being 'a briefless barrister on the Scottish Southern Circuit' to being Lord Chancellor of England, in the Whig interest. Before 1808 *The Edinburgh* was, however, not a politically partisan journal. Its remarkable impact was due to the fact that in politics and literature it offered a sharp and at times iconoclastic vein of criticism for which English-speaking opinion was ready. In 1816 the London *Times* had a daily circulation of only 8,000. *The Edinburgh* had a subscription list of 12,000 in 1813 and Jeffrey, its editor, was surely right in arguing that this represented at least 50,000 readers.

It was Brougham, a passionate humanitarian devoted to alleviating the lot of such human chattels as the negro slave or the British soldier, but in all other respects an unprincipled and conceited careerist, who pushed *The Edinburgh* over the top late in 1808 with an article (jointly written with Jeffrey) in which it was said that 'reforms in the administration of our affairs must be adopted, to prevent more violent changes'. In a sense, the question is why such a performance should have elicited so violent a Tory response. Brougham would cheerfully have enlisted under the Tory banner, if offered advancement for doing so. Accusations by a Tory MP in a pamphlet entitled *Remarks on the Jacobinical Tendency of the Edinburgh Review* were more or less routine and not at all convincing. The sheer lunacy of the more extreme forms of the 'Red Peril' parrot-cry as a means of smearing all opponents of the ruling clique was becoming obvious. By 1815 John Robison's theory of universal malignant conspiracy against all the decencies was being referred to with something akin to levity in the pages of the *Transactions of the Royal Society of Edinburgh*. Henry Dundas, to the very end of his life, automatically accused anyone in Scotland who would not knuckle under his political will of embracing the unmentionable excesses of the French Jacobins. It was a charge doubly hollow when applied to the ducal house of Hamilton in the age of that conservative military dictator Napoleon Bonaparte. Brougham's wilder statements of near democratic theory were every whit as offensive to the conservative wing of the Whigs as to the Tories.

Yet Walter Scott, culturally the rising hope of the stern unbending Tories, found the defeatism of *The Edinburgh*'s comments on the British campaigns in Spain unendurable and not only withdrew from occasionally contributing to it, but also sponsored the launching in 1809 of the rival, militantly Tory *Quarterly Review*, backed by many of the staff of an ultra-rightwing paper, the *Anti-Jacobin*, which had ceased publication in 1798. Scott, the son of a Writer to the Signet and the eldest daughter of John Rutherford, Professor of Medicine in the University of Edinburgh, was nothing if not committed to the Tory cause. Called to the Scots Bar in 1792, he married the daughter of a French Royalist refugee in 1797, and in 1799 was preferred, through the influence of the Duke of Buccleuch to the post of Sheriff-depute of

Selkirkshire, a job which left plenty of free time for literature. The
years 1802−3 saw the publication of the three volumes of his superb
Minstrelsy of the Scottish Border, which brought to fulfilment his
obsession with Border balladry. Long narrative poems of high adventure like 'The Lay of the Last Minstrel' (1805), 'Marmion' (1808), and
'The Lady of the Lake' (1810), sold astonishingly well and made his
literary name. In 1811 Scott purchased the beginnings of the estate on
the Tweed he called Abbotsford. He was approaching Olympus; nay
he was personally hovering on the verge of the divinity which hedged a
Scottish laird well in with the Melville interest.

    The Scotch Whigs were by comparison a pathetic sight. Their old
leader Lauderdale was drifting steadily to the right at a rate of knots
calculated to carry him out of the Whig haven altogether. Such was
the state of Whiggery in North Britain that for several years it had to
be led by an Irish earl, Lord Moira, an intimate of the Prince of Wales
who was appointed Commander-in-Chief Scotland in 1803 and in
1804 married a Scottish heiress, Flora Countess of Loudon in her own
right. The couple lived at Duddingston House and were deservedly
popular, but after failing to achieve high political office in 1807 and
1812, Moira was kicked upstairs by his fat friend the Prince Regent in
1813, when he went off to achieve lasting fame as Governor General of
India and Marquis of Hastings. In 1806 Walter Scott was appointed
one of the Principal Clerks of the Court of Session. Henry Erskine's last
hopes of legal preferment evaporated in 1811 when Charles Hope was
appointed Lord President of the Court of Session over his head.
'Harry' Erskine had had enough. He retired to the solace of his country
seat, his garden, and his violin. What then did the Tories fear? Fundamentally they seem to have sensed what Henry Cockburn, a relative of
Dundas but a Whig, described in his *Memorials Of His Time* as 'a
great though as yet a silent change' in the 'mind of the lower, and far
more of the middle, class'. Peace, with its economic problems and
release from the wartime pressures for patriotic solidarity, could only
accelerate that change.

    The conservative reaction in Scotland had been too successful. It
was part of a general British revulsion from the radicalism of the
French Revolution which found its supreme expression in the Irishman Edmund Burke's *Reflections on the Revolution in France* (1790).
Burke there argued from prescription, defending the *status quo* on
the ground that its survival proved its worth. He virtually, if not
absolutely, closed the door to constructive reform. James Mackintosh,
a young Scot educated at Aberdeen and Edinburgh Universities,

produced in 1791 in *Vindiciae Gallicae* a brilliant refutation of Burke which, among others, deeply influenced Robert Haldane of Airthrey. Yet Mackintosh, like Haldane, subsequently withdrew from articulate opposition to the sharp swing to the right among the ruling classes. Inevitably that swing went to extremes. In a world where the Dundas interest seemed to have obliterated serious opposition, Lord Braxfield was so foolish at the trial of Thomas Muir in 1793 as actually to say that government was 'just like a corporation; and in this country, it is made up of the landed interest, which alone has a right to be represented'. Given the infamous state of Scottish municipal corporations, which belied even the most ingenious attempts by government sycophants to argue that parliamentary representation in some mysterious way reflected the property and intelligence of the land, it was a singularly injudicious analogy. Arrogance was depriving the authorities of their capacity for some of the central techniques of the British Establishment such as the avoidance of confrontation, the use of urbane prevarication rather than open refusal, and above all the making of ambiguous or inconsequential concessions in order to preserve their grip on the significant decision-making process. As the agitations of the 1780s resumed after 1815 it was to become clear that only the Whigs had the ability fully to deploy such weapons in defence of the established social and political order. English Tories did indeed try to adopt a more flexible, empirical attitude from the early 1820s, but paid a heavy price in terms of internal conflict and fission. Scotch Tories, always an extreme case, inhabited a world in which politics had been reduced to interlocking patronage rackets and social hysteria. Flexibility was beyond them. Immediately after the outbreak of peace Henry Cockburn unerringly identified the emerging swing of opinion among the propertied classes. Radicalism of the United Scotsman type might be dead but Whigs were now emerging 'from despised dissenting congregations, from half liberated corporations, from shops, from the law, and which was a better sign of the current, even from medicine, and, what was the best symptom of all, from the aristocracy of the lower orders'. To such people the Whigs offered a prospect of reform of the more outrageous and indefensible abuses in Scottish public life without any accompanying threat to property rights or the principle of hierarchy in social relationships.

7

Structural Change in an Era of Political Immobilism 1790 – 1815

Within the framework of order provided by the landed ascendancy, Scottish society was changing rapidly by the late eighteenth century, and changing in ways which ultimately were to erode the bases of that ascendancy. Fully to understand what was happening, it is essential to look more closely at the forces changing the face of the Lowlands and convulsing parts of the Highlands, where Gaelic society was to pay a heavy price for its almost total subordination to Anglo-Saxon values. Fortunately we have, in *The Statistical Account of Scotland* a unique contemporary source sponsored and organized by the improving laird and politician Sir John Sinclair of Ulbster (1754–1835), whose estates lay in the northern but not Highland county of Caithness. Using his own resources and the help of the clergy of the Church of Scotland, he produced 21 volumes of a survey, as well as a digest of those volumes, and more specialized surveys of agriculture.

From these works, it is clear that from about 1770 onwards change had become fairly general in the countryside and that the prime mover in this complex process was nearly always landlord demand for higher rents, related initially more often to a simple need for money to sustain higher standards of living than to any systematic investment in improvement as such. Sinclair reckoned the landlord class as encompassing well under 8,000 individuals. He calculated that there were 396 persons owning large properties worth £2,500 sterling or more in rent per annum; 1,077 proprietors of estates worth between £600 and £2,500; and some 6,181 proprietors of small estates worth less than £600 of annual rent. This gave a total of 7,654 estate owners, to which had to be added 144 estates belonging to corporate bodies. Though in certain areas, such as the small county of Kinross, there were significant concentrations of working farmers who were owner-occupiers, most of Lowland Scotland had the 'three-decker' rural social structure characteristic of most of England. Below a small proprietorial class the land was worked by tenant-farmers and their families, usually with the aid of a low-status class of labourers.

The world of the labourers was itself hierarchical and complex. Their origins varied enormously from one region to another. In the Lothians, where commercial farming was most highly developed, the skilled labourer or hind was landless but was paid half or more of his wage in grain. This inflation-proof element was supplemented by a money wage which to a skilled ploughman in 1815 might be £15–20 a year. On the other hand, the unskilled 'day labourer' was physically segregated from the regular workforce in a hut or bothy and paid purely in cash. Many small farmers in hill areas like the Sidlaws or Ochils seem to have lost their holdings in the course of landlord con- solidation of farms; to have lacked the capital to set up on their own account; and to have ended up as labourers, either on improved farms in fertile areas or in towns, where they could still move out seasonally to take agricultural work such as reaping or shearing. In Aberdeen- shire, where there was a substantial Scots-speaking crofter population, it was traditional for the crofters to send bachelor sons to be living – in servants on the improved farms. Elsewhere, in fertile areas such as the Carse of Gowrie on the north side of the Tay or the Carse of Stir- ling, there were significant concentrations of people known as cotters. They had a house and garden, but not enough land to live off. Rather, they had a dwelling and a means of occupying themselves during the quieter periods of the agricultural year whilst keeping themselves available for unskilled labour at the busy seasons. Robert Burns, him- self an Ayrshire tenant farmer, immortalized and sentimentalized such a household in 'The Cotter's Saturday Night', but like other small tenants they seem to have been increasingly squeezed out in favour of hired hands as the eighteenth century progressed.

By 1814, after 20 years during which landlords undoubtedly had invested quite heavily in their estates, it was reckoned that the land- rent of Scotland was increasing by a steady £100,000 to £200,000 per annum, but Scottish landlords would not have been able to obtain these continually higher rents as leases fell in and were renewed by public auction if prospective tenants had not been confident that they could expand their output and yet receive good prices for their produce. Throughout much of previous history increased output simply meant lower prices, at least in local markets. One explanation of the new confidence in farming was population growth. After being probably no higher in 1755 than in 1690, Scottish population entered a phase of steady expansion, increasing by a quarter by 1801, when it was on the threshold of even more rapid retained growth. The next decade saw an annual population increment averaging 1.5 per cent, and that was the highest ever seen, before or since. The usual natural checks which had reversed or flattened population growth curves in all previous time, ceased to operate. The years 1740–2 were the nearest eighteenth-century Scotland came to a national mortality crisis, and it was not one. In 1782 there was a severe food shortage over much of Scotland due to harvest failure. Nevertheless the evidence is that those extensive regions of Scotland affected by the shortages simply coped, without famine, political convulsion, or the panic emigration so common in previous eras. Malting could be abandoned by agreement, thus releasing significant grain stocks for consumption. Stores were of course consumed. In some counties increases in mortality rates of up to 13 per cent amongst the lower orders cut the demand for grain, while early reaping and substantial imports eased the final stages of the crisis. Imports were particularly significant, because they were evidence of accumulated capital which could be used to stave off demographic collapse.

Scottish farming, which had probably reached its climatic limits of expansion under existing techniques by about 1750, had clearly passed through a major transition to more intensive farming sustained by increasing commercialization and higher levels of investment. Investment was much encouraged by the effect of war after 1793. In 1795, for example, a poor harvest and restrictions on imports of grain from Europe led to a leap in wheat prices from 50 shillings to 81s. 6d. a quarter in some Scottish markets. In 1796 prices as high as 96s. a quarter can be found, while in 1812 payments for wheat as high as 126s. 6d. a quarter occurred. The rôle of wheat must not be exaggerated and overall statistics are usually confounded by the partial nature of our records and the scale of regional variations, but it is quite clear that the war gave a great stimulus to agricultural prices in many different sectors of production. The droving trade in cattle to English markets is an excellent example. War had always been good news for it, mainly because it implied a huge government demand for salt beef for the Royal Navy, and the French Revolutionary and Napoleonic Wars were extremely protracted. In 1786 the average price of beasts crossing from Skye to the mainland was £2 to £3. In 1794 it went up to about £4. Towards the end of the war in 1814 prices peaked at as much as £18 a head.

Market mechanisms were thus transmitting the effects of high protective barriers and soaring state expenditure to individual farmers. So profitable were markets that landlords were willing to invest in social overhead capital for its indirect effect on their rent rolls. Though coastal shipping should never be underestimated, turnpike roads were a prime example of the landlord contribution to the creation of an improved transport system. These toll roads were largely funded by the landed interest at a construction cost estimated to be in the region of £5,300 a mile. In the 20 years up to 1814 between £2 million and £3 million sterling was sunk in Scottish roads in this way. Between 1750 and 1814 as much as 3,000 miles of new roadway may have been built. Yet by 1821, with a few exceptions like the Inverurie turnpike in Aberdeenshire, Scottish turnpikes were financially in a mess, usually barely capable of servicing interest and upkeep charges, quite incapable of repaying the large debts representing initial construction costs. Over-optimism during the turnpike boom is only a partial explanation of this situation. The gains expected from turnpikes were always in large measure indirect and measured in enhanced rents for agricultural land or quarries, as much as in dividends.

Another example of this kind of landlord investment was the planned village. Hundreds of them were built by enlightened landlords in Scotland between 1730 and 1830, and the tradition of establishing such new nucleated settlements only died with the stagnation of agricultural rents in the so-called 'Great Depression' of the late nineteenth century. From early examples such as Ormiston in East Lothian, laid out by John Cockburn of Ormiston around 1740, a whole range of types of village developed. Many represented the clearing of an old village from the vicinity of a noble seat. Thus, between 1803 and 1808 the Earl of Mansfield not only completely rebuilt Scone Palace outside Perth, but also erased Old Scone village, and built New Scone a mile and a half off. The Dukes of Argyll had been engaging in a similar operation at Inverary from 1740s, albeit with far higher architectural standards for the new burgh of Inverary. Other planned villages were meant to be centres of industry and population, facilitating the commercialization of surrounding agricultural areas. Some failed totally. Others flourished.

Until cheap tile drains were introduced on a large scale by such innovating landlords as Sir James Richardson of Pitfour in the Carse of Gowrie near Dundee in the 1820s, the absence of efficient low-cost drainage was a grave problem. Huge quantities of lime were used on the fields to sweeten and fertilize the sour, wet soils. The latter half of the eighteenth century saw a spectacular expansion in lime production and the creation of lime quarries and kilns on a scale never seen before. An expert (Robert Bald) writing in 1808 remarked that the lime industry 'may be said to be only in its infancy'. Lothian with its coal, advanced agriculture, and carboniferous limestone had many lime kilns. A battery of kilns on the Earl of Morton's estate at Raw Camps near East Calder was producing up to 20,000 bolls of lime annually around 1800.[1] By 1837 there were more than two dozen large commercial limeworks in the region around Edinburgh. Nor was this sort of development limited to Lothian. The parish of St Cyrus on the Angus coast south of Montrose had two very large commercial limeworks.

Though some aspects of agricultural change, such as the gradual spread of potato culture after 1750, were relatively cheap, most forms of improvement required significant investment. Even pure reorganization, with abolition of running, amalgamation of tenancies, and improvement of lay-out on larger farms, involved heavy costs, including surveying costs. Indeed between 1740 and the coming of the Ordinance Survey a century later lay the history of the land surveying profession in Scotland. Yet tenant farmers as well as landlords were latterly willing to invest in new methods, which is why improved implements such as James Small's lightweight horse-drawn swing plough with iron wearing parts spread so rapidly after 1763. Farmers could obtain credit to embark on improvements because of the sophistication of Scottish banking.

Due to chronic shortage of specie Scottish banks had by 1750 encouraged the use of notes far further than in any other European country and had made of them the dominant element of the money supply. Adam Smith remarked that by the 1760s Scotland had new banking companies in virtually every considerable town 'and even in some country villages'. Credit had always been available on the security of heritable landed property, but after the suspension of cash payments by banks in 1797, credit accounts for tenant farmers became common. Fewer farmers produced more food which sold at higher prices. The principal victims of radical reorganization were those displaced from the land; the *Statistical Account* of Perth described their fate:

The poor are very numerous. Some of the heritors maintain any

---

[1] A boll was standardized at 10 stones or 140 lb. in 1824. Prior to that date it varied by region and commodity.

who may be upon their estates. The great resort of the poor, from all parts of the country, is to Perth. Some of them make a shift, perhaps for 3 years, to maintain themselves, and then when they fall into distress, or their cart horses die by which they gained their daily bread, they apply to the public for relief.

At least in the Lowlands there were expanding towns like Perth capable of absorbing displaced rural population, and the economic structure of farming was in the long run strengthened by the changes taking place. The Highlands were a very different story and perhaps a classic illustration of the inadequacy of any theory of economic growth which suggests that rational organization and efficiently enforced property rights are by themselves adequate guarantees of long-term development. The lack of development in the Highlands was a matter of concern to bodies like the Commissioners for the Forfeited Annexed Estates and the Highland Society of London (established in 1775) long before 1800. Publicists like Dr James Anderson were arguing with passion in the 1770s and 1780s that Highland development, especially in fisheries and the woollen manufacture, ought to be a priority. With the swing to internal colonization after the loss of America this view gained ground and the London Scot John Knox elaborated in several books a whole programme of improvements ranging from establishing towns to transport facilities such as the future Caledonian and Crinan canals. Gone was Adam Smith's cautious scepticism as to whether the Highlands could be successfully modernized on a commercial basis.

In 1786 'The British Society for extending the Fisheries and improving the Sea Coasts of this Kingdom' was founded in London, patronized by Highland magnates like the Duke of Argyll and Lowland lairds like George Dempster of Dunnichen. Contemporaries were very anxious to stop what they saw as an alarming wave of emigration which set in after 1770 when many tacksmen preferred to sell up and emigrate, with their dependents, rather than be continually rack-rented. At least 12,000 left the Highlands between 1782 and 1802, despite bodies like the British Fisheries Society which tried to develop new fishing towns in the Highlands and Islands. Despite limited success at Tobermory and Mull, it was clear by 1806 that the Society was never going to effect a major economic transformation. To an aristocratic régime increasingly paranoid about social upheaval, the loss of 'simple', 'loyal', Highland peasant stock was an unfortunate development underlined by the obvious inability of the region after 1793 to produce the regiments it had supplied for previous wars. The fact that

Highland regiments also had a distinguished tradition of mutiny stretching from 1743 to 1804 was conveniently forgotten in loud lamentations about the need to keep up Highland units with Lowland recruits.

But as the embodiment of the image of the 'Noble Savage' the Highlander marched on, for that image fed on a cult of the primitive and an optimism about the inherent moral potential of mankind that were pervasive in polite circles in Europe in the eighteenth century. That historian's abstraction known as the European Enlightenment contained many intellectual strands, some of which had been present in previous ages, and many of which were hardly consistent with one another. Alongside the cultivation of universalist, classical values there went, in the later eighteenth century, a rising tide of enthusiasm for folk poetry. In the English-speaking world the best-remembered literary milestone along this latter road was the publication in 1765 of Thomas Percy's *Reliques of Ancient English Poetry* with a dedication written by Dr Johnson which stressed that the poems were presented 'not as labours of art, but as effusions of nature, shewing the first efforts of ancient genius'. Several years before this interest had helped to rocket to fame a young Gaelic-speaking schoolmaster and tutor from Ruthven near Kingussie. This was James Macpherson, a burly, sour, and consumingly ambitious man with strong familial Jacobite connections who secured introductions to leading literary figures in Edinburgh through his fellow-Gael Professor Adam Ferguson. Nothing better demonstrates the disintegration of social and moral structures in the Highlands than the career of James 'Fingal!' Macpherson, as impudent and brazen a liar as the Celtic Twilight ever sent to plague the Anglo-Saxon world before the rise of David Lloyd George in the twentieth century.

Encouraged by men like John Home, the clerical author of the now unreadable tragedy 'Douglas', the Reverend Doctor Alexander 'Jupiter' Carlyle, and the Reverend Doctor Hugh Blair, not to mention David Hume and Principal Robertson, Macpherson foisted on the world what purported to be translations of two ancient Gaelic epics by the poet Ossian, *Fingal, an Ancient Epic Poem, in Six Books* (London and Edinburgh, 1761), and *Temora, an Ancient Epic Poem, in Eight Books* (London, 1763). Though Macpherson at various points did use scraps of authentic Gaelic tradition, the whole operation appears to have been dishonest from the very start and was primarily a means of gaining access to the patronage which would lift Macpherson from poverty and neglect to fame and fortune. *Temora* was too much for many even of his supporters. David Hume experienced grave doubts, while a strong school of opinion in London denounced Macpherson as a shameless forger. That he was, but he brazened it out with all and sundry save the formidable Dr Johnson, never a one to use a rapier where a bludgeon would do, who alone forced the odious Caledonian to crawl away from a literary dog fight with all the dignity of a well-beaten cur. The Highland Society of Edinburgh was still publishing an elaborate report on the Ossianic controversy in 1805 long after the real author of that bard's works had been laid, with great pomp, in 1796 in his grave in Westminster Abbey, near to the sepulture of the irascible, and presumably rapidly rotating, Johnson. After 1764 Macpherson had plunged deep into the seamier aspects of imperial politics, from west Florida to India. He was at one stage London agent for the Nawab of Arcot, an Indian potentate whose debts and shark-like British creditors were one of the great contemporary scandals, and he helped his kinsman, Sir John Macpherson, another egomaniac devoid of principle or scruple, to intrigue his way into the position of Governor General of British India.

In Europe Voltaire cackled with malevolent insight over the whole Ossian episode, but in both Italy and Germany the impact of the Ossianic literature was widespread, profound, and reached writers of the stature of Goethe and Herder. In Britain Macpherson was always something of a wry commentary on contemporary social and intel-lectual values. He eventually retired to an estate which had belonged to the Macintoshes of Borlum, and derived twisted satisfaction from making the local lairds treat his children, every one a bastard, as equals. However, it must be said that even the infamous Macpherson undoubtedly gave a massive impetus to the growing interest of both the British people and the British government in the Scottish Highlands.

Government action was directed mainly towards roads in the High-lands. For half a century expenditure on military roads there had been a recurring feature of the state budget, and the mileage created by General Wade before the '45 was expanded up to about 1,000 miles by his successors, but these were purely military roads, useful to Bonnie Prince Charlie in 1745, but not really designed to facilitate commer-cial intercourse, and the 800 miles or so of them still usable towards the end of the century were increasingly dilapidated and neglected. The British Fisheries Society employed as its surveyor Thomas Telford (1757–1834), perhaps the greatest of all civil engineers. He had started out a Scots apprentice mason in the service of the Duke of

Buccleuch, moving as building booms attracted him from Edinburgh to London and then to Portsmouth Docks. The patronage of Sir William Pulteney, who had been born a Johnstone of Westerhall and had changed his name when he married the heiress to the Earl of Bath, helped to make him surveyor of public works in Shropshire. Like the architect Robert Adam, Telford returned to Scotland with a reputation made outside it. In 1801 the Treasury commissioned him to survey the potential for road, canal, and fishery development in the Highlands.

An act of 1803 created a Commission, funded by public money 'for making Roads and building Bridges in the Highlands of Scotland'. Under its aegis, with the Commission paying half the cost and local heritors the other half, the modern road pattern of the Highlands was laid down as 900 miles of road were created between 1803 and 1821 and another 300 miles of road substantially upgraded. Strategic bridges were a vital part of the achievement and their construction endorsed the insight of the Commissioners for the Forfeited Annexed Estates, who had latterly directed their funds towards, amongst other objects, bridges.

In 1802 Telford recommended the construction of the Caledonian Canal from Inverness to Fort William, along the line of the Great Glen. Opened belatedly in 1822 with a mere 12 feet of water in the cuts, 15 in the locks, it was a financial white elephant useful mainly for fishing boats. The Crinan Canal across the Mull of Kintyre opened in 1801 with a modest 10 foot depth, but by 1817 financial straights had placed it under the commissioners responsible for the Caledonian Canal. Though by 1750 some Highland lairds were said to have 'screwed their rents to an extravagant Height', the traditional agriculture of the Highlands simply could not compete with improved Lowland farming. Specialization rather than general development attracted proprietors whose patriarchal qualities showed more in London ballrooms than on estates which they saw mainly as sources of rent.

Demand for wool and mutton was so buoyant around 1800 that Blackface and Cheviot stock sheep, managed by southern graziers, had already displaced black cattle as the main surplus Highland product south of the Great Glen, and as wool prices continued to soar extensive sheep farming spread inexorably into Inverness-shire, Rose-shire, Sutherland, and the Hebridean islands. Extensive reorganization of farming and tenurial relationships was essential to create big commercial sheep farms. Cleared from the interior the old tenants were to be settled on small plots or crofts near the shore whence, as the surveyor who planned the much-resented reorganization of Lord Macdonald's estates in Skye and North Uist around 1800 remarked, 'immense sums may be drawn, equal at least, if not passing, the produce of the soil'. The reference was to the kelp manufacture, a process of collecting and burning seaweed in simple kilns to produce an alkaline extract used in soap and glass manufacture. Kelp prices had been just over £2 a ton in the 1760s, soaring to about £10 a ton in the 1790s when the war cut off imports of Spanish barilla, the main rival industrial alkali, and briefly doubling thereafter. It was believed in the early 1800s that Hebridean landlords alone made a profit of £70,000 on an annual export of 15,000–20,000 tons of kelp.

Paying as they did a mere pittance to their labour force, Highland landlords naturally tried to preserve and expand it. They supported the Passenger Vessels Act of 1803 which they hoped would obstruct emigration by raising shipping standards and therefore costs. Social constraints on early marriage were dissolved. Between 1801 and 1821 population soared by 20 per cent in Argyll, by 24 in Inverness-shire, by 29 in Caithness, and by 22 in Ross and Cromarty. Kelp alone does not explain all this. Population rose in Skye, where kelping was less important, and in Shetland by 30 per cent, partly due to the stimulus of the labour-intensive 'haf fishery'.

Seen against this general background, the obsession of many historians with the clearances on one utterly a-typical estate may appear deeply misleading. The ducal house of Sutherland was in the early nineteenth century the richest noble family in Britain. Elizabeth, Countess of Sutherland in her own right, married in 1785 the heir to the vast landed and industrial wealth of the Marquis of Stafford in the English Potteries. With over a million acres, comprising most of the county, the Sutherlands set out with the guidance of their principal man of business James Loch, a kinsman of the Adams of Blair Adam near Kinross, to transform Sutherland into a profitable, viable estate.

The programme was a variation on the standard one. The Sutherlands were mildly Whiggish in politics. Loch was an Edinburgh intellectual, a friend of Edinburgh Whigs like Henry Brougham and Henry Cockburn, and a devotee of Smithian political economy. His policies were more articulate than most. He even wrote a book in 1820, *An Account of the Improvements on the Estates of the Marquis of Stafford*, to defend them, but they were compounded of fashionable platitudes. As local agents of change, forcing landward tenants out to make way for sheep, and trying to compel people to be industrious crofters on the shores instead, two Morayshire capitalists William Young and Patrick Sellar became obnoxious to contemporaries and historians alike. As one local minister could see by 1818, the whole enterprise failed to create a more viable economy. It was not worth the cost to the landlords, nor the trauma to the people, but at least the Sutherland concept of development was not a reckless over-expansion of population and kelping. Like the Reverend T. R. Malthus, Loch had an obsession about the tendency for population to outgrow the means of subsistence.

Elsewhere, and especially in the Hebrides, the collapse of kelping before foreign imports and synthetic substitutes after 1820 led to new waves of clearance and emigration. The fact was that all Scottish landlords, Highland and Lowland, were becoming dependent on the changing pattern of demand generated by a new industrial society, a society which ultimately was to undermine the political ascendancy of the landed classes, but without whose buoyant demand the latter could scarcely have weathered the huge burden of war taxation between 1793 and 1815. Industrialization in Scotland in this period was undoubtedly textile-led, though other non-agricultural activities such as coal-mining also throve. Heavy investment in machinery in the linen trade, the first spectacular growth area in Scottish textiles, was long confined to the finishing stages of manufacture, so for several decades industrial growth was closely linked with dispersed cottage industry.

The spread of mechanization, because initially it was dependent on good water-power sites, did not at first break this pattern of interwoven industrial and agricultural developments. Vertically-mounted water-powered four-bladed rotors were invented to scutch flax by breaking the woody parts of its stem prior to their removal by heckling or combing, and by 1772 there were 252 of these lint mills in Scotland. Much more significant was the opening in 1788–9 of the first water-powered roller spinning mill for linen yarn in Scotland, at Brigton in Angus. By 1760, with the general adoption of the 'flying shuttle', one hand loom weaver needed five or six hand spinners to supply him. Now the spinning bottleneck was broken.

Already linen had totally outstripped the traditional Scottish woollen manufacture, though a small commercial woollen trade survived in Clackmannan, Stirlingshire, and Aberdeenshire, and woollen tweed manufacture was by 1800 expanding in Border towns like Jedburgh, Hawick, and Galashiels. However, the scale of linen manufacture may be judged by the fact that in 1778 there were 4,000 linen looms in and around Glasgow, as well as another 1,360 in nearby Paisley. Dundee at that time had some 2,000 linen looms weaving mainly coarser fabrics.

The truly explosive growth sector in Scottish textiles after 1780 was cotton. The first cotton-spinning mill was set up at Penicuik in 1779, followed by one at Rothesay in 1780. By 1834 there were 134 cotton mills in Scotland and apart from some big ones in Aberdeen and one at Stanley on the Tay near Perth, they were almost all in Glasgow or within a 25-mile radius of that city. Great noblemen like the Duke of Atholl, landlord of Stanley, tended merely to lease land to cotton spinners, but lesser lairds were often active partners in cotton mills, as were Clydeside West India merchants, who imported the original sea-island long-staple cotton. By 1812 Sir John Sinclair believed that the Scottish cotton industry employed 151,300 people, many working in their own homes, and was producing £6,200,000 of output per annum.

Mechanizing the delicate weaving process proved more difficult. Indeed, steam power was applied to spinning long before mechanical weaving became practical. Urbanization of industry was the inevitable consequence of the coming of steam power, however incompletely. There were, of course, exceptions such as the Scottish paper industry which remained in rural surroundings, albeit usually near places like Aberdeen, Glasgow, and Edinburgh whose demand helped it to grow from 9 per cent of UK output in 1800 to 22 per cent in 1850. Few manufacturers needed so many millions of gallons of water as paper-makers.

The not very efficient Savery and Newcomen pumping engines developed in England had been slowly adopted by Scots mines for drainage work. Only with the invention of the separate condenser by the young Glasgow instrument maker James Watt was the efficiency of the steam engine dramatically increased. Watt's break-through seems to have owed less to the academic theories of his Glasgow mentors, such as Professor Joseph Black, than to patient empirical experiment, both in Scotland and in Birmingham, where Watt went into partnership with the English industrialist Matthew Boulton. To Watt's separate condenser were added a centrifugal governor and a device furnishing rotary motion. Though widely used in mines, the despatch of Bolton and Watt engines, in small numbers, to Scottish textile mills in the 1780s and 1790s was most significant. When Watt's patents expired after 1800, the manufacture of improved engines became widely dispersed throughout Scottish foundries and the early 1820s in particular saw a surge in the rate of installation of engines in urban works.

One consequence was an additional stimulus to the rise in coal prices which were already soaring under pressure of domestic and industrial demand. Between 1790 and 1795 coal in Glasgow went from 5s. 5d. to 10s. 10d. a bag. After 1780 there was a boom in coalmining, with rapid growth of the waggonway systems along whose wooden rails horses pulled coal trucks to navigable water. Despite their servile status, men faceworkers in the pits doubled their wages between 1715 and 1785, and more than doubled them again by 1808. By 1799 collier and salter bondage had been abolished — to encourage cheap labour to flood into the pits.

Close connections with England, and marginal but decisive cost advantages, explain a great deal of Scottish industrial growth around 1800, but the Scottish iron industry is rather an exception. Had not transport costs protected its domestic market from Welsh competition, it would almost certainly have been in dire trouble. Eric Svedenstierna, a Swedish official who visited Britain in 1802–3 and toured the major Scottish ironworks, has left an account of them including the Wilsontown works in Lanarkshire wholly owned by John Wilson of London. Svedenstierna could see that it was the scale of production of iron and steel spades mainly from scrap metal which made the Cramond works outside Edinburgh so competitive. He could see that David Mushet (1772–1847), the foundry manager who identified huge native resources of black-band ironstone in central Scotland, was congenitally incapable of the precise costing needed for commercial success. Svedenstierna could not see as clearly as historians can in retrospect that the undercapitalized Scottish ironworks were desperately dependent on war demand. Carron works was founded during the Seven Years War; Wilsontown during the American War; and four more just before and four during the Revolutionary and Napoleonic Wars. By 1820 over-capacity was an acute problem.

Only in the chemical industry can it be convincingly argued that the academic teaching of science in Scotland was a necessary, though not of course by itself a sufficient cause of early-nineteenth-century industrial growth. The textile industry's need for bleaching agents more efficient than sunshine and sour milk led to the establishment of the Prestonpans sulphuric acid works in 1749. By 1815 a dozen or so establishments around Edinburgh and Glasgow were producing the acid. Its commercial use had been publicized by the lectures and writing of academics like Dr Francis Home (1719–1803) of Edinburgh. Key entrepreneurs had usually learned the indispensable minimum of chemistry at lectures in Scottish university medical schools. However, it was with Charles Tennant's success in taming the new gas chlorine by combining it with lime to produce bleaching powder that Scottish chemical manufactures really made the decisive leap forward.

Tennant established the St Rollox Works in Glasgow near the Monkland Canal. By 1830 the works covered 10 acres and produced bleaching powder, sulphuric acid, soaps, and industrial alkali. Though patented by Tennant the chlorine powder had actually been invented by Charles Macintosh, son of a dyestuff manufacturer. Charles joined the Glasgow University Chemical Society which had been founded under the inspiration of Dr William Irvine, who held conjoint lectureships in Chemistry and *Materia Medica* between 1769 and 1787. Several other members joined Macintosh in his first independent venture — the manufacture of the mordant required to 'fix' textile dies, from aluminous shales in Renfrewshire near Paisley.

In what was undoubtedly a bonanza atmosphere around 1800, the chemical industry inevitably spawned eccentrics like the 9th Earl of Dundonald who tried to repair a ravaged family fortune by distilling coal tar, pioneering gas lighting, synthesizing salt and industrial alkali, and even manufacturing cheap bread from potatoes. Financially, if not chemically, he was a failure, but he had his revenge on respectable mediocrity with his son Thomas, Lord Cochrane, later 10th Earl of Dundonald. Inventor, swashbuckling admiral, and pugnacious Whig MP, Lord Cochrane went off to be a hero of Latin American independence after being convicted in 1814 of participation in a stock-exchange swindle. He was almost certainly rightly exonerated later. His villainous uncle Andrew Cochrane-Johnstone seems to have misled and manipulated him.

Any country producing members of the ruling class like the Cochranes was unstable as well as vital. The Britain of which Scotland was a part was moving along a path of inflation, growth, and cyclical economic instability. Between 1780 and 1815 urban and agricultural wages were said to have risen two and a half to three times. Generalization is misleading, but that increase rather outstripped the overall rise in food costs. However, there were many less fortunate, as well as the fortunate, and between January 1799 and April 1800 Edinburgh meal prices went from a shilling a peck[2] to 3s. 7d — a 358 per cent price rise

[2] A peck was 1/16 of a boll.

in 15 months. Meal riots were, hardly surprisingly, endemic in Scottish burghs between 1783 and 1813. Industrial strike action was not unknown, especially amongst weavers and seamen. Even the isolated Highland tenants whom the 8th Earl of Selkirk (1771–1820) considered ground down by greedy landlords and ruthless factors, to the point where he encouraged them to emigrate to Canada, did occasionally riot against clearances. The Commander-in-Chief Scotland, Lord Adam Gordon, was clear that riots in Ross and Sutherland in 1792 proceeded not from political radicalism, but well-founded fear of expulsion in favour of sheep.

The lower orders looked back to a patriarchalism their betters preached but did not practice. In 1812 Glasgow weavers did secure a court ruling that the local JPs had a statutory duty to fix adequate wages. The JPs refused to enforce the wages they set at a time of falling wage rates, and secured repeal of the relevant legislation in 1813. A massive weavers' strike in the western Lowlands in 1812–13 failed completely. The ability of the ruling élites to force the principal victims of change to pay the price for it remained as unshaken as the massive self-righteousness of the propertied and powerful.

8

The Twilight of the *Ancien Régime* 1815 – 1827

By 1815 it was clear that on top of all its other problems the Tory ascendancy in Scotland faced an identity crisis. The attempt to reduce Scotland and England to North and South Britain, explicit in the Act of Union of 1707, had at the level of nomenclature failed, less because the Scottish ruling class rejected North Britain than because their English equivalents simply could not swallow South Britain. The incorporation of the Loyal and Brave Highlander into the officially-countenanced mythology of the British Army rendered the problem of identity even more acute. The Black Watch (the 42nd Regiment of Foot) fought heroically throughout the Napoleonic Wars from Egypt under Sir Ralph Abercromby; to Corunna in Spain in 1809 under another famous Scottish name, Sir John Moore; to the final climacteric of Waterloo where they fought under that long-nosed Irishman the Duke of Wellington who expressed so laconically the cult of devotion to the early-nineteenth-century British state. Savagely pounded by Marshal Ney's cuirassiers at the Battle of Quatre Bras two days before, the Black Watch did not bear a prominent rôle at Waterloo, but they lined the hedges through which the Scots Greys galloped in a famous and destructive charge, encouraged as they went by the shouts of the Black Watch, 'Scotland for Ever!'.

Nobody embodied the Scottish crisis of identity of the period in more intriguing form than the man who arranged a dinner for the Black Watch in the Assembly Rooms after their triumphant return to post-war Edinburgh. That man was Walter Scott who had on 7 July 1814 published anonymously his first novel *Waverley* with its significant sub-title *Or 'Tis Sixty Years Since*. Scott has been perceptively described as 'a great novelist with a weak aesthetic conscience'. He had been willing to acknowledge his authorship of poetry but the anonymity with which he masked his relationship with *Waverley* was an expression of a deep-seated doubt whether scribbling novels was compatible with the dignity of a landed gentleman or a man of business.[1] Yet *Waverley* is a great novel and a milestone both in Scott's personal career, and in the history of world literature. That the novel is about the '45, the last Jacobite rising in Scotland, does not render it in any way parochial, for like all the greatest of Scott's novels it is essentially a study of social and ideological conflict, as reflected in the dramatized lives of specific individuals. On the other hand, the Scottish context was quite vital for Scott to find full scope for both his enormous antiquarian erudition, and for the perhaps not always fully articulate tensions and contradictions within his personality which gave urgency and complexity to the major themes of the work. The idea of exploiting national characteristics and traits in dramatized prose was something Scott always generously admitted he had derived from a study of the work of the Irish lady novelist Maria Edgeworth whose first novel *Castle Rackrent* had appeared in 1800.

Scott produced the less successful novel *Guy Mannering* in 1815. In 1816 he published the first two titles in his 'Tales of my Landlord' series, *The Black Dwarf*, and *Old Mortality*, thereby underlining the extent to which man was for him a social animal. The latter is one of his greatest books, while the tale of the misanthrope dwarf is a disaster. He returned to the Jacobites again in 1818 with *Rob Roy*, producing also in the same year his most ambitious novel *The Heart of Midlothian*. Eighteen nineteen saw *The Bride of Lammermoor*, his most overtly political novel where the Whigs are the villains of the piece, and *A Legend of Montrose*. By 1820 *Ivanhoe* a 'rattling good yarn', skilful and lively but stuffed with clichés and pseudo-medieval nonsense, gave warning of worse to come, though as late as 1824 in *Redgauntlet* he could revert to his most impressive vein. Written, usually in three volumes (of which the third was often blatantly padded to reach the required length), the novels were sold in unprecedented numbers to a predominantly middle-class market. The three small duodecimo volumes of *Waverley*, for example, were priced at a guinea (21 shillings) and the first thousand went in under a week.

In itself the market for the 40-odd novels Scott produced was an irony. Scott, the arch-Tory despiser of the bourgeois virtues of thrift and caution, made his money out of the bourgeoisie. Then there was the additional irony that by his achievements in both verse and prose Scott was seen in retrospect as a Father of European Romanticism. The very term Romantic is so imprecise as to create doubts about its usefulness, but in practice it is one of those unsatisfactory terms which

---

[1] He first publicly acknowledged his authorship of the novels as late as 1827.

has to be used because to eschew it would be to commit the folly of refusing to recognize a major shift or series of shifts in the sensibility of modern man. Romantic literature sprang from the new liberal, secular view of man evolved mainly in pre-Revolutionary and Revolutionary France, though it could derive inspiration as much from revulsion against the implications of that view as from sympathy with it. Above all, Romanticism shifted the emphasis from man as a social being to man as an individual, man wrestling with his emotions, be they in his own heart or the result of communion with nature. Naturally Romantic writers were attracted by extreme forms of emotional experience. None of this fits Scott. So uninterested was he in depicting the raw emotion of sexual attraction that a reconciliation between a hero and a (usually insipid) heroine in his pages almost invariably symbolizes a compromise between major historical processes. Although Scott repeatedly called himself an 'incorrigible Jacobite', there is precious little savouring of maudlin emotion for its own sake in his major Jacobite novels. They are extraordinarily sensible, fair, and balanced. They shame the appalling excesses of those nineteenth-century Romantic propagandists in the American South or Nationalist Ireland who thought of themselves as literary disciples of 'the Wizard of the North'. They expressed their extremism in a parody of Scott's 'big Bow-Wow strain', but their simplistic and intolerant outlook in no way reflected his complex response to the concept of nationality.

Scott was an eighteenth-century man in terms of his formal values. Extremists in his works all die or retire into monasteries or convents. It is always the reasonable man in the middle, who can see both points of view, who survives, and survival is implicitly recognized as a major virtue. It is true that Scott is emancipated from one major delusion of the neo-classical Augustan school of literature which dominated the eighteenth century. He could see that no society could claim final validity for its culture or standards, and that cultures change over time creating different psychological types in different generations. He admired the feudal virtues of loyalty and panache, but he dreaded the tradition of anarchic violence which he thought accompanied them. For him the defeat of the Jacobites, with all the traditional virtues of which some of them were capable, was inevitable, and the triumph of the house of Hanover was right and a step forward in human history. Ardent supporter of the Act of Union that he was, Scott jumped at the chance to express his Toryism, his monarchism, and his Unionism, as well as his antiquarianism, by stage-managing the visit that George IV paid to Edinburgh in a typical foggy, wet, and windy Scottish August in 1822. The former Prince Regent had lost none of his zest for expensive and exotic clothing, buying no less than £1, 354 18s. 0d. worth of Highland dress and accoutrements for the trip. The 2nd Viscount Melville, who had been strongly in favour of the visit, was, like Scott, quite delighted at its success in countering the spread of radical ideas by evoking 'determined and deep rooted monarchical feeling'.

Yet the visit also obviously evoked a heightened sense of Scottish identity on the part of all participants. Had this not been so, it is difficult to see why George IV bothered to drape his portly figure in the kilt, or why his millionaire crony and companion Sir William Curtis did the same, even if the pink pantaloons worn underneath the kilt rather spoiled the total effect. There was a heavy stress throughout the proceedings on the Highlands, with what were assumed to be their traditions of clanship and loyalty. Sir Walter, who had been instrumental in restoring to the light of day the long-mislaid Honours of Scotland (the Scottish crown jewels), even arranged a royal procession from Holyrood to Edinburgh Castle along the Royal Mile 'for the purpose of calling up, as exactly as might be, the time-hallowed observance of "the Riding of the Parliament " '. Given that one of the objections raised in 1780 to the proposal to establish a Society of Antiquaries in Scotland had been that it was not 'consistent with political wisdom, to call the attention of the Scots to the ancient honours and constitution of their independent Monarchy', times had clearly changed. Or had they?

Partly, the explanation for this heightened sense of Scottishness was the way in which Scottish national characteristics had ceased to constitute a serious political problem and had become, with changing artistic fashions, a source of visual or literary stimulus. Scott's novels were the best example of this, but a similar trend can easily be discerned in the visual arts. Sir Walter's baronetcy had been the first creation of the reign of George IV who, with all his faults, was a munificent and discerning patron of the arts who sincerely admired Scott's work and who had commissioned a portrait of the novelist by Sir Thomas Lawrence for the great gallery of Windsor Castle. Also present in court dress at Holyrood House when George IV held court there as the first Hanoverian monarch ever to do so was the painter David Wilkie. A good friend of Sir Walter Scott and an artist whose use of Scottish materials offers parallels with Scott's literary career, he was the third son of the Reverend David Wilkie, Minister of Cults, a parish on the River Eden in Fife.

Wilkie was a product of the Drawing Academy set up in Edinburgh in 1798 under the auspices of the Board of Trustees for Fisheries and

Manufactures in Scotland and taught mainly by the history painter John Graham. Previous Scottish academies of fine art such as the Academy of St Luke in Edinburgh between 1729 and 1731, or the Foulis Academy in Glasgow between 1753 and 1775, had been financially unstable and had failed to establish a tradition. Graham, though working on a shoe-string, proved a great teacher, producing amongst his earliest students David Wilkie and William Allan and in the years up to his death in 1817 a remarkable percentage of the main names in Scottish art in the next generation. Wilkie was a more than competent portrait painter but he made his name as 'the Scottish Teniers' which implied, correctly, that he had much in common with the Dutch and Flemish genre painters of the seventeenth century. He attracted the attention of his first aristocratic patron, Lord Mansfield, with his picture of 'Pitlessie Fair' and despite his poor health and shy manner he went on to a glittering career which progressed through an acquaintance with the Prince Regent, for whom he painted 'Blind-Man's-Buff', one of his best-composed genre pieces, to the companion piece 'Penny Wedding' completed in 1819 when George IV was already on the throne. By 1822 it was Wilkie who was chosen to record the royal junketings in Edinburgh in a canvas only finished much later, 'The King's Entry Into Holyrood', which finds a prominent place for Walter Scott. Limner to the King for Scotland from 1823, Wilkie became in 1830 'Principal Painter in Ordinary to the King' in England and was so close to the Tory leadership (Sir Robert Peel was a personal friend) that it was considered a mark of grace on the part of a Whig administration to sponsor his knighthood at the hands of William IV in 1836.

Though Wilkie resented being categorized as a genre painter, his attitude to the fast-fading distinctively Scottish peasant society which he loved to paint is historically most significant. Scott had precious little sensibility in the field of painting, but in the Scots dialect of the peasant dialogues in his novels he was doing exactly the same — trying to render permanent by his art something vanishing swiftly before his eyes. This sense of loss was very widespread in articulate circles in Scotland. Mrs Grant of Laggan, writing from Edinburgh to a friend in Glasgow in 1812, remarked how profoundly anglicized Edinburgh was as compared with Glasgow, and then added that 'our spoken nationality decays so fast, that I feel a kind of pain at its departure'. Despite Scott's lack of discrimination in the pictures on his dining room walls at Abbotsford, he was important in involving artists in the task of fixing images of the Scottish past. William Allan is a good example. Returning from an extended stay in Russia in 1814, Allan was all set for a career as a painter of exotic subjects, producing fascinating canvasses full of Circassian princes and captives, not to mention Turkish Bashaws. However, he was employed by the publisher Constable to illustrate Scott's novels when they were issued as a set in 1820, and encouraged by Scott and Wilkie, he developed into a history painter specializing in Scottish topics like 'The Murder of Archbishop Sharpe' or 'Knox Admonishing Mary Queen of Scots'. He never abandoned his exotic interests but when in the 1840s he turned to battle scenes 'Prestonpans', the Jacobite victory of 1745, preceded 'Waterloo', and he died with 'Bannockburn' unfinished in his studio.

Incomparably the best example of linkages between literary and pictorial artists in the common endeavour to preserve lively images of a way of life clearly threatened with extinction was John Galt, the novelist, who began to write in 1813 a book which eventually appeared in 1821 as *Annals of the Parish*. What makes him such a good example is his self-consciousness. After seeing Wilkie's 'Village Politicians' and 'Blind Fiddler' at a Royal Academy exhibition in London, Galt had written to Wilkie on 12 May 1807 virtually associating himself with a campaign to delineate the traditional Scottish peasant world before it altogether vanished.

Born in Irvine in Ayrshire, Galt was brought up after the age of 10 in the busy port of Greenock, where his father was in the West India trade. Educated for a commercial career, Galt moved to London in 1804, seeking wider opportunities of which he singularly failed to take advantage, for he failed miserably and repeatedly in business. He survived by becoming a successful hack writer, using numerous pseudonyms. Another venture into business as the Gibraltar agent for the great Glasgow merchant Kirkman Finlay, who maintained an elaborate organization for smuggling British goods into Europe past Napoleon's attempt to exclude them by his Continental System, necessarily came to an end with the war. Only as a writer was Galt ever much of an entrepreneur, but it was his good luck in 1819 to establish a special relationship with one of Scotland's most enterprisng publishers – William Blackwood. Like that other thrusting Tory publisher Archibald Constable, who produced the *Quarterly Review*, Blackwood had party ends as well as profit in view when he launched *Blackwood's Magazine* in 1817, for that was the year in which the unmistakably pro-reform newspaper *The Scotsman* first appeared, and *Blackwood's* was designed as massive reinforcement for the Tory counter-attack on the Whig press. By 1819 Galt was contributing regularly to *Blackwood's* and indeed a series of connected articles he started to produce for it grew into a major novel – *The Ayrshire*

Legatees. In 1821, with Galt solidly entrenched at the heart of the
Tory reaction, *Annals of the Parish* deservedly made his literary name
for him. The next two years saw a burst of high-level creativity such as
Galt never again matched and which gave to the world books such as
The Provost, *The Entail*, and *Ringan Gilhaize*.

As late as 1832 Galt produced an important political novel, *The
Member*, based on his characteristically unsuccessful experiences
when he was employed by the directors of the Edinburgh and Glasgow
Union Canal to lobby at Westminster on behalf of a bill which was to
have empowered them to raise more funds. Like Scott, Galt's supreme
ambition was to live the life of a country gentleman, an ambition all
the more tantalizing in that he actually achieved it temporarily in the
1820s in Canada as the resident agent of a predictably unsound
Canadian land development company. However, it is the achievement
represented by the six novels in Ayrshire Scots which Blackwood kept
in print for a hundred years as 'The Works of John Galt' which has left
an enduring mark on Scottish letters. The free use of dialect rather
shocked Edinburgh *literati*, not excluding Walter Scott who found
some of Galt's language 'vulgar'. *The Last of the Lairds*, a not
altogether successful novel which Galt published in 1826, was
thoroughly bowdlerized by Dr D.M. Moir, at Blackwood's request,
before publication, and the original text only appeared in print as late
as 1976.

Henry Mackenzie, by sheer longevity, was able to submit the now
archly Scottish literary productions of the ruling ascendancy in North
Britain to the anglicizing norms which much the same ascendancy had
embraced half a century before. He claimed that he could not even
understand the language spoken by Galt's characters. Mackenzie had
not moved with the times. Scottish national consciousness symbolized
by the broadswords of Jacobite gentlemen as late as 1746 had threatened the *status quo*. Tamed, provincialized, and fading, a vernacular
culture could in 1820 be used to buttress the *status quo*. Galt's half-
remembered, half-invented Irvine was ultimately a stable hierarchy,
threatened by radical influences from outside, but ultimately
unshakeable under shrewd, pawky Tory leadership. Not for nothing
had a Mr Brown of Dundee so commended himself to Henry Dundas
in the 1790s by an anti-reform pamphlet archly entitled *Look before
Ye Loup*, that Dundas promptly made him editor of a new govern-
ment-sponsored newspaper entitled the *Patriots Weekly Chronicle*.
The first decades of the nineteenth century were in fact the period
when Carolina Oliphant, a retiring member of Sir Walter Scott's
Edinburgh social circle, wrote many of the 'traditional' Jacobite

ballads like 'Wi' a hundred pipers' or 'Will ye no come back again'. They were sung with approval in circles devoid of a flicker of disloyalty to the house of Hanover. Indeed in 1822, on the occasion of the visit of Holyrood duly recorded by Wilkie, George IV was presented with a petition drawn up by Sir Walter Scott praying him to restore the titles of attainted Jacobite families which, unlike their estates, had not been returned, and it was the granting of this request by legislation of 1824 which turned Carolina Oliphant or Nairne into Baroness Nairne, when her husband Major Nairne, an Assistant Inspector of Barracks, became Lord Nairne.

A logical corollary of this change in the attitude of the ruling élite towards Scottish culture was a new attitude towards the Scottish past. The old distrust of Scottish history, the feeling that it should be dis-countenanced 'for fear of awakening the Old National Grudge, that should now be sopited and industriously forgotten', as Francis Pringle the Professor of Greek in St Andrews said in 1736, had long passed. Principal Robertson had found Scottish history a convenient vehicle for the launching of his career, though he jettisoned it with his usual urbane egotism when he wished to become an international celebrity. Robertson had little time for emotionalism. He even thought Burke's *Reflections* on the French Revolution excessively emotion-charged. By 1790, when the *Reflections* appeared, Robertson was out of step with official opinion. Sir Walter Scott believed that there was strong prac-tical utility in studying the continuity of the Scottish historical past. With his prodigious energy and zest in the tradition of convivial club-manship which was so central to the eighteenth-century Edinburgh social and intellectual scene, Walter Scott was able to institutionalize his concern for the Scottish past by being instrumental in the founda-tion in 1823 of the first of the Scottish historical publishing clubs — the Bannatyne Club.

Scott was not, of course, conjuring new forces into creation when he helped to found the Bannatyne. There had always been a strong anti-quarian tradition already several centuries old running alongside the grand 'philosophical history' tradition of the eighteenth century. Writers like David Hume simply assumed that human nature and indeed human society, in every aspect save the purely technological, were essentially unchanging. As Hume put it in his *Enquiry Concern-ing Human Understanding*, 'The same motives always produce the same actions, the same events follow from the same causes'. The anti-quarian tradition was far readier to study the past on its own terms, and as a result had a vastly great interest in the study of primary sources. It was scholars in the antiquarian tradition like Thomas Innes and James Anderson who had by 1740 introduced all that was best in European developments in palaeography and diplomatic into the stream of Scottish scholarship. It is no accident that Scott gives a sympathetic if humorous portrait of the old scholar Jonathan Oldbuck, the eponymous hero of Scott's *The Antiquary*. However, in the work of Sir David Dalrymple, Lord Hailes, a law lord who lived from 1726 to 1792, the purely antiquarian and the more philosophical traditions in Scottish historiography came together in a fashion which enabled Walter Scott to describe Hailes as 'the father of national history'. The principal work produced by Hailes was his *Annals of Scotland From The Accession of Malcolm Canmore*, in which, as well as in a number of tracts originally published separately, he subjected the sources of medieval Scottish history to salutary scrutiny. When William Creech, the most important Edinburgh bookseller of the day and an old friend of Lord Hailes, published the latter's collected works in three volumes in 1797, he could compare them favourably with Voltaire's *Annales de l'Empire*, saying that they had 'all the philosophic reflection of the latter, with a superior acuteness of critical investigation'. It was no mean boast, even if it has not worn well.

Scotland was already by 1788 endowed with the earliest purpose-designed record repository in Britain in the handsome shape of Register House in Edinburgh, designed by Robert Adam in a unique blend of Roman Imperial grandeur and English neo-classical palladian taste. It was this commission which confirmed Robert Adam's reputation in Scotland. In London the appearance of a similar complex, Somerset House, designed by his deadly rival Sir William Chambers (himself the son of a Scottish merchant trading in Sweden) almost instantly overshadowed Adam's achievement. It was in Edinburgh, with Register House, Charlotte Square, and his work for the University of Edinburgh, that Robert Adam left a monumental mark on a metropolis. However, a fine repository is not necessarily a guarantee of a flourishing 'national history'. It was equally important that after the bulk of the national archives had been transferred from the Laigh Parliament House to the new depository, they be made accessible to historians by the creation of a repertory and catalogues, and by the publication of the more important series in scholarly editions. The official legally responsible for the oversight of the Scottish records was the Lord Clerk Register. In 1806 the holder of this post, Lord Frederick Campbell, earned the eternal gratitude of historians by appointing a Deputy Clerk Register in the shape of a young advocate who was a former secretary to Lord Hailes, and a close friend of Walter Scott. This man was Thomas Thomson who, under the

absentee but benign sway of the Lord Clerk Register, laid the foundations of modern Scottish archival methods. Thomson succeeded Scott
in the presidency of the Bannatyne Club and in association with men
like Robert Pitcairn and Cosmo Innes assumed a leading rôle in its
publication work. In fact Thomson was careless in accounting for
public moneys and incorrigibly dilatory in producing volumes for
publication in such official series as the *Acts of the Parliaments of
Scotland* (left incomplete when he left office in 1841), with the result
that he demitted office under a cloud, but the foundations of scholarship he laid well.

There was a broad spectrum of support for all these efforts to make
the sources of Scottish history available. Geographically, it became
clear that the Bannatyne, with its considerable social status connected
with a limited membership, would be imitated outside Edinburgh
when in 1829 the Maitland Club was established in Glasgow. It shared
members, like Scott and Pitcairn, with the Bannatyne, but was
predictably more mercantile in membership than its lawyer-domi-
nated Edinburgh counterpart. As the nineteenth century progressed
many Scottish cities were to participate in the historical publishing
club adventure. Whigs as well as Tories were founder-members of
clubs. Yet politics did creep in to the hotly-contested elections for
membership to these rather exclusive bodies. In 1830 Scott was furious
when the normal sequence of candidates coming up for election to the
Bannatyne was overturned to admit the Whig MP for the Ayr burghs,
Thomas Kennedy of Dunure, in preference to Scott's friend the Tory
Lord Medwyn. Cosmo Innes, a great record scholar of the next generation to Thomson was so strong a Whig that the passing of the Reform
Act of 1832 represented a major career opportunity for him. Under
sympathetic governments he was appointed Lord Advocate Depute in
1833 and Sheriff of Moray in 1840. Nevertheless, it is not going too far
to argue that the core of the revival of interest in Scotland's past was
unmistakably Tory. The protean genius of Scott lay at the very heart
of the movement. The only substantial multi-volume *History of Scotland* which emerged in this period (its first two volumes came out in
1829) was that of Patrick Fraser Tytler, who literally boasted of not
having a drop of Whig blood in his veins. His fine scholarship failed to
compensate for his hostility to post 1832 governments, which cost him
every official post he aspired to.

A new emphasis on the old and the local was part of the response of
the traditional ruling classes of Scotland to what they saw as a mounting threat to their long-entrenched political ascendancy. They had
been shaken by what they saw as the corrosive impact of cocksure

Jacobin radicalism on the social and governmental structures of the France of the *Ancien Régime*. After 1815 they saw a similar threat in the increasingly strident and confident Whig propaganda against the existing pattern of political power in Scotland. There was a growing conviction in circles in Scotland opposed to significant political change that the superficial rationalism inculcated in the elementary classes in Scottish universities might well prove the solvent of those bonds of deference on which their prescriptive right to rule rested. That there was truth in some of the conservative strictures on the Scottish universities, and merit in the new directions which the conservative reaction could give to intellectual enquiry, is amply demonstrated by the career of another friend of Walter Scott, the Seceder clergyman John Jamieson. Born in Glasgow in 1759, the son of the pastor to one of only two Seceder congregations then established in that city, Jamieson was predestined to the priesthood of his denomination more or less from birth. His higher education was therefore absurdly premature. Admitted to the first Humanity (Latin) class at the University of Glasgow at the ripe age of 9, he studied logic at 11, and sat at the feet of the venerable Thomas Reid, the 'Father of the Common Sense School' a year later, at an age which Jamieson himself thought rendered the exercise ridiculous. The Associate Presbytery of Glasgow admitted him a student of theology when he was 14, and licensed him to preach at 20. Settled, not very happily, at Forfar, he became friendly with George Dempster of Dunnichen, and married the daughter of a laird. It was at Dempster's residence that he met the Danish Professor of Antiquities Thorkelin who persuaded him to embark on his great *Dictionary Of The Scottish Language* of which two quarto volumes appeared by subscription in Edinburgh in 1808, and two comparable volumes of *Supplement* in 1825. Latterly Jamieson had been translated to a charge in Edinburgh. He was a regular visitor to Scott's Abbotsford and pursued his hobby of angling in Border streams until his death in 1838.

Apart from the accident of belonging to a Seceder levitical dynasty, Jamieson was a well-integrated, if relatively humble, member of the ruling group in Scotland, with all that implied in terms of access to patronage for his seven sons. Alas, the dreadful mortality of the period ensured that only one of them outlived him, but it is significant that three of them died in the corn kist of Scotland, India. An even more remarkable example than Jamieson of Scott's ability to patronize creatively a very Scottish character of humble origins and to build him into the Tory literary establishment was James Hogg. He was born in 1770, the son of a shepherd in a remote part of Ettrick Forest in the Borders.

After a few months of formal schooling, he educated himself by sheer determination and labour, becoming well read to the point where his longer poems contain substantial echoes of Milton and Pope and his *Poetic Mirror* contains inspired parodies of, amongst others, Scott, Byron, and Wordsworth. Though he was familiar with traditional Scots balladry and not ignorant of the late-medieval Scots poets known as the Makars, Hogg was also steeped in the formal English of the Authorized Version of the Bible. His lifelong friendship with Walter Scott dated from 1802 when Scott contacted him during researches for the third volume of his *Minstrelsy of the Scottish Border*. By 1810 Hogg, an unsuccessful farmer, had become a professional writer in Edinburgh, achieving overnight fame in 1813 with his poem 'The Queen's Wake'. By 1815 he was in possession of a life tenancy rent-free of a farm in Yarrow on the Borders, gifted to him by the Tory magnate the Duke of Buccleuch. The gift mitigated the effects of Hogg's financial mismanagement, which remained chronic.

It was felt in aggressive Tory circles that the *Quarterly*, for all its merits, was scarcely smiting the iniquities of the Whig *Edinburgh Review* hip and thigh, so in 1817 William Blackwood, a pushing Tory bookseller-publisher who had taken the unprecedented step of quitting the old haunts of his profession on the High Street for Edinburgh's fashionable New Town, launched in April his *Edinburgh Monthly Magazine*. Betrayed by his editors, who were removed, Blackwood stepped into the breach himself, supported by a group of friends including John Gibson Lockhart, the future son-in-law and biographer of Walter Scott; James Hogg; and John Wilson, better known by his soubriquet of 'Christopher North' and a future Professor of Moral Philosophy in the University of Edinburgh. With its seventh issue, *Maga* as it became affectionately known burst into the literary scene with a vituperative virulence which became its hallmark, savaging Archibald Constable, the rival printer who had suborned the original *Maga* editors, Francis Jeffrey of the *Edinburgh*, and indeed most of the city's leading Whigs, in mock Old Testament language in a very funny article entitled 'Translation from an Ancient Chaldee Manuscript'. Deemed so blasphemous that it had to be omitted in reprints of the number, the piece produced exactly the sensation needed to make people buy future numbers. From 1822 to 1835 Blackwood's ran an extraordinary series of articles in the form of a dialogue between 'Christopher North' and a figure obviously based on Hogg, to the point where the figure's name 'The Ettrick Shepherd' became Hogg's soubriquet. Wilson's was the master-hand, and his treatment of Hogg, whom he exploited, used, and in mephistophelean fashion occasionally abused behind his back, was as twisted as it was a literary triumph. Hogg himself was a complex character, writing four versions of an autobiography, none very reliable, and producing in 1824 in his masterpiece *The Private Memoirs And Confessions Of a Justified Sinner* a novel which is arguably the most compelling exposition of the power of evil in the literature of the English-speaking peoples. It was published anonymously and the posthumous edition of 1837 (by which time the authorship was known) was expurgated to appease High Calvinist opinion.

Hogg greatly assisted the *Blackwood's* group in attacking the Whig leadership, amusingly, but at times unfairly, viciously, and vulgarly. Hogg's stature as a 'true national poet', Whig newspapers like the *Scotsman* and the *London Magazine* protested, was being prostituted to serve the purposes of 'the guilt and filth' of *Blackwood's*. Nor was this mere literary badinage. John Scott, the young editor of the *London Magazine*, was actually killed in a duel with Lockhart's friend Christie. It is therefore hardly surprising that when in 1819 John Gibson Lockhart produced his *Peter's Letters to his Kinsfolk*, an extended commentary mainly on the Edinburgh scene, he made serious efforts to tone down the personal bitterness in his writing and even to apologize indirectly to some, like the rising Tory divine Thomas Chalmers, whom he had attacked recklessly and mistakenly. Nevertheless, *Peter's Letters* scored a considerable *succès de scandale* when it appeared, partly because, despite the less acerbic tone of its prose, it was permeated by a strongly partisan tone, and partly because in making sure that the Whig dogs had the worst of it Lockhart necessarily developed a critique of polite Edinburgh culture which was both serious and significant. For years Walter Scott had been the only Edinburgh literary figure of stature who was also a committed Tory. Now Lockhart, fresh from savouring at Abbotsford in the company of Scott and the 2nd Viscount Melville a neo-feudal lifestyle which was nothing if not intensely Scottish, could point out that the Whig tradition as embodied in the *Edinburgh* was blind to some of the most important cultural developments of the day, notably to the greatness of Wordsworth and to the theme of nationality which was so central to the work of Scott.

Romantic Toryism drew strength from cultural currents running far beyond the shores of Britain, and notably from Germany. In the early 1790s Walter Scott himself had become 'German-mad'. The first signs of serious interest in German literature in Scotland followed Henry Mackenzie's 'Account of the German Theatre' read to the Royal Society of Edinburgh on 21 April 1788, and published in its

Transactions two years later. Alexander Fraser Tytler, the father of Patrick Fraser Tytler, had translated Schiller's *Die Räuber*. Scott never achieved the exact scholarly knowledge of German possessed by, say, his friend James Skene of Rubislaw, who had lived in Saxony, but he acquired enough of the language to plunge deep into German ballads and to translate pieces by Burger and Goethe. With the coming of the French Revolutionary Wars German '*Sturm und Drang*' literature was increasingly identified in Britian with radicalism and Godlessness. Indeed the Reverend James Macdonald, minister of Anstruther Wester in Fife from 1799 to 1804, and a man who had lived in Germany, and who not only propagated a knowledge of German literature in Scotland but also pioneered the introduction of the poetry of Burns to German readers, was moved to try to organize criticism of John Robison's *Proofs of a Conspiracy against all the Religions and Governments of Europe* around 1800, on the grounds that it stoked a needless and irrational prejudice against German culture. In practice romanticism had no necessary political bias. It could be used to serve the end of either reaction or radicalism. Its only inherent hostility was to the aesthetics of neo-classical culture. After 1815 it was therefore natural for conservatives in Scottish cultural life to draw once more on the reserves of sympathetic material available in contemporary Germany. From 1817 to 1828 *Blackwood's Magazine* ran a series of '*Horae Germanicae*' designed to widen its readers' acquaintance with German literature. Blackwood himself in 1817 financed Lockhart's summer holiday in Germany, in the course of which Lockhart went to Weimar and met Goethe. Blackwood also commissioned a work of translation from the German from Lockhart, and it is revealing that the latter chose to translate the *Geschichte der alten und neuer Literatur* of Carl Wilhelm Friedrich von Schlegel, who after a career as the *enfant terrible* of radical romanticism had swung to the opposite extreme. Converting to Roman Catholicism and the Austrian public service, he had acquired those nationalistic and reactionary views discernible in much of his later work including the translated *On the History of Literature* which Lockhart published in 1818.

The cultural counter-offensive by the defenders of the political *status quo* in Scotland, whilst itself a symptom of insecurity, was thus impressive in its width, vitality, and quality. Lockhart's *Peter's Letters*, that biography of a national culture, was probably justified in its claim that the great weight of talent in 1819 in literary circles in Scotland was on the Tory side. Yet it is clear that the erosion of the Tory grip on Scottish life continued, if not at a pace which threatened revolution, at least at a pace which deeply disturbed Tories, and it is important to ask why this should have been so. The answer seems to lie in a combination of positive and negative factors. The latter may briefly be summed up as a set of reasons why the Tory reaction was more impressive than convincing, and to these reasons it is logical to turn first.

In a preface to his novel *Quentin Durward*, dated December 1831, Scott remarked that this book, set mainly in late-medieval France, had proved more popular both at home and on the Continent than some of its predecessors. This was true. Scott rapidly reached a regular print run of 10,000 copies for the first impression of a novel and Lockhart reckoned his annual income from fiction, or 'works of mere amusement' as Scott called them, at £10,000, after the first four novels. However, increasingly careless and diffuse writing led eventually to well-deserved failures such as *The Abbot*, and once the magic spell was broken to undeserved failures such as *Redgauntlet*, which was poorly received, so it was obviously a fillip to Scott that *Quentin Durward* revived a measure of his old success, the more so as its implicit 'message' was so close to Scott's heart. The 'message' which Scott spelled out, was the danger involved in the total loss of the feudal virtues of honour, constancy, and loyalty in the face of the socially disruptive machiavellian egotism of a ruler like Louis XI. Yet Scott's own neo-feudalism was bogus and unstable. Lockhart, whose biographical technique, polished on lives of Robert Burns and Napoleon, involved an artistic blending of the man and his myth, carefully concealed in the official biography of Scott the extent to which Scott was responsible for the financial disaster which overwhelmed both him and his business associates in 1826. Lockhart set up as the villains of the episode the Ballantyne brothers who between them served as Scott's copy-editors, printers, and literary agents, but in fact the Ballantynes and Archibald Constable, Scott's publisher, were the victims of the bad business judgement and total financial irresponsibility of Scott, with whom their finances were hopelessly and to some extent secretly intertwined.

Already, in a lengthy preface to *The Fortunes of Nigel*, Scott had felt obliged hotly to defend himself against the charge that he wrote too much too fast in an attempt to collect a maximum amount of copy money in a minimum time. The charges were perfectly true but greed was not the motive. Rather was it desperation to keep intact a bubble of credit which finally burst late in 1825. The collapse itself was in the long run clearly inevitable, but its dating was closely linked to a traumatic downturn in the business cycle in Britain which involved a run on the banks which was itself rendered more disruptive by a credit-squeeze imposed by the Bank of England. James Ballantyne and Company had been hopelessly insolvent for some time. When the crash came Scott was responsible for no less than £116,838 11s. 3d. worth of their debt, almost all of which had been contracted on his initiative. Archibald Constable and Company went bankrupt with a deficiency of £256,000, and their valuable assets had to be sold for a fraction of their true worth to satisfy desperate creditors. That Scott, with the assistance of generous creditors, coped heroically with this terrible debacle and literally buckled down to writing off his debts, to the point where he had drafted his last novel, unpublished before the twentieth century, during the Mediterranean holiday which ended in his death, was less significant than the collapse of his make-believe world.

Scott was by no means the only man living in that world, though he was by far the most remarkable inhabitant of a cosmos which Atlas-like he did so much to sustain. In the field of the visual arts Henry Raeburn also upheld a deeply romantic vision of Scotland. Raeburn's portraits of swashbuckling Highland chiefs like the MacNab, and that by no means dissimilar character Alastair Macdonnell of Glengarry, show all the penetration, masculine vigour, and authority of which the painter was capable. After 1798 Raeburn had no serious rival as a portrait painter in Edinburgh. He was of middle-class origin, the son of a textile manufacturer, and his portraiture was particularly effective when its subject was a member of the professional classes. His brush has recorded such academic figures as Professor John Robison. With the aristocracy he had a struggle to establish himself, and he failed in a tentative bid to set up as a fashionable London portrait painter in 1810. Like Scott, he was latterly hounded by problems of debt due to unsuccessful business deals. Always a trifle suspect for slapdash finish and deficient anatomical knowledge, he had few official commissions for portraits in the Grand Manner, despite being willing to produce them at less than half the rate demanded by the leading London portrait painter of the early 1800s — Sir Thomas Lawrence. Raeburn died in 1823, having been knighted by George IV during that monarch's visit to Scotland which in many ways was the final celebration by a virile but doomed provincial ascendancy of their extraordinary neo-feudal romantic self-justification, so compellingly limned by the brush of Raeburn in his Highland portraits, and so persuasively preached by Scott in his numerous novels.

Beneath the glamorous, if sometimes gimcrack surface of events the old ruling groups were undoubtedly loosing their grip in Scottish society. High agricultural prices and rents during the Napoleonic wars had enabled the aristocracy to indulge in massive building schemes. Their new castles, as befitted intellectual fashions in the best circles, were often in that castellated style first developed by Robert Morris at Inveraray and further developed by Robert Adam in a whole series of Scottish castles such as Mellerstain and Wedderburn in Berwickshire, Seton in East Lothian, Airthrey in Stirlingshire, and perhaps most spectacularly at Culzean in Ayrshire. At Abbotsford Sir Walter Scott and the architect William Atkinson created after 1816 the prototype building for the Scottish baronal style which was to sweep Scotland after the mid century. Meantime, magnates like the Earl of Breadalbane were building vast castellated palaces like Taymouth Castle in Perthshire which was begun by the architects Archibald and James Elliot in 1806 and extended by William Atkinson after 1818. Gothic revival was clearly in the air, a selfconscious cultivation of pseudo-medieval religiosity which made the Elliots call the arcade girdling the basement at Taymouth a cloister, and caused patrons like the Earl of Mansfield to build medieval touches into every room in the new Scone Palace built under William Atkinson's supervision between 1803 and 1812. At Crawford Priory in Fife after 1813 a rising young Scots architect, James Gillespie Graham, recased an eighteenth-century house in 'ecclesiastical gothic'.

Yet the religiosity was as unconvincing as the feudal postures. Scott patronized Episcopalian churches occasionally to underline his dislike of the Presbyterian Kirk, but his real religious commitment appears to have been as tepid as that of the elder Dundas. The old Moderate ascendancy in the Kirk By Law Established was undoubtedly the most convenient arrangement in the field ecclesiastic for those who managed Scotland in the Dundas interest, but by 1820 it was clear that the peace in church—state relations created by that ascendancy was under threat from two irresistibly growing forces — Evangelical sentiment within the Church of Scotland and dissenting denominations without.

The Original Secession of the 1730s had been led by men of ability and character. Its cause commanded widespread sympathy because of opposition to lay patronage and fear that the fundamentals of the Faith were in danger from fashionable theology. Only the difficulty of furnishing qualified ministers for its congregations prevented very rapid expansion in its numbers. Nevertheless, by 1737 the original 4 Seceder congregations had increased to 15, and three years later it was 36. From 1742 they were active in Ulster and by 1760 there were 99 Seceder congregations in Scotland alone. To the considerable glee of their opponents they were increasingly riven by faction, dividing in

1747 into Burghers and Anti-Burghers over the licitness of the terms of an oath necessary for those assuming the status of burgess in Scottish burghs. In 1795 a serious dispute over the standing of the seventeenth-century Westminster Confession of Faith further divided Seceders between Auld Lichts and New Lichts, and underlined the extent to which new currents of thought were disturbing them. Yet the very divisions of this cantankerous religious tradition led to expansion, especially in the towns where the Seceding groups made a very strong appeal to the manufacturing and commercial middle classes. They also appealed to lower middle class and artisan groups in town and country, and never lost a strong following amongst small tenant farmers.

Much more radical before 1800 in both theology and in their approach to the church—state relationship were the members of a third Presbyterian tradition which in 1761 set up what was called the Relief Presbytery. It owed its existence to a very remarkable man, Thomas Gillespie of Garnock. Deposed from his charge in the Church of Scotland, he never exhibited any bitterness towards it, and indeed all his life shunned the very face of the religious controversy on which Seceders throve. He held communion with all sincere Christians of any denomination. For his day this was a very radical step. Gillespie opposed not only patronage but also the church—state connection. Despite this he was a reluctant member of the Presbytery of Relief and eventually urged his own congregation to return to the Church of Scotland, which they did. Yet the denomination which this unworldly and saintly man so reluctantly founded went on after his death, liberal in its theology, unaggressively radical in its politics.

As early as 1765 it had been said that 100,000 people in Scotland adhered to non-established denominations. In 1795 the Lord Advocate, Robert Dundas of Arniston, thought the figure was 150,000. Almost certainly he exaggerated. Dr James Hall, a Burgher minister in Edinburgh, was able in 1797 to exploit the Lord Advocate's neurosis to collect £300 a year, secretly, for acting as Westminster's 'agent' among the Scotch Seceders. Only in 1807 did a new Prime Minister, Spencer Percival, put a stop to this discreditable confidence trick. Seceders were not Jacobins. However, they were outwith the scope of positive management by the politicians, and they drifted in more rather than less radical directions with time. For example the Original Secession left the Church of Scotland still committed to the principle of a state church. It simply objected to the precise nature of the relationship between church and state in Scotland in the early eighteenth century. By the early nineteenth century the bulk of Seceding opinion was moving towards the disestablishment principles expounded by the Relief Kirk. One result of this development was a further spasm of schism which gave birth to the greatest single achievement in the writing of ecclesiastical history in nineteenth-century Scotland – the *Life Of Knox* (1811) and the *Life of Melville* (1819) in which Thomas McCrie, that most conservative of Seceders, demonstrated beyond any shadow of doubt that the absence of a religious establishment had never been acceptable to the Fathers of the Scottish Reformation.

The Reverend Doctor Thomas McCrie, to give him his full title, also turned his warm indignation against what he saw as Walter Scott's denigration of Scottish Presbyterianism in *Old Mortality*, to such effect that Scott felt obliged to defend himself at length in an article in *The Quarterly Review.* Like Scott, McCrie was ultra-conservative. The inability of the two greatest Scottish men of letters of their day to agree was inevitable: they held radically antagonistic views as to precisely what kind of heritage needed to be conserved. At least their visions had this in common; neither was universally acceptable, though both had enduring emotional appeal. McCrie was wholly out-with the main currents of Seceder history which in 1820 carried the two New Licht groups towards a union.[2]

More significant, from the point of view of the rulers of Scottish society, was the mounting Evangelical offensive within the Church of Scotland. Moderates disapproved in principle of the stress upon an intensely personal, emotion-charged conversion experience which was characteristic of the Evangelical school, but Evangelical and Seceder never became synonymous terms. The 'Cambuslang Wark' of 1742, a tremendous religious revival of a highly emotional kind centred on Cambuslang (a Clydeside parish with Covenanting traditions and on bad terms with its patron), owed much to the English Calvinistic Methodist George Whitefield, but it was associated with ministers of the Established Kirk. Evangelicals were bound to be unhappy about the implications for vital religion in a parish of an unbridled right of patronage in the hands of a patron whose commitment to the Faith might be tepid or non-existent. The Evangelical Party of the early nineteenth century was, until his death in 1827, under the extremely conservative leadership of the Reverend Sir Henry Moncrieff Bart, of St Cuthbert's Edinburgh, but even at its most conservative that party was bound to want to restrict patron's rights (never in Scottish eccle-siastical law deemed absolute), and from restriction to abolition was

[2] Joined in 1847 by the Relief Church to constitute the United Presbyterian Church.

always a possible mental leap. Above all, Evangelicals had positive ideas about adapting the Established Kirk to meet the new challenges of a changing Scotland.

Of necessity this would have involved active co-operation and concessions from a state whose masters regarded Scottish politics as an exercise in buying individuals to ensure that Scottish problems were not even raised, let alone added to the long list of problems which Westminster was actively wrestling with, not always with success. It therefore added greatly to the potential difficulties of government when in 1809 the most dynamic and forceful personality produced by the Church of Scotland in the nineteenth century, Thomas Chalmers, experienced a conversion which turned this young minister of Kilmany in his native Fife from a typical Moderate into a conservative but bustling Evangelical. Evangelical revivalism was in the air in Scotland to the point where there was no emotional gap, as in England, for Methodism to fill, and this fact, allied to financial mis-management by Valentine Ward, the leading Methodist preacher active in Scotland between 1811 and 1819, ensured that Scottish Methodism always remained small. Lay evangelism which eventually contributed to the creation of Baptist and Congregational communities did exist and was sponsored between 1798 and 1810 to the tune of over £70,000 by the remarkable brothers James and Robert Haldane of Airthrey in Stirlingshire, but the main preoccupation of the embattled Moderates remained the duel with the Evangelicals during elections for representative elders to sit in the General Assembly.

During his tenure of a St Andrews professorship Chalmers was returned to the Assembly neither by his hyper-conservative university or by the local presbytery. Forced to canvass his native burgh of Anstruther Easter, Chalmers had to pay the usual price in food and drink for the votes which returned him. Despite his election as Moderator of the General Assembly in 1832, the Moderate grip held until 1834. It was based on a landed and legal block in the Assembly which between 1820 and 1832 still accounted for about 80 per cent of the elders. Among the lawyers (50 to 60 per cent of elders in the Assembly in this period), 97 to 98 per cent were usually of Edinburgh provenance. However, the Moderate dam was clearly strained to breaking-point by the Evangelical pressure behind it before 1832, and this is all the more impressive in that the social composition of General Assemblies changed little.

Again and again the existing political ascendancy was falling foul of forces in Scottish life which represented the wave of the future, whether in the field of opinion, or in the changing balance of economic power. Nowhere was this more true than in the towns where the rapidly-expanding commercial and manufacturing middle classes, very often Seceder or if Established Kirk Evangelical in persuasion, were face to face with the oligarchical cliques which monopolized urban government. The management of burgh finances was always secretive, usually incompetent, and not infrequently dishonest. By 1817 the long moribund agitation for burghal reform had started to life again under one of its old leaders, Archibald Fletcher. A new reforming press had come into existence since 1800 and now strongly supported demands for a clean up of an urban government system so disreputable that reformers of every hue were at one in denouncing it. *The Dundee Advertiser* was one of these radical papers and had been established in 1801. *The Aberdeen Chronicle* was another which had come into being in 1806. *The Scotsman* was born in Edinburgh in January 1817 as a direct result of the experience of William Ritchie, an Edinburgh solicitor, in trying to publicize facts he had ascertained about the gross mismanagement of Edinburgh Royal Infirmary.

Burghal reform, to most of its supporters, was a common-sense rather than an ideological commitment, though their opinion of the London government inevitably declined when it became apparent that it was not prepared to countenance any meaningful reform. An old technique of securing a royal warrant for an election of the town council by a poll of all burgesses was reactivated in 1817 in Montrose by reform sympathizers who deliberately engineered irregularity in the council election, but the government soon made it clear it would issue no more such warrants. In 1819 Lord Archibald Hamilton secured a parliamentary inquiry which showed that Edinburgh, Aberdeen, Dundee, and Dunfermline had been virtually bankrupted by corrupt practices. Between 1818 and 1821 petitions from the royal burghs of Scotland demanding reform rained in upon the House of Commons, which referred them to a select committee. Its *Report* (ordered to be printed 14–15 July 1821) admitted that the almost total breakdown of pre-1707 legal and accounting controls over the burghs had led to scandalous goings-on. It singled out Inverurie in Aberdeenshire as an extreme case of the improprieties which accompanied the practice of having absentee councillors, and Cupar in Fife as an infamous example of the sale of council office. Apart from the submission of public annual accounts and better audit procedures, the *Report* recommended no change. Nay, it flatly stated that any infringement of vested rights was too dangerous a precedent.

Yet in the burghs of Scotland the *Ancien Régime* was inexorably wasting away. Bankruptcy was staring Edinburgh in the face by 1825 when a further government loan of £240,000 was only secured by pledging most of the council's real-estate assets, including the docks in the subject port of Leith, on which great sums had been spent. Council plans to recover some ground by increasing already high port charges after selling the docks to a private company consisting mainly of councillors led to a major row and the transfer by legislation of control of Leith Docks to 21 commissioners, representing several interests as well as Edinburgh town council, which by 1833 was declared bankrupt. Dundee passed through a similar struggle as local textile manufacturers, acutely aware of the vital importance to them of dock facilities for coastal and other shipping in a pre-railway age, fought to keep control of harbour developments out of the hands of the urbane but rascally Provost Alexander Riddoch and his council cronies who undoubtedly hoped to impose increased levies on a growing flow of trade through an improved harbour, in order to service existing and dubiously acquired council debts.

Significantly, it was in the course of their struggle over the harbour that Dundee radicals like Robert Rintoul, editor of *The Dundee, Perth and Cupar Advertiser*, enlisted the support of a local laird George Kinloch of Kinloch, a man of very strong character who in 1816 actually dared to oppose the main motion at a county meeting of noblemen and freeholders at Perth presided over by the Duke of Atholl. The motion was simply the standard uncritical panegyric beloved of British governments then and since and expected from 'sound' organs of opinion. It said that His Majesty's Government was making the best of a difficult job and that all reasonable men recognized that even its least popular policies were the only possible ones. Kinloch unsuccessfully suggested that the alternative to the only possible policy was to do something different and that in particular taxes were too high. William Maule, MP for Forfarshire and a member of an ancient house which had long rebuffed the insolence of the upstart Melvilles, helped Kinloch and his allies to secure legislation establishing Dundee Harbour Commissioners. Kinloch had to flee abroad to avoid a charge of sedition in 1819 but he returned in 1822, was pardoned in 1823, and lived to serve briefly as Dundee's Whig MP between 1832 and his death in 1833.

With such support, reform could hardly be equated with anarchy, hard as the government tried. One of the few cards in government hands when the support of the bulk of the urban middle classes was at stake was the natural fear of 'the middling sort' for the social radicalism of 'the lower orders'. In certain cases this fear was well developed, almost to the point of paranoia. Kirkman Finlay, the Glasgow merchant-prince and cotton manufacturer is a case in point. He was a notable opponent of the monopoly of the India trade held by the Honourable East India Company and after·being elected MP for Glasgow in 1812 had the immense satisfaction of assisting in the destruction of that monopoly in 1813 (John Company kept its legal monopoly of British trade with China until 1833). Immediately, Kirkman Finlay freighted and first ship direct from the Clyde to India — the 600 ton *Buckinghamshire* which sailed for Calcutta. However, the great man's fear of revolution drove him in a steadily more conservative direction. The Glasgow crowd which had dragged his coach along the Trongate in triumph in 1812 to his house in Queen Street, returned in March 1815 to find him not at home, so they smashed all his windows to express their wrath at his support for the new Corn Law of 1815 which, by prohibiting the sale of foreign grain in Britain until the home price reached 80s. a quarter for wheat and 40s. and 27s. respectively for barley and oats, aimed at keeping up domestic grain prices. It was only very marginally successful in so doing, but it became a great symbol of landed privilege, denounced by street orators as well as by academic economists who believed in free trade, like David Ricardo.

By 1816 Kirkman Finlay was actively trying, in co-operation with a worried London government, to erect an intelligence network capable of penetrating any seditious radical conspiracies. There was certainly a lot of wild talk around in the Lowlands, where the period between 1815 and 1822 was one of sustained depression and hardship for working-class Scotsmen with few redeeming features. The singularly ungenerous so-called 'Old Scots Poor Law' had been firmly rivetted on the countryside, though less successfully on the burghs. On the other hand, it was precisely in the burghs that the scale of the problem of poverty was becoming simply unmanageable. Nor was it mitigated by countervailing pressures from organized labour, for the failure in 1812—13 to sustain judicial settlement of wages by either legal or strike action took the heart out of any incipient trade union movement. Post-war depression came swiftly after 1815, exacerbated by massive demobilization and a flow of poverty-stricken migrants from the countryside. Black cattle prices fell as soon as peace broke out, while kelp prices at once entered a long period of decline deeply debilitating to the Highland economy but inevitable due both to pressure from renewed imports of foreign organic-derived industrial alkali and to the competition of inorganic alkali produced by factories like the St Rollox Works in Glasgow.

Political awareness amongst hard-hit sections of the working classes was undoubtedly fanned by the activities of two Englishmen – William Cobbett the journalist, and Major John Cartwright, a veteran radical agitator. Both men preached drastic parliamentary reform as a panacea for the troubles of the day. For Cartwright, who toured Scotland extensively in 1815 to promote the cause of radical Hampden Clubs, this meant annual parliaments, equal electoral districts, the secret ballot, and payments to MPs. It was no accident that Cartwright went to important centres of the hand-weaving industry like Paisley, Dunfermline, Forfar, Perth, Dundee, and Glasgow. Power looms were coming into use in Scotland. There were 1,500 of them in 1813, a figure which rose to 2,000 in 1820 and to 10,000 in 1829, but most of these were cotton looms in or near Glasgow. In 1833 Kirkman Finlay argued that the unsuitability of steam looms for fine weaving made hand looms perfectly competitive for many fabrics. Certainly in 1831 there were only 15,127 steam looms in and around Glasgow as compared with 32,000 hand looms. Wartime levels of income for handloom weavers working on the plainer fabrics, and these were the vast majority of such weavers, fell sharply immediately after Waterloo and never recovered. Admittedly the wages of the most skilled weavers, such as those whose handlooms produced fine Paisley shawls, held up for another decade, but then they too fell.

A certain amount of secret oath-taking undoubtedly occurred in radical circles. Alexander Richmond, later anathemized as 'the spy', a man who had been an active radical weaver in 1812, became drawn into the intelligence system operated by Kirkman Finlay and his allies such as Samuel Hunter (1769–1839) who was a colonel in the Glasgow Yeomanry as well as editor of the violently conservative *Glasgow Herald*. The government, headed by Lord Liverpool since 1812, authorized state prosecutions of leading Scottish radicals arrested in 1817. The upshot was a fiasco. Truth and paranoid delusion were so confusingly intermingled that Whig lawyers like Jeffrey and Cockburn were able to secure acquittals or nominal sentences for the accused and the principal state prosecutor, Lord Advocate Maconochie, looked so foolish that he had to be kicked upstairs as Lord Meadowbank by the already venerable tradition of appointment to the Court of Session as a reward for political loyalty, if not necessarily political intelligence. By suspending *habeas corpus* and passing further restrictive legislation known as the Six Acts the government had heightened an already tense atmosphere which in Scotland finally erupted in the strangely pathetic 'Radical War' of 1820. That a minority of the unenfranchised were prepared to use violence to challenge the government is clear. In the 1830s champions of peaceful reform like the journalist Peter Mackenzie suggested that the conspiracies were entirely engineered by *agents provocateurs* like Richmond. This just does not seem to be true. Richmond was not employed as a government agent after 1817. What is clear is that only a tiny minority of reformers were ready to use physical force in 1820 when placards in Glasgow called on them to support a not very visible 'Provisional Government'. Weavers came out in a political strike, but a rising by radicals at Strathven in Lanarkshire simply petered out, while a huge horde consisting of 35 Glasgow radicals marching on Carron was gallantly defeated by government cavalry – hussars and yeomanry – at Bonnymuir near Falkirk.

Apart from the trial of 47 men arrested and the execution of three of them, that was the end of physical force reform in Scotland and in most cases of any serious middle-class fear of revolution. Eighteen nineteen had been the culmination of an appalling trade recession exacerbated by poor harvests, high grain prices, and the most savage deliberate deflation by government in modern times. When in August 1819 a survey was made of an area, excluding Paisley, within a five mile radius of the centre of Glasgow, it revealed that of the 18,537 looms only 13,281 were working and 5,256 people were unemployed. Thomas Chalmers, who had been inducted to the crowded parish of the Tron Kirk in central Glasgow in 1815, had no sympathy with political radicalism, deeming 'the spirit of a factious discontent with the rulers of our land' to be 'unscriptural'. At various points he, as much as Walter Scott, was convinced that society was teetering on the brink of the abyss of revolution. Yet even Chalmers was by December 1819 convinced that the menace of political agitation was so reduced that 'the repeal of the Corn Bill' could be represented as a concession from strength. He insisted in a letter to his fellow-Evangelical the great William Wilberforce that repeal would in no way harm the landed interest and that nothing could be more effectual in 'recalling our people to loyalty and quietness'.

9

North Britain and Cockburn's Millenium

It is difficult to study the events leading up to the passage of the Scottish Reform Act in the summer of 1832 without seeing them through the distorting lenses provided by the writings of that most engaging of Scotch Whigs, Henry Cockburn. In the phrase of Thomas Carlyle, Cockburn, the son of a staunchly pro-Dundas father, was 'small, solid and genuine'. He was born in 1779. His father, partly owing to the influence of Dundas, rose to be a Baron of the Exchequer and a Judge Admiral. Despite the fact that his Whiggish proclivities were already known, Henry Cockburn was himself appointed Depute Lord Advocate by his imperious uncle Henry Dundas in 1807. Three years later, to his own relief, he was dismissed from the post for political insubordination. Cockburn was a conservative Whig who distrusted the wilder men of his party. He thought Brougham 'morally, as well as intellectually, mad'. Cockburn was in favour of extending the parliamentary franchise to the significant section of the well-off and the educated hitherto excluded, in order to avert the risk of revolution. In pursuit of his limited aims he was endearingly pugnacious. He was also a delightfully human character reflecting the many emotional and cultural currents of his period in a peculiarly graceful way epitomized by his regular journeys from his classical town house in Edinburgh to his beloved baronial retreat, Bonaly Castle in the Pentlands.

Oddly enough, Cockburn's literary reputation is almost totally posthumous. In his lifetime he published (in 1852) a competent two-volume *Life Of Lord Jeffrey With a Selection From His Correspondence*, but the books on which Cockburn's fame rests like the *Memorials Of His Time*, his so-called *Journal*, and his *Circuit Journeys*, were all published after his demise, by his trustees. It is now clear that in selecting material to make up the *Memorials*, the trustees bowdlerized the manuscripts at their disposal. However, the

Memorials derived from records which Cockburn began to keep about 1821 and the printed versions reflect accurately enough his tendency to depict the contemporary Scottish scene as a sharp dichotomy between two great political parties, the Whigs and the Tories. Naturally he saw himself and his fellow Whigs as striving to raise Scotland from the depths of political degradation, and at the very end of the *Memorials* (which close in 1830) stands the assertion that in this connection 'In the abuses of our representative and municipal systems alone, our predecessors have left us fields in which patriotism may exhaust itself'. Though true up to a point this statement has done much to encourage a profoundly misleading perspective on the sequence of events which apparently culminated in 1832.

For a start, it insinuates a grossly exaggerated view of the rôle of parliamentary elections in that decision-making process which may be described as the British political system. Certainly since the passing of the Septennial Act in 1717, which lengthened the permissible life of a parliament to seven years, elections have never been intended to exert any serious influence over what historians call the 'High Politics' of major decisions. Secondly, Cockburn compounds this error by overstressing a two-party model of contemporary politics which is itself over-simplified and which employs an extremely ambiguous nomenclature. To take the very last point first: such terms as 'Tory' have been used to describe political groupings in first English, then British politics over three centuries, but in fact the history of such groupings or parties is fragmentary and totally non-continuous. In Scotland in 1747 a Tory could either be a rank Jacobite or a throw-back to the English Toryism of the days of Queen Anne – an Episcopalian country gentleman of extreme conservative and 'country' views. By 1810 Tory in Scotland was a term of abuse applied by people like Jeffrey and Cockburn to supporters of the contemporary holders of power at Westminster, all of whom, incidentally, along with their Scottish supporters, would have ranked as rabid Whigs in terms of the politics of 1747 or indeed 1688.

Simply to give shape to the discussion, the terms Tory and Whig have been used in this present study from about 1794 when at least it can be said that the dichotomy between government and an identifiable, committed opposition is clear. The opposition called itself Whig for the same reason that modern southern Irish political movements literally fight one another over some dead hero's grave – to try to monopolize the prestige associated with a (usually specious) claim to continuity with an honoured name. However, to label the government and its supporters as Tory is to obscure the central and obvious fact that the administrations of the Younger Pitt and of Robert Banks Jenkinson, second Earl of Liverpool (1770–1828), who effectively succeeded Pitt as principal Man of Business to the British Establishment, were very much non-party 'broad-bottom' administrations endorsed in their hey-day by all but a small, a-typical, disgruntled minority of the ruling classes. The first major politician within the ruling consensus who was willing to call himself a Tory was George Canning. He too was desperate to establish himself as a representative of an historic and legitimate political tradition. The emptiness of his claims to be the natural leader of the ruling classes may be measured by the fact that his accession to power as premier in 1827, after Liverpool's resignation due to ill-health, marked the beginning of the end of the consensus so laboriously constructed by the Younger Pitt and the urbane, conciliatory Liverpool.

In Scotland daily political life was dominated by the huge presence of the Melville interest, a political machine built on the sheer scale of the patronage at the disposal of the British government, and on the gross venality, even by eighteenth-century standards, of the Scottish ruling class, which was basically the landed interest and its urban sycophants. However, party struggles in the constituencies need not imply, indeed in British politics very rarely imply, party government at Westminster. Cockburn might say, rightly, that by the 1820s all that was best in the intellectual life of Edinburgh, apart from the bankrupt and ailing Scott, was Whig and of the Tories that 'their political influence now depended almost entirely on office'. Office was enough. There is absolutely no evidence that either Cockburn and his friends, let alone any more radical and popular movement, were capable of shaking the ascendancy built up by the Melvilles, itself essentially a re-creation of the sort of machine run by the Earl of Islay at an earlier period. The existing order could only break up from within, and that is what it did from 1827 onwards.

Major questions in British politics, even after 1835 when political parties completed their conquest of the House of Commons, and became accepted as the organizations whose relative strength should determine the composition of the government, tend to be resolved within parties. Radical policy choices almost always involve party splits during high political manoeuvres which recast the ruling group or the patterns of thought fashionable within it. The decision-takers usually succeed in turning any electoral process into a confirmatory validation exercise after the big decision has been taken. The changes

validated by the election which followed the passing of the Reform
Acts had been in progress since 1822 and signs of the splits in the
central political élite which heralded the coming of change had been
apparent earlier than that.

Submerged social and political tensions can often find an outlet in a
highly personalized form, which because of its stress on personalities
obscures any incipient radicalism in the issue. Thus even James
Boswell was able to surmount his usual panic-stricken social conservatism and support the 'popular' side in 'The Douglas Cause', a legal
cause célèbre of the late 1760s when Archibald Douglas or Steuart,
whose own paternity was not beyond question, successfully and to the
great glee of the Edinburgh mob, asserted his right to succeed to the
vast inheritance of the late Duke of Douglas, in despite of the furious
efforts of the Duke of Hamilton to arrest the process of succession, on
grounds of devious fraud by the father of the claimant, the rascally
Jacobite Colonel John Steuart. The equivalent of this bizarre episode
in the early nineteenth century, at a much higher level, of course, was
the vulgar drama of Queen Caroline, whom George IV, her undutiful
spouse, regarded with total loathing. Brougham had corresponded
with her during her lengthy exile on the Continent but when she
elected to return to England in 1820 she rapidly came under the influence of the extreme London radical Alderman Wood. Brougham
disapproved of her provocative behaviour, and stalled the announce-
ment of his appointment as Queen's Attorney General as long as he
could in the hope of being bought off by the government, but in fact
his defence of his unsavoury client when George IV badgered his
unhappy ministers into legal action against her was perhaps his
greatest forensic achievement. Public opinion, alienated by a spoiled,
self-indulgent monarch and his aloof, unsympathetic government,
revelled in an orgy of Queenite enthusiasm, much of it violent and all
of it spiced by the prurient details of Caroline's relationship with
Bartolommeo Pergami, on which George IV hoped to build a case for
divorce. A prince of cross-examiners, Henry Brougham more than
any other man compelled the government to abandon its case in
November 1820, and won for himself and his Whig aristocratic political associates a degree of popularity which they never quite lost.

The Queen's early death and George IV's partially successful
counterbid for popularity via provincial progresses, such as that to
Edinburgh in 1822, eliminated Queenite agitation from the political
agenda. However, an increasingly harried government was by 1822
embarking on a new course of liberalization in economic policy

associated with the name of William Huskisson (1770–1830), under whose régime at the Board of Trade freer trade, a simplified fiscal system, and a new stress on economy became platitudes shared by the rival government factions headed by Canning and the Duke of Wellington. Such views did not, of course win over radicals like the Scotch nabob Joseph Hume who after making a fortune in India sat as a radical MP for Aberdeen (1818–30), Middlesex (1830–7), Kilkenny (1837–41), and eventually for Montrose burghs (1842–55). Opposed to the Corn Laws and obsessed with economy to the point where he virtually painted 'Retrenchment' on the Whig banners, Hume was irreconcilable, as any man willing to inflict over three hours of his own continuous didacticism on the House was likely to be. However, government support was further fractured when it became clear that even the accession of Wellington to power as premier in 1828 marked no reversal of the gradual government drift towards economic liberalism, to which Wellington was every bit as committed as Huskisson.

The single most decisive development in the process whereby the heirs of Liverpool divided against one another without reconciling the hard core of the Whig opposition was undoubtedly the passing of Roman Catholic emancipation in 1829. In Scotland leading figures in pro-government and opposition circles combined to support the measure, alongside eminent divines like Thomas Chalmers, but even the sympathetic Cockburn had to admit that this legislation was profoundly unpopular. Twice as many Scots petitioned against it as for it. To some extent this may have been a reaction to the new stream of Irish Roman Catholic immigrants who after 1800 abruptly reversed the long, gradual decline of that communion in Scotland. In 1791 the immigration of Roman Catholic Highlanders into Glasgow had been encouraged by promises from local manufacturers of employment and facilities for worship. In 1793 in pursuance of the last promise, a distinguished Highland priest was established in Glasgow. By 1831 it was said there were nearly 27,000 Roman Catholics in Glasgow and about as many again in the surrounding area, most of them of Irish origin. To employers they represented a vital reinforcement of cheap labour for the labour market. So confident were radical political economists like Joseph Hume and Francis Place of the ability of market forces to make trade unions ineffective that in 1824–5 they were instrumental in securing the repeal of Pitt's 1800 Combination Act on the grounds that by adding the spice of illegality to their existence it was delaying the demise of unions. When a Catholic Schools Society was founded in Glasgow in 1817 it was supported by Protestant

manufacturers like Kirkman Finlay who, in the teeth of popular Protestant resentment, persisted in his view that education was the least he
owed to workers without whom his manufactures could not have been
carried on.

Yet the feelings stirred by Roman Catholic emancipation ran much
deeper than crude nativist hostility to immigrants. Sir Thomas Dick
Lauder of Fountainhall, a friend of Cockburn and a well-known
champion of the picturesque style of romantic taste, records an
episode which underlines this. In his *Account Of The Great Floods Of
August 1829, In The Province Of Moray* (Edinburgh, 1830), he
reported that a waterspout, a harbinger of the future massive floods,
had on 12 July 1829 totally devastated the lands and crops of a hamlet
in the parish of Contin in Ross-shire, and continued:

> This waterspout did not extend beyond two miles on each side of
> the village, a circumstance that led these simple people to consider
> their calamity as a visitation of Providence for their landlord's vote
> in Parliament in favour of Catholic emancipation.

The truth was that the curious political structure which governed
Britain derived its, ultimately exorbitant, claims to sovereignty
directly from the English Reformation under Henry VIII in the sixteenth century, and its claim for popular support on a vague but
emphatically Protestant interpretation of freedoms secured by the
Glorious Revolution of 1688. Politicization could not be widespread in
Scotland outside the major cities because of the restricted intellectual
life of most of the country. While we perhaps tend to underestimate
the mental life of a provincial capital like Perth around 1800, with its
very large printing industry (whose leading family, the Morisons,
actually produced an *Encyclopaedia Perthensis*), the fact remains that
as late as 1787 there was no bookseller between Aberdeen and Inverness. On the other hand, the humblest Highland peasant knew by the
end of 1829 that the 'Protestant Constitution' he had been taught to
revere was no more.

Also gone was any coherence in the groups which had supported
Liverpool and Pitt before him. The second Viscount Melville was not
prepared to swallow Catholic emancipation. He resigned, logically
enough, for the political divisions he had been used to were in full dis-
solution. The Earl of Lauderdale, no admirer of Queen Caroline and
for a Whig unfashionably critical of some of the ideas of Adam Smith
and Ricardo, had rapidly moved into a position of real influence with

the government in the latter years of Liverpool. However he in his turn found the pace and direction of change more than he could take. For example, proposals to reduce the number of judges in the Court of Session, to use the salaries saved to enhance the remuneration of those left, and to reorganize the court in order to increase its efficiency, had provoked a storm of protest in the late eighteenth century, on the grounds that this constituted parliamentary violation of the Act of Union. Many critics opposed to yet another assertion of parliamentary omnicompetence of a kind which had provoked both an American and an Irish crisis insisted that what was needed was rather an enhancement of the rights of juries in criminal cases in Scotland and the introduction of jury trial in civil cases. Even Walter Scott saw the need for reform of the procedure of the Court of Session which was effected by legislation sponsored by the second Melville in 1808 and 1825. Civil jury trial was introduced in 1816, with Scott's friend the very conservative Whig William Adam of Blair Adam as the, outstandingly successful, Lord Chief Commissioner of the Jury Court. However, by 1830 legislation finally did reduce the Court of Session to 13 judges, 8 sitting as an Outer House and 5 in the Inner House. Lauderdale's last speech in the Lords in July 1830 was against the second reading of the Court of Session Bill. He voted by proxy against the second and third Reform Bills.

With Melville's resignation, the classic managerial régime in Scotland ended. As early as 1826 Sir Walter Scott had warned a correspondent in England against the dangers of permitting extensive liberalization in Scotland on the grounds that 'Scotland, completely liberalized, as she is in a fair way of being, will be the most dangerous neighbour to England that she has had since 1639'. It was a curiously misguided comment, presuming as it did that Scotland was capable of generating a political culture independent of the prevailing pattern of power at Westminster. There was no likelihood that Scotland's political allegiances would change except in step with changes at the centre of power. Even with Melville gone, and with the political élite in London deeply divided over the argument that some measure of meaningful reform was essential to eliminate the long-term danger of political and social revolution, pro-government candidates fared remarkably well in Scotland in the general election of 1830. *The Scotsman* acidly remarked that in Scotland 'men would enlist under Beelzebub's banners, if he were First Lord of the Treasury'. The precondition for change in Scotland was the passing of a measure of reform so substantial as to underline a major shift of power and opinion in parliament.

With the fall of Wellington's administration in November 1830, that shift began. Sheer insensitivity did more than anything else to bring the Hero of Waterloo down. As his most sympathetic and percipient biographer has remarked, geniality and willingness to make real concessions was something which he and his colleagues in government seemed to find natural only when dealing with foreigners. Even so, the eventual passage of the so-called Great Reform Bill by the government headed by an old champion of Queen Caroline, Earl Grey, was a saga involving a struggle with the House of Lords and with William IV. Agitation there certainly was all over Britain, reaching a crescendo in the wild Days of May in 1832, but the burgh of Elgin was typical of all of Scotland, and much of England, in that the agitation only began with the process which culminated in the passing of the legislation. Isaac Forsyth, the local bookseller and antiquary, was prominent in the agitation despite the extreme hostility of his old friends the Duke and Duchess of Gordon, and he was assisted by such local worthies as Sir Andrew Leith Hay, the first MP for Elgin Burghs after the passing of the Reform Bill; Admiral Duff of Drummuir; and Dr John Paul. In Scotland there was no unconnected but contemporary upheaval like the widespread revolt of farm labourers which disturbed rural areas in southern and central England in 1828–30. These convulsions do not in fact appear to have been politically motivated but by coincidence they ensured that the political tension in England was heightened by all the horrors of arson, machine-breaking, and mobbing, culminating in ferocious repression directed by the Whig Home Secretary Lord Melbourne. Lowland Scotland was a classic example of a mixed farming area and not a specialized cereal area like those parts of England where the labourers' revolt was at its worst. Because of the need for labour all round the year, long hires were common in Scotland, where most farm servants were hired for six months or a year, and this stability was further enhanced by a substantial element of payment in kind in Scottish farm wages, which had the effect of minimizing wage erosion by inflation. Though a bothy system of housing single male workers in crude barracks known as bothies did exist in a few a-typical areas such as Kincardineshire, the Carse of Gowrie, or the Laigh (or coastal plain) of Moray, Scottish farmers did not normally keep the pool of under-employed, miserably paid, seasonal workers which existed in, say, Kent. Seasonal workers in Scotland tended to come in from the Highlands or Ireland.

Inevitably the bulk of attention at Westminster was bestowed on the

English Reform Bill, to the relative neglect of the parallel Scottish and Irish measures. The Scottish measure, drawn up by Lord Advocate Francis Jeffrey, Solicitor General Henry Cockburn, and their friend and ally T.F. Kennedy of Dunure, certainly pleased its authors. Cockburn insisted that the measure 'is giving us a political constitution for the first time'. Its overall impact could not but be dramatic once it became clear that Grey and his colleagues were bent on a franchise extension so generous as to stabilize the situation indefinitely and kill any further demand for changes which might affect the basic decision-taking process of government which Grey was determined to keep as secretive and oligarchic as ever. In 1820 there had been only 2,889 county electors in Scotland. Adding to these the burgh electors still gave a total of only 4,239, and of these only a fraction were truly independent. At the first reformed election in 1832 there were 65,000 voters. Quantitatively it was a much more drastic change than the one in England.

In the burghs in Scotland change was even more drastic. The franchise monopoly of the old town councils vanished. A £10 household franchise was uniformly applied instead. The number of burghs seats was increased from 15 to 23, a process which allowed a breach in the parliamentary monopoly of royal burghs by the granting of an MP to non-royal burghs such as Paisley and Greenock. Other burghs of this kind such as Falkirk were added to existing groups of burghs. Grouping sustained the average Scottish burgh electorate at a respectable average of over 1,300 voters each, even when Aberdeen, Dundee, and Perth were withdrawn from their respective groups to return an MP apiece and Glasgow was similarly withdrawn to return two MPs. Edinburgh received an additional MP to match Glasgow with two. Obviously the self-perpetuating town council was doomed, and burgh reform legislation in 1833 introduced the £10 householder as the municipal elector. Already special commissioners for harbours and above all police commissioners, elected under private legislation to deal with a wide range of municipal functions including paving and lighting as well as the maintenance of order, had introduced the urban middle classes to the problems of voting for local government bodies. The great success of the Whigs in the Scottish constituencies in the election of 1832 rested mainly on urban votes. They not only swept the burghs but in the Scottish counties also it was often urban votes which tipped the balance in favour of Whigs, as in Selkirkshire where the reform candidate, Robert Pringle of Clifton, lost in the purely rural vote but won the county on the strength of his support in the small burghs of Selkirk and Galashiels. The Whig government owed the £10 householder his municipal franchise after 1832, for services rendered.

Whig or Liberal ascendancy in the Scottish burghs never really wavered before the British political system entered major crisis in the mid 1880s. Between 1832 and 1886 Tory or Conservative candidates (as they usually called themselves in Scotland) won only 14 contests in Scottish burghs. This was what Cockburn and Brougham and Jeffrey expected. What was millenial about the Reform Act to them was that it rigged the franchise in such a way that the erstwhile Tory ascendancy was likely to lose elections in Scotland, for ever. The prosperous middle classes were enfranchised. They voted overwhelmingly Whig or Liberal. Nobody in circles which mattered in 1832 intended to enfranchise the working classes. *Chamber's Edinburgh Journal* which was founded in 1832 by William Chambers, a staunch Whig supporter of the Reform Bill, was typical of Scotch Whiggery in eschewing any nonsense about democracy and offering the labouring classes not political power but political economy of the kind which lauded punctuality, assiduity, and thrift and utterly deplored unions and strikes. James Stuart of Dunearn, another stalwart Whig who received and gave hard knocks in the approach to the Reform Bill, was a man of the same kidney. He actually shot and killed a scabrous Tory journalist (Sir Alexander Boswell, the son of the biographer of Johnson), but despite this and some little local difficulties over his bankruptcy, he achieved in 1833, with the help of Brougham who was now Lord Chancellor of England, his first government post. It was connected with the royal commission on the employment of children, and on that body, as in his subsequent career as an early factory inspector, Stuart displayed consistently bloody-minded prejudice in favour of employers. The millenium was meant to make the political world safe only for Whigs.

It was therefore a measure of the sheer incompetence of which the leading Whigs in North Britain were capable that they botched the job of fixing the county constituencies. The number of these constituencies remained at 30, but the old practice of pairing small counties, with alternative right to representation, was abolished by accepting the need to fuse counties for electoral purposes. The new county franchise was supposed to eliminate the old jobbery inspired by a franchise based on feudal superiority and substitute the simple minimum criterion of effective control of property worth £10 per annum. Alas, the task of drafting a watertight definition of which tenants qualified under this rule proved quite beyond the authors of the bill. In

December 1832 the Whigs romped home with 43 out of 53 Scottish seats. Thereafter in the counties the old supporters of the Melville interest, like the Duke of Buccleuch, picked themselves up and realized that slipshod draftsmanship and the collapse of old checks on corruption had opened a marvellous vista on cut-price manipulation. As Sheriff John Cay said in 1838, 'never . . . had there been a statute vulnerable on so great a number of points, and those of so delicate a description'. With no secret ballot, and splendid opportunities to manufacture voters, the old discredited Tory magnates could count on their superior advantages in land, money, and tenants to gradually regain the upper hand. By 1840 they had done so in all but a minority of constituencies where Whig aristocrats, using similar devious means, had established their own local ascendancy. Between 1841 and 1868 there were very few contests in Scottish counties. After 1832 what was by contemporary standards an infamous state of affairs in the Scottish burghs was rectified: power now roughly corresponded with property. In the counties, within a few years, remarkably little seemed to have changed except that voters were more numerous and cheaper. At Westminster the great majority of Scots MPs were still broadly in support of the government for as the diarist Greville said at the end of the first session of the reformed legislature: 'matters remain pretty much as they were, except that the Whigs have got possession of the power which the Tories have lost.'

The decisive confrontation between Whig and Tory over parliamentary reform was in fact brief. For about three years before 1832 Scottish Tories tried to resist a strong current of opinion in favour of reform. Tory motives were largely self-interested. However by 1831–2 pressure for change was overwhelming. In Glasgow even the Merchants' House, the seat of financial and social power in the city, petitioned for parliamentary reform in 1831. Virtually all other organized bodies in Glasgow, from the Incorporated Trades to the lawyers in the Faculty of Procurators, followed suit. Once defeated and relieved of their fear of social upheaval, Tories abandoned their opposition to changes the country clearly wanted. Inevitably Toryism paid a heavy immediate price for its selfish intransigeance in terms of electoral defeat. Over much of rural Scotland the Tories' eclipse proved temporary, though they never recovered equally strongly in the Scottish burghs.

By 1832 Scotland was poised on the verge of momentous changes in her economic life. An era of industrial development based on water power and textiles was about to merge into a second wave of industrialization based on steam power and heavy metallurgy. The first successful river steamboat in Europe was built and engined in Glasgow. This was Henry Bell's *Comet* which in 1812 started to run on the much-dredged and deepened Clyde between Glasgow, Greenock, and Helensburgh. In 1818 she opened the steamship route to Fort William via the Crinan Canal. On land the horse-drawn colliery or quarry waggonways started to evolve into locomotive-using railways like the Monkland and Kirkintilloch railway authorized in 1824 and opened in 1826. The eccentric Dundee and Newtyle railway, which started in 1826 and was completed in 1832, lacked a mineral hinterland and was never very successful, despite a bold use of stationary engines and rope haulage to overcome severe gradients, but the Glasgow and Garnkirk railway, which opened in 1831, proved that a railway could successfully compete with the nearby Monkland Canal.

Metallurgical expansion hinged on two discoveries. One was the discovery in 1801 by David Mushet of a vast reserve of raw material in the shape of black band ironstone near Glasgow. The other was the invention by James Beaumont Neilson, manager of the Glasgow Gas Company, of the huge saving in cost effected by heating the air blast sent through an iron smelting furnace. Adopted by William Baird at his Gartsherrie works in 1828, hot blast was widely recognized as a success after 1835, and cheap iron became the foundation of an ever-expanding Clydeside heavy engineering complex.

Expansion and immigration bred problems and neuroses. In 1812 the Edinburgh authorities reinforced the social order by hanging three teenage youths who had beaten and robbed middle-class Hogmanay revellers outside the Tron Kirk. Another public execution in Edinburgh, in 1828, was that of William Burke who with his fellow Irish immigrant William Hare had murdered many victims to supply dissection subjects for a third rising local entrepreneur, the anatomy teacher Dr Robert Knox. What is clear is that tensions were social and sectarian rather than nationalistic. As early as 1820 it became obvious that even the most radical of Caledonian reformers wanted to work closely with their English counterparts. The Reform Act of 1832 is best seen as an episode in a continuing debate in Britain as to the techniques and ideology best suited to the needs of the propertied classes in a rapidly-changing industrial society. Francis Jeffrey, one of the framers of the Scottish Reform Act said flatly 'The real battle is not between Whigs and Tories, Liberals and Illiberals and such gentleman-like denominations, but between property and no-property — Swing and the law.' 'Captain Swing' was the mythical symbol of the revolt of the English farm labourers in the period 1831–2, a revolt much marked by incendiary attacks on property.

Curiously, the intellectual roots of the two rival ideologies competing to control the response of the British Establishment to 'Swing' were deeply embedded in early-nineteenth-century Scotland. Presumably this fact, like other precocious aspects of Scottish social thought, derived from the stimulus provided by the experience of a dramatic and telescoped modernization of Scottish society after 1750. Certainly by 1818 *Blackwood's*, the widest-selling of the quarterlies, was articulating a full-blown neo-feudal Tory aristocratic reaction against what it saw as destructive and excessive social and intellectual change. It held up a vision of a paternalistic, aristocratically-led, vertically-integrated society, and lambasted the tribe of liberal, free-trade, laissez-faire economists of the classical school as socially disruptive. *Blackwood's* vision of the conservative value of ancient loyalties was very much that of Walter Scott. It was Scott's social conservatism which made him so bitter about 'the late disposition to change everything in Scotland to an English model.' He defended the Scottish pound note in 1826 against attempts to abolish it with the same zeal he had supported the Dundas interest.

However, the rival set of values represented by what has been called 'the entrepreneurial ethic' was already well on the way to victory before 1832 set the seal on its triumph. The predominantly aristocratic ruling class was profoundly penetrated by commercial values and attracted by a school of classical political economists who rationalized a repudiation of responsibilities to the poor. Absentee landlords, Whig lawyers, and collusive judges in the Court of Session had conspired by 1834 to write into the textbooks a largely bogus, and incredibly mean, 'Old Scots Poor Law' under which any attempt to lay on a local assessment to assist 'able-bodied labourers in time of dearth' was deemed illegal. Such legal chicanery was reinforced by white-hot Evangelical passion in the shape of that arch-Tory the Reverend Dr Thomas Chalmers who in a famous experiment in his Church of Scotland parish in Glasgow tried to 'prove' that the poor could adequately be coped with by voluntary contributions, mainly from the poor themselves. In 1837, long after Chalmers had left Glasgow, his experiment was wound up as hopelessly inadequate.

Nevertheless, Evangelical religion, puritanical and individualistic, went well with a puritanical and atomistic social ethic. The increasingly confident and powerful middle classes could preach their gospel of self-help from more places than just the pulpit. They could preach through the press. J.R. McCulloch was not only a classical economist convinced that the working classes should abandon 'violent and unjustifiable proceedings' like strikes, but also a sometime editor of *The Scotsman*. Parochial education in Scotland was scarcely dynamic in 1832. Schoolteachers received their first pay rise since 1696 only in 1803, and then mainly as a reward for political conservatism. In 1836 the Reverend George Lewis of St David's parish Dundee published a pamphlet entitled *Scotland a Half Educated Nation*. By 1826 it had become clear that anachronistic constitutional arrangements were seriously obstructing the ability of the Scottish universities to respond to changed circumstances. However, a host of new educational devices ranging from lantern lectures to the Mechanics' Institutes set up in many towns propagated the ideology essential to the creation of that new and viable class society which was progressively ousting the old aristocratic ethos. Thomas Dick of Methven, Secession clergyman, popular author, pioneer of Mechanics' Institutes, saint and astronomer, summed up in himself many of the strengths of the new society.

That in the politics of the burghs after 1832 the Tories were often cast in the rôle of the Demon King in the emotional pantomime which recurringly validated the new Whig or Liberal ascendancy, should not obscure the fact that the new order was based on a consensus over basic issues. Yet the harsh impersonality of a market society, shaped by class relationships, was hard for a man of imagination and sensitivity to stomach. Landscape painters like Alexander Nasmyth (1758–1840), and Sir Walter Scott's friend the Reverend John Thomson of Duddingstone (1778–1840), limned a vision of Scotland as a non-industrial 'Land of the mountain and the flood'. Like Scott's evocation of a safely-dead pre-Union Scotland, this vision was ultimately less a tourist lure than an emotional salve for North Britons uneasily conscious of also being Scots.

A Note on Further Reading

General

The outstanding general survey of this period is the relevant section of
W. Ferguson, *Scotland 1689 to the Present*, the Edinburgh History of Scotland, vol. IV (Edinburgh, 1968). No other general survey merits mention
though social history is elegantly served by T.C. Smout's *A History of the
Scottish People 1560–1830* (London, 1969). The work of Henry Grey
Graham, *The Social Life of Scotland in the Eighteenth Century* (1st edn, 2
vols., 1899; and many subsequent editions) is downright misleading and best
ignored. Rosalind Mitchison's *Life in Scotland* (London, 1978) is rather slight.
Its author's talents are better appreciated in her many important and stimulating articles. General surveys of Scottish economic history which cover this
period include R.H. Campbell, *Scotland Since 1707* (Oxford, 1965), S.G.E.
Lythe and J. Butt, *An Economic History of Scotland 1100–1939* (Glasgow,
1965), and B. Lenman, *An Economic History of Modern Scotland 1660–1976*
(London, 1977).

There is a useful collection of documents in R.H. Campbell and J.B.A.
Dow, *Source Book of Scottish Economic and Social History* (Oxford, 1968)
which despite its title is almost entirely post 1707 in content and indeed mainly
post 1770. Demography is well represented by M. Flinn (ed.), *Scottish
Population History* (Cambridge, 1977). A regional study of classic stature is
M. Gray, *The Highland Economy 1750–1850* (Edinburgh, 1957), while
A. Slaven, *The Development of the West of Scotland 1750–1960* (London,
1975) is a survey of the most important of Scotland's industrial regions. Business history is not well covered as yet but P. Payne (ed.), *Studies in Scottish
Business History* (London, 1967) contains a good survey of the sources plus a
couple of relevant articles for this period. S.G. Checkland, *Scottish Banking: A
History, 1695–1973* (Glasgow, 1975) is basic, as is B. Duckham, *A History of
the Scottish Coal Industry*, vol. 1 (Newton Abbot, 1970).

In a separate category are books by geographers such as R.N. Millman's
disappointing *The Making of the Scottish Landscape* (London, 1975) and I.H.
Adams, *The Making of Urban Scotland* (London, 1978). A convenient summary of new work is M.L. Parry and T.R. Slater (eds.), *The Making of the*

Scottish Countryside (London, 1980). It is clear that geographical science and historical studies have grown apart in method over the last few decades to the point where it is difficult for anything written on one side of the divide wholly to please those on the other. Fortunately this is less true of other disciplines which overlap with the fields of interest of the historian, and art history is a particularly good example. D. and F. Irwin, *Scottish Painters At Home and Abroad 1700–1900* (London, 1975) is a major work of historical scholarship as is J. Dunbar's *The Historic Architecture of Scotland* (London, 1966; 2nd revised edn, 1978).

Specialist themes are dealt with in D. Johnson, *Music and Society in Lowland Scotland in the Eighteenth Century* (London, 1972), R.K. Marshall, *Women in Scotland 1660–1780* (Edinburgh, the National Galleries of Scotland, 1979), and T.M. Devine (ed.), *Lairds and Improvement in the Scotland of the Enlightenment* (Proceedings of the 9th Scottish Historical Conference, Glasgow, 1979). There is at last a competent synthesis of Scottish ecclesiastical history in the shape of A.L. Drummond and J. Bulloch, *The Scottish Church 1688–1843* (Edinburgh, 1973). Literary history is conveniently covered in two contrasting and complimentary works: D. Craig, *Scottish Literature and the Scottish People 1680–1830* (London, 1961), and M. Lindsay, *History of Scottish Literature* (London, 1977). Finally mention must be made of a unique venture in comparative history which contains several relevant and helpful articles, L.M. Cullen and T.C. Smout (eds.), *Comparative Aspects of Scottish and Irish Economic and Social History 1600–1900* (Edinburgh, 1977). A. Hook, *Scotland and America 1750–1835* (Glasgow, 1975) is a study of literary relations.

Chapter 1   Scotland After the '45: The Structure of the Economy and of Society

J.A. Symon's, *Scottish Farming Past And Present* (Edinburgh, 1959) is useful but dated. I. Whyte, *Agriculture and Society in Seventeenth-Century Scotland* (Edinburgh, 1979) is essential for an understanding of eighteenth-century developments. I.H. Adams has written extensively on land surveyors in works like *The Mapping of a Scottish Estate* (University of Edinburgh, Department of Educational Studies, 1971) and *Papers on Peter May Land Surveyor 1749–1793* (Scottish History Society, 4th series, vol. 15, Edinburgh, 1979), ed. I.H. Adams, but it is worth drawing attention to Dr Adam's brief article 'Economic Process and the Scottish Land Surveyor', *Imago Mundi* 27 (1975), pp. 13–18, where in a few pages, reinforced by histograms, the general significance of this specialized work is far better illustrated than in any other place. A.J. Durie's, *The Scottish Linen Trade in the Eighteenth Century* (Edinburgh, 1979) is a fine book which at last renders A.J. Warden, *The Linen Trade, Ancient and Modern* (2nd edn, Dundee, 1867) outdated (though still well worth reading). David Steel's 1975 St Andrews Ph.D. thesis on 'The Development of the Fife linen industry in the late 18th and 19th centuries' is an excellent regional study. E. Gauldie's work on bleachfields is most accessible in her article 'Mechanical Aids to Linen Bleaching In Scotland' in *Textile History* I, no. 2, Dec. 1969, pp. 129–56. R.H. Campbell has edited *States of the Annual Progress of the Linen Manufacture 1727–1754* (Edinburgh, HMSO, 1964).

Chapter 2   The Age of Islay 1746–1761
H. Hamilton's pioneering scholarship in *The Industrial Revolution in Scotland* (London, 1st edn, 1932; reprinted 1966) retains much of its freshness. T. Devine's work on the tobacco trade is summed up in *The Tobacco Lords* (Edinburgh, 1975), but his articles on 'Glasgow merchants and the collapse of the tobacco trade, 1775–1783', *Scottish Historical Review (SHR)* 52 (1973), pp. 50–74, and 'Glasgow Colonial Merchants and Land, 1770–1815', in *Land and Industry*, ed. J.T. Ward and R.G. Wilson (Newton Abbot, 1971), pp. 205–44), are also worth consulting as they modify very significantly the views of chapter 9 of H. Hamilton, *An Economic History of Scotland in the Eighteenth Century* (Oxford, 1963), which is otherwise a useful, if staid survey. R. Mitchison's 'The Making Of The Old Scottish Poor Law', *Past and Present* 63 (1974), pp. 58–93, sparked off an interesting controversy between the author and R.A. Cage. It can be followed in the same journal no. 69 (1975), pp. 113–21. Another extremely important article by Mrs Mitchison is 'The Movements of Scottish Corn Prices in the Seventeenth and Eighteenth Centuries', *Economic History Review*, 2nd series, 18 (1965), pp. 278–91. R.H. Campbell's *Carron Company* (Edinburgh, 1961) is a good study of a very a-typical company. J. Lindsay's *The Scottish Poor Law* (Ilfracombe, 1975) is useful but not as good a book as the same author's *The Canals of Scotland* (Newton Abbot, 1968).

The fundamental work on eighteenth-century Scottish politics after 1745 is A.J. Murdoch *The People Above* (Edinburgh, 1980), a published version of his excellent 1978 Edinburgh Ph.D. thesis ' "The People Above": Politics and Administration in Mid-Eighteenth-Century Scotland'. John M. Simpson, 'Who Steered the Gravy Train, 1707–1766?' in *Scotland in the Age of Improvement*, ed. N.T. Phillipson and R. Mitchison (Edinburgh, 1970), pp. 47–72, is important for Islay. Two older articles show the detailed workings of a constituency – W.L. Burn, 'The General Election of 1761 at Ayr', *English Historical Review* 52 (1937), pp. 103–9, and W. Ferguson, 'Dingwall Burgh Politics and the parliamentary Franchise in the Eighteenth Century', *SHR*38 (1959), pp. 89–108. Using insights provided by modern research, it is possible to reinterpret evidence provided by older standard works of reference like M. Wood, *The Lord Provosts Of Edinburgh 1296 to 1932* (Edinburgh, privately printed 1932), or A. Heron, *The Rise and Progress of the Company of Merchants of the City of Edinburgh 1681–1902* (Edinburgh, 1903).

There is no satisfactory book on the Scottish Enlightenment comparable to more general studies such as Norman Hampson's *The Enlightenment* (Penguin ed.) or P. Gay, *The Enlightenment: an interpretation* (London, 1967). This may be a commentary on the extreme difficulty of the task.

J. Rendall, *The Origins of the Scottish Enlightenment 1707–1776* (London, 1979) is competent but limited. Anand C. Chitnis, *The Scottish Enlightenment: A Social History* (London, 1976) is, as its title says, a solid and useful study of the social foundations rather than of the intellectual superstructures. It has an excellent bibliography listing all the important articles including those by N. Phillipson and the less well known but very distinguished group of papers by J.B. Morrell on the scientific aspect of the academic achievement of the period. The latter should be supplemented by A.L. Donovan, *Philosophical Chemistry in the Scottish Enlightenment* (Edinburgh, 1975). On Hume there is a vast literature, much of it very technical. The standard biography is E.C. Mossner, *The Life of David Hume* (Oxford, 1970). Hume's correspondence is available in J.Y.T. Greig (ed.), *The Letters of David Hume*, (2 vols., Oxford, 1932; reprinted 1969), and in the older *Letters of Eminent Persons Addressed to David Hume* (Edinburgh, 1849). Hume's writings are available in scores of editions. Good short introductions to his strictly philosophical work are D.G.C. MacNab, *David Hume: His Theory of Knowledge and Morality* (London, 1951) and T. Penelhum, *Hume* (London, 1975). D. Forbes, *Hume's Philosophical Politics* (Cambridge, 1975) is basic. H.T. Dickinson, *Liberty and Property: Political Ideology in Eighteenth Century Britain* (London, 1977) provides the broader British context for Hume's political attitudes. Also worth consulting are F. Watkins (ed.), *Hume's Theory of Politics* (London, 1951) and J.B. Stewart, *The Moral and Political Philosophy of David Hume* (London, 1963). Two articles give some idea of the position of the Moderate party in the Kirk: Henry Sefton, 'Lord Islay and Patrick Cumming: A Study in Eighteenth Century Ecclesiastical Management', *Scottish Church History Society Records* 19 (1977), pp. 203–16, and I.D.L. Clark, 'From Protest to Reaction: The Moderate Régime in the Church of Scotland, 1752–1805', in N.T. Phillipson and R. Mitchison (eds.), *Scotland in the Age of Improvement*.

Chapter 3   Growth, Enlightenment, and Integration 1760–1775
Early examples of successful Scottish professional careers in eighteenth-century London are chronicled in B. Little, *The Life and Work of James Gibbs 1682–1754* (London, 1955) and C. Tweedie, *James Stirling: A Sketch of his Life and Works along with his Scientific Correspondence* (Oxford, 1922). For Scots on the Grand Tour see Basil Skinner's elegant little *Scots in Italy in the 18th Century* (Edinburgh, 1966). For the Adams family J. Fleming, *Robert Adam and his Circle in Edinburgh and Rome* (London, 1962) is a good introduction. Of the many books on Robert Adam D. Yarwood, *Robert Adam* (London, 1970) has the virtues of compactness and clarity. Philip Gaskell's, *A Bibliography Of The Foulis Press* (London, 1964) provides a splendid introduction to its subject while D.W. Doughty, *The Tullis Press Cupar, 1803–1849* (Dundee, Abertay Historical Society Publication no. 12, 1967) shows something of the achievements of printers outside Glasgow and Edinburgh, a topic further illumined by R.H. Carnie's, *Publishing In Perth*

Before 1807 (Abertay Historical Society Publication no. 6, 1960). The best introduction to the social thought of the eighteenth-century Scots *literati* is still Gladys Bryson, *Man And Society: The Scottish Inquiry of the Eighteenth Century* (Princeton, 1945). Duncan Forbes edited Adam Fergusson's, *An Essay on the History of Civil Society 1767* for Edinburgh University Press in 1966 and a paperback version came out in 1978. W.C. Lehmann, *Adam Ferguson and the Beginnings of Modern Sociology* (New York, 1930) remains important. Of two recent biographies of Kames, A.E. McGuinness, *Henry Home Lord Kames* (New York, 1970) and I.S. Ross, *Lord Kames and the Scotland of his Day* (Oxford, 1972), the latter is fuller but oddly blind to its subject's rôle as practical Improver. Annette Smith's essay on 'The Administration of the Forfeited Annexed Estates, 1752–1784' in *The Scottish Tradition*, ed. G.W.S. Barrow (Edinburgh, 1974), pp. 198–210, is a reminder how far aspiration could outstrip reality in the world of Improvement, as is S.G.E. Lythe, 'James Watt and the Strathmore Canal Project', *Transport History*, 1, no. 1 (1968), pp. 67–70. The same author's 'The Tayside meal mobs 1772–3', *SHR* 46 (1967), pp. 26–36 brings out the pre-class nature of the mentality of his meal mobs.

For upper-class careers in diplomacy D.B. Horn's *The British Diplomatic Service 1689–1789* (Oxford, 1971) can be supplemented by Karl Schweizer, 'Scotsmen and the British Diplomatic Service, 1714–1789', *Scottish Tradition* 7–8 (1977–8), pp. 115–36. Basic to an understanding of Principal Robertson's career is Jeremy J. Cater, 'The Making of Principal Robertson in 1762', *SHR* 49 (1970), pp. 60–84, while Edmund Heier in 'William Robertson and Ludwig Heinrich von Nicolay, his German Translator at the Court of Catherine II' in *SHR* 41 (1962), pp. 135–40, shows that Robertson's reputation in polite circles stretched — like the polite circles — from the Atlantic to the Urals.

Chapter 4   A Loyal Province and the Crisis of the State 1775–84
The ideological context of the American Revolution can be studied in D.S. Lovejoy, *The Glorious Revolution in America* (New York, 1974) and in two books by Bernard Bailyn, *The Ideological Origins of the American Revolution* (Cambridge, Mass., 1967) and *The Origins of American Politics* (Cambridge, Mass., 1967).

The basic article on Scottish opinion and the war is Dalphy I. Fogerstrom 'Scottish Opinion and the American Revolution', *The William and Mary Quarterly*, 3rd series 11 (1954), pp. 252–75. Both for this chapter and for the previous one J.S. Shaw's important unpublished thesis 'Civic Leadership and the Edinburgh Lawyers in Eighteenth Century Scotland with Special Reference to the Case of Andrew Fletcher, Lord Milton', Stirling University, 1980, is fundamental. Caroline Robbin's article ' "When it is that Colonies may turn Independent": An Analysis of the Environment and Politics of Francis Hutcheson (1694–1746)' in *The William and Mary Quarterly*, 3rd series 11 (1954), pp. 214–51, examines a liberal viewpoint. Much more characteristic of contemporary Scottish opinion were the extremist views of that charming man, Allan Ramsay, which are brought out, with much else, in A. Smart, *The Life and Art of Allan Ramsay* (London, 1952). Scottish regiments in the American War may be traced in Colonel David Stewart of Garth's *Sketches of the Character, Manners, and Present State of the Highlanders of Scotland with details of the Military Service of the Highland Regiments* (2 vols., Edinburgh, 1822) and in action in B.G. Moss, 'The Rôles of the Scots and Scotch-Irishmen in the Southern Campaigns in the War of American Independence, 1780–83', St Andrews unpublished Ph.D. thesis, 3 vols., 1979. There is a convenient article on 'The Yorkshire Association, 1780–4: A Study in Political Organisation' in I.R. Christie, *Myth and Reality in Late-Eighteenth Century British Politics and Other Papers* (London, 1970).

Chapter 5   Patronage and Enlightenment during the Consolidation of the Dundas Ascendancy 1784–93

The standard life of Henry Dundas is Holden Furber, *Henry Dundas First Viscount Melville 1742–1811* (Oxford, 1931). On the Earl of Buchan, James Gordon Lamb's 'David Steuart Erskine 11th Earl of Buchan: A Study of his Life and Correspondence', unpublished University of St Andrews Ph.D., 1963, is fundamental. Some notion of what went on on the Forfeited Annexed Estates before they were returned to the original possessing families in 1784 may be gathered from V. Wills (ed.), *Reports on the Annexed Estates 1755–1769* (Edinburgh, HMSO, 1973). J.N.M. Maclean, *Reward is Secondary* (London, 1963) is important for the career of the odious Lauchline Macleane. It is excellent on his Westminster and Indian interests but not at all convincing on his Jacobite motives. *The Oxford History Of India*, by V.A. Smith (3rd edn, ed. Percival Spear, Oxford, 1970), is a useful introduction. More specialized are P.J. Marshall, *East India Fortunes* (Oxford, 1976); P. Nightingale, *Trade and Empire in Western India 1784–1806* (Cambridge, 1970); and E. Ingram (ed.), *Two Views of British India: The Private Correspondence of Mr Dundas and Lord Wellesley 1798–1801* (Bath, n.d.). H.T. Fry, *Alexander Dalrymple and the Expansion of British Trade* (London, 1970), provides an account of the hydrographer brother of Lord Hailes. For the anti-slavery movement, C. Duncan Rice, *The Rise And Fall Of Black Slavery* (London, 1975) gives very adequate coverage to the Scottish contribution to anti-slavery agitations but can usefully be supplemented by Folarin Shyllon, *James Ramsay: The Unknown Abolitionist* (Edinburgh, 1977).

Adam Smith is an industry as well as a person. The principal research tool in Smith studies is now the Glasgow Edition of the Works and Correspondence of Adam Smith, of which the following are particularly relevant: R.H. Campbell, A.S. Skinner, and W.B. Todd (eds.), *An Inquiry into the Nature and Causes of the Wealth of Nations* (Oxford, 1976); D.D. Raphael and A.L. Macfie (eds.), *The Theory of Moral Sentiments* (Oxford, 1976); Andrew

Skinner and T. Wilson (eds.), *Essays on Adam Smith* (Oxford, 1975); E.C. Mossner and I.S. Ross (eds.), *The Correspondence of Adam Smith* (Oxford, 1977). J.M. Lothian's edition of a student's notes of Adam Smith's *Lectures on Rhetoric and Belles Lettres* (Edinburgh, 1963) has great charm while two monographs are most helpful in elucidating Smith's views: T.D. Campbell, *Adam Smith's Science of Morals* (London, 1971), and D. Winch, *Adam Smith's Politics* (Cambridge, 1978). Smith's neglected predecessor has been rescued from undeserved obscurity by Andrew Skinner who has edited *Sir James Steuart: An Inquiry into the Principles of Political Oeconomy* (2 vols., Edinburgh, 1966). The same scholar has produced a handy Pelican Classic edition of Adam Smith, *The Wealth Of Nations Books I–III*.

Scottish medical teaching can be studied in the ponderous but very useful J.D. Comrie, *History Of Scottish Medicine* (2nd edn, 2 vols., London, 1932) as well as in university histories such as J.D. Mackie, *The University of Glasgow 1451–1951* (Glasgow, 1954), and D.B. Horn, *A Short History of the University of Edinburgh 1556–1889* (Edinburgh, 1967). What can be said in defence of St Andrews in this context is said in R.G. Cant's *The University of St Andrews: A Short History* (Edinburgh, 2nd edn, 1970). S.R. Gloyne, *John Hunter* (Edinburgh, 1950) is an excellent introduction to the theme of the teacher of medicine as entrepreneur.

Henry Mackenzie's *The Man of Feeling* is available in an excellent edition by Brian Vickers in the Oxford English Novels series (London, 1967). It should be read by anyone trying to understand fashionable literary taste in this period. The best brief introduction to Burns is D. Daiches, *Robert Burns and his World* (London, 1971). The standard edition of *The Poems And Songs Of Robert Burns* is by J. Kinsley (3 vols., Oxford, 1968). J. De Lancey Ferguson (ed.), *The Letters of Robert Burns* (2 vols., Oxford, 1931) holds the field pending a new Oxford edition by Professor G. Ross Roy. The problem of the early editing and biographical study of Burns is dealt with by R.D. Thornton, *James Currie the Entire Stranger and Robert Burns* (Edinburgh, 1963). Dr Robert Chambers, *Life And Works Of Robert Burns*, revised by William Wallace, (4 vols., Edinburgh, Chambers, n.d.) is by no means entirely superceded. M. Lindsay, *The Burns Encyclopedia* (3rd edn, New York, 1980) is extremely helpful. For Allan Ramsay see B. Martin, *Allan Ramsay: A Study of his Life and Works* (Cambridge, Mass., 1931), and J.W. Oliver, B. Martin, A.M. Kinghorn, and A. Law, *The Works of Allan Ramsay* (Edinburgh, 1974). Finally, no discussion of the cultural context of Burns can neglect the contentious and provocative little work by D. Daiches, *The Paradox of Scottish Culture: The Eighteenth-Century Experience* (London, 1964).

Chapter 6 Political Attitudes during the French Revolutionary and Napoleonic Wars 1793–1815
Holden Furber's biography of Dundas remains basic. H.W. Meikle, *Scotland And The French Revolution* (Edinburgh, 1912; reprinted London, 1969) is less comprehensive than it should be. Alexander Fergusson, *The Honourable*

Henry Erskine Lord Advocate For Scotland (Edinburgh, 1882) is appallingly diffuse. Alexander Haldane's, *The Lives of Robert Haldane of Airthrey and of his Brother, James Alexander Haldane* (London, 1853) is important for both political and religious history. K.J. Logue, *Popular Disturbances in Scotland 1780–1815* (Edinburgh, 1979), and N. Murray, *The Scottish Hand Loom Weavers 1790–1850: A Social History* (Edinburgh, 1978), ch. 9, 'Radical Attitudes And Activities', are important. For the *Edinburgh* see J. Clive, *Scotch Reviewers: The 'Edinburgh Review' 1802–1815* (London, 1957) and J.A. Greig, *Francis Jeffrey Of The Edinburgh Review* (Edinburgh, 1948). C. Tennant, *The Radical Laird: A Biography of George Kinloch 1775–1833* (Kineton, 1970) studies a minor Scotch Whig. For the Whigs as a British party consult F. O'Gorman, *The Whig Party And The French Revolution* (London, 1967), and L.G. Mitchell, *Charles James Fox and the Disintegration of the Whig Party 1782–1794* (Oxford, 1971).

Chapter 7   Structural Change in an Era of Political Immobilism 1790–1815
The father of the *Old Statistical Account* is the subject of R. Mitchison, *Agricultural Sir John: The Life of Sir John Sinclair of Ulbster 1754–1835* (London, 1962). J.E. Handley, *Scottish Farming in the Eighteenth Century* (London, 1953), and the same author's *The Agricultural Revolution in Scotland* (London, 1963) are important surveys from a point of view which requires modification. R.A. Dodgshon, 'Farming in Roxburghshire and Berwickshire on the eve of Improvement', *SHR* 54 (1975), pp. 140–54, is a good introduction to revisionist views, referring in footnotes to most of the other significant articles. The Highlands now possess in James Hunter's *The Making of the Crofting Community* (Edinburgh, 1976) an excellent general survey from the eighteenth century. A.J. Youngson in his *After the Forty-Five: The Economic Impact on the Scottish Highlands* (Edinburgh, 1973) surveys the political economy of schemes for Highland development in a fascinating but not totally successful book. J. Dunlop, *The British Fisheries Society 1786–1893* (Edinburgh, 1978) is definitive. E. Richards, *The Leviathan Of Wealth: The Sutherland Fortune in the Industrial Revolution* (London, 1973), is both invaluable in its own right and a guide, in its footnotes rather than in its bibliography, to many areas of controversy. R.J. Adam has edited John Home's *Survey of Assynt* (Scottish History Society, 3rd series, vol. 52, Edinburgh, 1960); and *Papers On Sutherland Estate Management 1802–1816* (Scottish History Society, 4th series, vols. 8–9, Edinburgh, 1972). For an interesting contemporary view see John Knox, *The Highlands and Hebrides in 1786* (London, 1787; reprinted Edinburgh, 1975). Highland roads have a literature of their own in this period. A.R.B. Haldane, *The Drove Roads of Scotland* (London, 1952) and *New Ways Through the Glens* (London, 1962), and W. Taylor, *The Military Roads in Scotland* (Newton Abbot, 1976), may all be recommended. For matters Ossianic see A. Gillies, *A Hebridean In Goethe's Weimar* (Oxford, 1969), and J.N.M. Maclean, 'The Early Political Careers of James "Fingal" Macpherson (1736–1796) and Sir John Macpherson, Bart.

(1744—1821)', unpublished Edinburgh Ph.D., 1967.

Though brief Donald Fleming's 'Latent Heat and the Invention of the Watt Engine', *Isis* 43 (1952), pp. 3—5 is a most important article. A. and N. Clow, *The Chemical Revolution: A Contribution to Social Technology* (London, 1952) is seminal, but A. Clow's typescript 'Scotland's Contribution to Industrial Development through the Application of Chemical Science since the Seventeenth Century' (University of Aberdeen Blackwell Prize Essay, 1944) may still be read with profit, as may A. Kent, *An Eighteenth Century Lectureship in Chemistry* (Glasgow, 1950), and J.H. Smith's *The Gordon's Mill Farming Club 1758—1764* (Edinburgh, 1962), which illustrates one early type of relationship between academic circles and changing technology. The career of one of the most eccentric offspring produced by a chemically-inclined family is chronicled in D. Thomas, *Cochrane: Britannia's Last Sea-King* (London, 1978) and Ian Grimble, *The Sea Wolf: The Life of Admiral Cochrane* (London, 1978). Eric T. Svedenstierna, *Svedenstierna's Tour of Great Britain 1802—3*, ed. M. Flinn (Newton Abbot, 1973), gives in ch. 6 an industrial spy's hurried survey of Scottish industry in 1803, metallurgical rather than chemical in bias.

A supremely self-confident aristocratic Improver of the old school is engagingly revealed in A. and H. Tayler (eds.), *Lord Fife and his Factor being the Correspondence of James Second Lord Fife 1729—1809* (London, 1925), while the multi-faceted activities of the house of Argyll can be traced in E.R. Cregeen, *Argyll Estate Instructions 1771—1805* (Scottish History Society, 4th series 1 Edinburgh, 1964) and I. Lindsay and M. Cosh, *Inverary and the Dukes of Argyll* (Edinburgh, 1973). J. Macaulay, *The Gothic Revival 1745—1845* (Glasgow, 1975) is important for the retreat from neo-classicism into a neo-feudal lifestyle. For the realities of social change in the countryside T.M. Devine, 'Social stability and agrarian change in the eastern lowlands of Scotland, 1810—1840', *Social History* 3 (1978), pp. 331—46 is important. Nor should the student fail to consult D. Fleming and B. Bailyn (eds.), *Perspectives in American History*, 7 (1973) for Malcolm Gray's characteristically fine and penetrating essay on 'Scottish emigration: the social impact of agrarian change in the rural lowlands 1775—1875'.

Chapter 8   The Twilight of the Ancien Régime *1815—1827*
Scott studies are a boundless sea. H.J.C. Grierson's Centenary Edition of *The Letters of Sir Walter Scott 1787—1932* (12 vols., London, 1932—7) must now be supplemented by J.C. Corson's splendid *Notes and Index to Sir Herbert Grierson's Edition of the Letters of Sir Walter Scott* (Oxford, 1979). W.E.K. Anderson has edited *The Journal of Sir Walter Scott* (Oxford, 1972). Scott's prose and poetry are available in myriad editions. E. Johnson, *Sir Walter Scott: The Great Unknown* (2 vols., London, 1970) is the standard biography. J.G. Lockhart, *Memoirs of the Life of Sir Walter Scott, Bart* (7 vols., Edinburgh, 1837—8)is also available in a handy one-volume Everyman format but should

be read alongside F.R. Hart, *Lockhart as Romantic Biographer* (Edinburgh, 1971). Other books on Scott I have found useful include Sir Herbert Grierson, *Sir Walter Scott, Bart* (London, 1938); R.C. Gordon, *Under Which King* (Edinburgh 1969); A.O.J. Cockshut, *The Achievement of Walter Scott* (London, 1969); D.D. Devlin, *The Author of Waverley* (London, 1971); A. Bell (ed.), *Scott Bicentenary Essays* (Edinburgh, 1973); A.M. Clark, *Sir Walter Scott: the formative years* (Edinburgh, 1969); E. Quayle, *The Ruin of Sir Walter Scott* (London, 1968); and A.N. Wilson, *The Laird of Abbotsford* (Oxford, 1980). For those of strong intellectual constitution there are two Scott bibliographies, J.C. Corson, *A Bibliography of Sir Walter Scott 1797–1940* (Edinburgh, 1943), and Jill Rubenstein, *Sir Walter Scott: a reference guide* (Boston, 1978), which goes up from 1932. On the very important question of the evolution of Scottish history in this period, in which Scott is an important figure, see B. Lenman, 'The teaching of Scottish history in the Scottish universities', *SHR* 52 (1973), pp. 165–90; *Scots Antiquaries and Historians* (Dundee, Abertay Historical Society Publication no. 16, 1972); and M. Ash, *The Strange Death of Scottish History* (Edinburgh, 1980). The *SHR* 53, part 2, no. 156 (October, 1974) is a number devoted to studies relating to the history of Register House and of the Scottish Records.

The best introduction to John Galt is C.A. Whatley (ed.), *John Galt 1779–1979* (Edinburgh, 1979). Galt's *Annals Of The Parish* is available in the Oxford English Novels series, edited with an introduction by James Kinsley (London, 1967). The Scottish Academic Press has published Galt's neglected political novel *The Member* (Edinburgh, 1975). The main Galt novels were published in 8 volumes in the nineteenth century (Blackwood, 1895) and in an illustrated 10-volume edition in the twentieth (Edinburgh, 1936). Douglas Mack has edited *James Hogg Selected Poems* (Oxford, 1970), and for the Scottish Academic Press *James Hogg Memoirs of the Author's Life and Familiar Anecdotes of Sir Walter Scott* (Edinburgh, 1972). The same publisher has an edition of Hogg's *The Three Perils of Man: War, Women and Witchcraft* (Edinburgh, 1972). *The Private Memoirs and Confessions of a Justified Sinner* is available ed. J. Carey in the Oxford English Novels series (London, 1969). L. Simpson, *James Hogg: A Critical Study* (Edinburgh, 1962) is sensible and helpful.

The fluctuating fortunes of religious parties and views may be followed in A. Fawcett, *The Cambuslang Revival* (London, 1971); in two articles in *Records of the Scottish Church History Society (RSCHS)* 20 (1978), I.F. Maciver, 'The Evangelical Party and the Eldership in General Assemblies 1820–1843', and W.R. Ward, 'Scottish Methodism in the Age of Jabez Bunting', pp. 1–13 and 47–64 resp. Also useful is I.D.L. Clark, 'The Reverend Andrew Lothian 1763–1831 United Secession Minister', *RSCHS* 20, part 2 (1979), pp. 143–62. Magnus Magnusson *et. al.* have written *The Glorious Privilege: The History of 'The Scotsman'* (Edinburgh, 1967), whose early pages are important for the history of conservative Whiggery. Radicals can be pursued in W.M. Roach, 'Alexander Richmond and the radical reform movements in Glasgow in

1816–17', *SHR* 51 (1972), pp. 1–19, an article which is an essential corrective
to P. Berresford Ellis and S. Mac A'Gobhainn, *The Scottish Insurrection Of
1820* (London, 1970). In ch. 2 of *From Esk to Tweed* (Glasgow, 1975), Bruce
Lenman tried to demonstrate the connection between port development and
Whig politics. The flavour of the unreformed corporations may be further
sampled in *Report from the Select Committee to whom the Several Petitions
from the Royal Burghs of Scotland, during the Years 1818, 1819, 1820 and
1821, were Referred etc.* (Ordered by the House of Commons, to be Printed,
14 and 15 June 1821).

Chapter 9   North Britain and Cockburn's Millenium
Henry Cockburn, *Memorials of his Time*, was largely written between 1821
and 1830. It was originally published in Edinburgh by his executors in 1856
and was most recently reprinted by the Mercat Press, Edinburgh, in 1971.
Harry A. Cockburn (ed.), *Some Letters of Lord Cockburn with Pages Omitted
from the Memorials of his Time* (Edinburgh, 1932) is an infuriating gloss on
the *Memorials*. Further posthumous works include Cockburn's *Journal* (2
vols., Edinburgh, 1874) and his *Circuit Journeys* (Edinburgh, 1888). Karl
Miller, *Cockburn's Millenium* (London, 1975) is great fun. Alan Bell (ed.),
Lord Cockburn A Bicentenary Commemoration (Edinburgh, 1979), is a
collection of scholarly essays. Brougham can be studied in A. Aspinall, *Lord
Brougham and the Whig Party* (Manchester, 1927), and Chester W. New, *The
Life of Henry Brougham* (Oxford, 1961). Lord Cockburn's own *Life of Lord
Jeffrey with a Selection from his Correspondence* (2 vols., Edinburgh, 1852) is a
compilation rather than a work of art, but a useful compilation. A provincial
Whig is described in Major-General Isaac Forsyth MacAndrew, *Memoir of
Isaac Forsyth Bookseller in Elgin 1768–1859* (London, 1889). An acid Tory
view of Edinburgh Whiggery can be read in J.B. Lockhart, *Peter's Letters to
his Kinsfolk* (Edinburgh 1819, new edn, ed. W. Ruddick, Edinburgh, 1977).
   There are two good books on the proto-radicalism of the Douglas Cause;
Lillian de la Torre, *The Heir of Douglas* (London, 1953), and *The Douglas
Cause*, ed. A. Francis Steuart (Glasgow, 1909). The nature of the long contro-
versy over jury trial is most clearly explained in I.D. Willock, *The Origins and
Development of the Jury in Scotland*, Stair Society, vol. 23 (Edinburgh, 1966).
N. Gash, *Aristocracy and People: Britain 1815–1865* (London, 1979) provides
a lucid political survey, very much from a government point of view. E.J.
Hobsbawm and G. Rudé, *Captain Swing* (London, 1970), is less deferential.
Christopher Hibbert, *George IV* (2 vols., London, 1972–3), is scholarly and
sympathetic. W. Ferguson, 'The Reform Act (Scotland) of 1832: intention and
effect', *SHR* 45 (1966), pp. 105–14, is a most important article for the
detailed working of the act. J.I. Brash has edited *Papers on Scottish Electoral
Politics 1832–1854*, Scottish History Society, 4th series 11 (Edinburgh, 1974).
For a profound analysis of the lack of relationship between elections and significant policy decisions see J.C.D. Clark, 'A General Theory of Party, Opposition
and Government, 1688–1832', *The Historical Journal*, 23 (1980),

pp. 295–325. A good city study which brings out the very limited local impact of the events of 1832 in Glasgow is D.A. Teviotdale, 'Glasgow Parliamentary Constituency 1832–1846', unpublished B. Litt. thesis, University of Glasgow, 1963.

William Burke has found his defender in Owen Dudley Edwards, *Burke & Hare* (Edinburgh, 1980). A.G. Ralston's 'The Tron Riot Of 1812', *History Today* 30 (1980), pp. 41–5, is a fascinating piece of social pathology. One unusual response to the economic and social stresses of the time can be examined in J. Butt (ed.), *Robert Owen: Prince of Cotton Spinners* (Newton Abbot, 1971). A. Tyrrell, 'Political economy, Whiggism and the education of working-class adults in Scotland 1817–40', *SHR* 48 (1969), pp. 151–65, is fundamental for the use of economic dogma as a form of social control. J.V. Smith, *The Watt Institution Dundee 1824–49* (Dundee, Abertay Historical Society Publication no. 19, 1978) is a neat local study. B. Gordon, *Economic Doctrine and Tory Liberalism 1824–30* (London, 1979) shows the political economists at work at Westminster. For the development of educational institutions in Scotland before 1872 J. Craigie, *A Bibliography of Scottish Education Before 1872* (London, 1970), is exhaustive to its own date of publication. Thomas Dick may be traced in W. Norrie's *Dundee Celebrities of the Nineteenth Century* (Dundee, 1873), though Dick should also be read in such editions as Collins Select Library which published *On the Improvement of Society* (Glasgow, 1860) and *The Christian Philosopher* (2 vols., Glasgow, 1860). The best introduction to the theme of the emergence of a class society is H.J. Perkin, *The Origins of Modern English Society 1780–1880* (London, 1969). The *SHR* 59 (1980) has two articles which develop this theme in a Scottish context: A. Dickson and W. Speirs, 'Changes in class structure in Paisley, 1750–1845', and J.A. Hassan, 'The landed estate, paternalism and the coal industry in Midlothian, 1800–1880', pp. 54–72 and 73–91 resp. For Chalmers the Reverend Robert Hanna, *Memoirs of Thomas Chalmers* (4 vols., Edinburgh, 1852–3), remains the basic source, though Drummond and Bulloch, *The Scottish Church 1688–1843*, ch. 8, gives some idea of the current radical reinterpretation of Chalmer's achievement. R. Mitchison 'The Creation of the Disablement Rule in the Scottish Poor Law', in T.C. Smout (ed.), *The Search for Wealth and Stability* (London, 1979), pp. 199–217, continues from her earlier articles study of a theme of central interest to Chalmers.

Sir Walter Scotts' fulminations against Westminster and Westminster's attempt at a reply may be conveniently read in *Sir Walter Scott 'Thoughts On The Proposed Change of Currency' and John Wilson Croker 'Two Letters On Scottish Affairs'*, with an introduction by D. Simpson and A. Wood (Shannon, 1972). Very important indeed as an introduction to the Scottish image is J. Holloway and L. Errington, *The Discovery of Scotland: The Appreciation of Scottish Scenery Through Two Centuries of Painting* (Edinburgh, The National Gallery Of Scotland, 1978). It can be supplemented by J. Cooksey's Introduction to *Alexander Nasmyth 1758–1840* (Exhibition Catalogue, Balcarres Gallery, St Andrews, 1979), and by A.A. Tait, *The Landscape Garden in Scotland 1735–1835* (Edinburgh, 1980).

Appendix: Chronological Table

1746   Battle of Culloden.
1747   The Abolition of Heritable Jurisdictions (Scotland) Act (20 Geo. II. Cap. 43).
1749   Prestonpans Sulphuric Acid Works established by John Roebuck and Samuel Garbett.
1755   Dr Alexander Webster's private census 'Account of the Number of People in Scotland, 1755'.
1756–63 The Seven Years War or 'the Great War for Empire'.
1759   Carron Ironworks founded near Falkirk by Roebuck, Garbett, and William Cadell. Robert Burns born near Ayr.
1760   Accession of George III.
1761   Death of Archibald Campbell, 1st Earl of Islay and 3rd Duke of Argyll, first great political manager of Scotland.
1761–3 Ministerial career of John Stuart, 3rd Earl of Bute and favourite of George III.
1766   James Craig wins the competition for the plan for the New Town of Edinburgh.
1767   Craig lays, in Rose Court, the foundation stone of the first house in the New Town.
1769   James Watt's first patent for an improved steam engine.
1771   Birth of Walter Scott in Edinburgh.
1772   Failure of the Ayr Bank.
1774   Major-General Simon Fraser granted the estates forfeited by his Jacobite father, Lord Lovat.
1776   Publication of Adam Smith's *An Inquiry into the Nature and Causes of the Wealth of Nations*.
1776–83 The War of the American Revolution.
1784   General Election confirms the administration of William Pitt the Younger and the importance of his principal Scottish ally, Henry Dundas, later 1st Viscount Melville. Remaining Forfeited Annexed Estates returned to the representatives of the forfeited families. Agitation for burgh reform in Scotland.
1788   Death of Charles Edward Stuart ('Bonnie Prince Charlie') in Rome.
1789   Outbreak of the French Revolution.
1790   Introduction of water-powered spinning machinery into Scotland.
1791   Henry Dundas becomes Home Secretary.
1792   Episcopalians' religious disabilities removed. 'General Convention

	of the Friends of the People in Scotland' meets in Edinburgh in December.
1793	France declares war on Britain in February. Third General Convention of the Scottish Friends of the People held in Edinburgh in October. In December it is forcibly dispersed by the authorities and its leading figures tried and sentenced to transportation.
1796	Death of Robert Burns.
1797	Extensive rioting in Scotland against the Militia Act. Professor Robison of Edinburgh University publishes his *Proofs of a Conspiracy against all the Religions and Governments in Europe*.
1800	Watt's basic patent rights over his improved steam engine lapse.
1801	William Pitt resigns as first minster of the Crown.
1802	Peace of Amiens with Napoleon's France. New opposition periodical, the *Edinburgh Review*, commences publication.
1803	Renewal of war with France.
1804	Pitt returns to office with Viscount Melville as First Lord of the Admiralty.
1805	Melville impeached and compelled to resign.
1806–7	So-called 'Ministry of all the Talents' headed by C.J. Fox and the Duke of Portland.
1809	Tory *Quarterly Review* commences publication.
1812	Great weavers' strike in Glasgow and the west of Scotland.
1813	'Tron Riot' in Edinburgh.
1814	Walter Scott publishes his novel *Waverley* anonymously.
1814–15	Defeat of Napoleon and European peace settlement. Radical Hampden Clubs set up in Scotland.
1816	Post-war business depression becomes severe.
1817	Series of political trials in Edinburgh and revival of agitation for burghal reform in Scotland. *The Scotsman*, a radical paper, established. *Blackwood's Magazine* appears as a Tory reply to *The Scotsman*.
1820	So-called 'Radical War' in the west of Scotland.
1822	King George IV's state visit to Edinburgh, stage-managed by Sir Walter Scott.
1824	Repeal of the Combination Acts through the agitation of Joseph Hume and Francis Place removes legal ban on trade union activity.
1825	Spectacular collapse of business boom decimates Scottish industry.
1826	Sir Walter Scott and his principal associates declared bankrupt.
1827	The second Viscount Melville resigns office.
1828	'Hot blast' iron-smelting process invented by James Beaumont Neilson.
1829	Catholic Emancipation.
1830	Fall of Wellington's Tory ministry. Whigs take office.
1832	Passing of the Reform Act (Scotland) largely shaped by Jeffrey, Cockburn, and Kennedy. Death of Sir Walter Scott.
1833	Burgh Reform Acts restructure Scottish burgh government.

Index